Getting and Staying Productive

All kinds of processes – those that make things or deliver services or operate companies – can be made more productive, and society's continued well-being requires it. This book is for all those with a stake in improving how companies run. It introduces the concept of "swift, even flow" and explains how that concept stands behind popular business tools such as "lean" principles and Six Sigma. More than that, it shows how swift, even flow can lead to deep, strategic insights and fresh ideas. The book uses many examples, both contemporary and historic, and 16 case studies from all sorts of business situations to demonstrate how swift, even flow can be applied. Services and manufacturing, supply chains and individual operations, product development and outsourcing, strategy and tactics, hourly workers and top level executives – all benefit from this fundamental rethinking of what it takes to become productive.

ROGER W. SCHMENNER is a visiting professor at the Judge School of Business, University of Cambridge. He is also Professor Emeritus of Operations Management and the former Randall L. Tobias Chair at Indiana University's Kelley School of Business. He has written three textbooks and consulted for over 80 companies.

Getting and Staying Productive

Applying Swift, Even Flow to Practice

ROGER W. SCHMENNER

Kelley School of Business
Indiana University
IUPUI Campus, Indianapolis, Indiana, USA
and
Judge Business School
University of Cambridge
Cambridge, United Kingdom

CAMBRIDGE
UNIVERSITY PRESS

CAMBRIDGE UNIVERSITY PRESS
Cambridge, New York, Melbourne, Madrid, Cape Town,
Singapore, São Paulo, Delhi, Mexico City

Cambridge University Press
The Edinburgh Building, Cambridge CB2 8RU, UK

Published in the United States of America by Cambridge University Press,
New York

www.cambridge.org
Information on this title: www.cambridge.org/9781107021327

First published 2012

Printed in the United Kingdom at the University Press, Cambridge

A catalogue record for this publication is available from the British Library

Library of Congress Cataloguing in Publication data
Schmenner, Roger W., 1947–
Getting and staying productive : applying swift, even flow to
practice / Roger W. Schmenner.
    p. cm.
Includes bibliographical references and index.
ISBN 978-1-107-02132-7
1. Industrial productivity.   2. Six sigma (Quality control standard)
3. Business logistics.   I. Title.
HD56.S345 2012
658.4′013–dc23
2011049121

ISBN 978-1-107-02132-7 Hardback

For Barbie and our years together

Contents

List of figures   *page* viii

List of tables   ix

Preface   xi

PART I   THE CONCEPT

1   The usual suspects   3

2   Swift, even flow   16

3   The old-fashioned way to make money   58

PART II   APPLICATION

4   Vision   93

5   Making a bad process better   131

6   Linking the supply chain   163

7   Amid uncertainty   193

8   Strategy   219

9   Resolving the paradox   247

Notes   264

Bibliography   274

Index   278

Figures

2.1	Wait time vs. capacity utilization	*page* 19
2.2	Process spectrum	20
2.3	A supply chain	33
2.4	A Biomet Vanguard® complete knee replacement	39
2.5	Swift, even flow and processes	44
2.6	Profit and uncertainty within the process matrix	47
2.7	Swift, even flow in services	48
2.8	The classic hybrid process	54
2.9	Cells feeding an assembly line	55
2.10	How cells can transform a process	56
3.1	A model of a Venetian galley	62
3.2	Arkwright's water frame, circa 1775	76
3.3	A close-up of Arkwright's water frame, showing the "clockworks"	76
3.4	The M1819 Hall rifle	81
3.5	A picture of the history of the mechanical clock and watch	85
5.1	"As is" process flow diagram for USA Services	134
5.2	"Should be" process flow diagram for USA Services	137
5.3	Average inventory declines when the review period shortens	155
6.1	The Barilla supply chain	175
7.1	A spectrum of product development organization	200
7.2	The process flow for Hot Wheels and Matchbox cars	209
8.1	Charters for Prentiss Products Europe's plants	235
8.2	Smaller, more frequent batches cut the average inventory carried	240
8.3	The heart of operations strategy	242

Tables

4.1	Lean Manufacturing Philosophy versus the "Received Tradition": 15 precepts	*page* 123
4.2	Allocating costs with throughput time	127
4.3	Traditional direct labor cost allocation	128
4.4	Throughput time allocated costs	130
6.1	A model of the supply chain – starting point	177
6.2	A model of the supply chain – completed	179
7.1	Comparing product development to manufacturing thinking	199
8.1	How simplicity and discipline support different needs for responsiveness	227

Preface

Productivity, with its potential and its paradoxes, has gnawed at me for years. For students of operations management, there is no greater issue. Its impact on society has been, and will continue to be, immense.

While the concept of swift, even flow grew, in fits and starts, out of my research over the past 30 years, the urge to apply it has grown out of my teaching and my years as a dean and an academic administrator. My students, mainly evening MBAs, deserved a point of view that they could bring to the nagging problems that they encountered in their day jobs. As a dean and as the chief of staff to the Chancellor at IUPUI, I preached that swift, even flow – which in the academic context means getting students through their degree programs on time – was what we owed them and ourselves. Upon returning to the classroom from my time as an administrator, it dawned on me how so many of the cases in the first-year MBA course could benefit from the perspective that the concept of swift, even flow could bring to them. The idea of a book that told the story of swift, even flow and then applied it relentlessly to a host of management problems took increasing hold of me.

As ever, I owe a debt of gratitude to Indiana University and its Kelley School of Business, on both the IUPUI and the Bloomington campuses, for providing me with the time and the opportunities for study and reflection. Over the years, my colleagues on both campuses have been wonderful. Special mention is due to Bob Hall, who has always been a fountain of stories and insight, and Morgan Swink, whose curiosity first challenged me to put my ideas on swift, even flow together. Bob Collins, of IMD in Lausanne, has been instrumental to my internationalization, a benefit both scholastic and personal. My gratitude extends as well to the Judge Business School of the University of Cambridge where I have been able, very pleasantly, to complete the writing.

PART I   **The concept**

I   The usual suspects

Your parents always wanted you to be a doctor. So, imagine that you are one, an orthopedic surgeon, in fact, specializing in knee and hip replacements. Life is good. The aging baby boomers will continue to need new knees and hips, assuring that you will always be in demand. Nevertheless, you know that healthcare's percentage of the gross domestic product cannot keep increasing, and that both the private insurance companies and the public system will surely be tightening up on their compensation for your surgical procedures.

How are you going to cut costs so that your annual income can be maintained? There are not a lot of options. The knee and hip implants themselves are billed separately by the hospital. The surgical instruments that you use are owned by the medical device company that supplies you with your knee and hip implants. You've got your surgical team to pay and the staff in your office. There are office expenses and insurance premiums, but your costs are overwhelmingly personnel costs and they aren't going down.

That leaves the option of adding to your revenues, and the easiest way to do that is to perform more operations in a week. But, you only have so much time in a day, especially only so much time when you are fit for holding a scalpel. You simply have to become more productive in the operating room; you have to do more operations in the same amount of time. But, how?

Productivity. It matters. In fact, over the long haul, it's about the only thing that matters.[1] It is the bedrock of our standard of living. When productivity increases, when we can get more output from the same resources, incomes can rise with no worries about inflation. Generations can live better than their predecessors. Poverty can be reduced and people can enjoy more arts and leisure. When productivity stalls, this march of progress comes to a halt.

Most of us no longer live on the farm, thanks to the advances made in that most productive sector of most rich nations' economies, agriculture. Just a small percentage of us can produce all the food that we consume, and then some, and do it so cheaply that the fraction of our incomes spent on food continues to decline. Many people bemoan the loss of jobs in manufacturing, often attributing the reduction to outsourcing. Yet, productivity advance is, by far, the more important explanation. In a country such as the United States, the value of manufactured products, in constant dollars, continues to climb. It is the great productivity of the manufacturing sector that explains why that increased value can be produced by fewer and fewer employees.[2]

The breadth and diversity of the service sector in the industrialized countries and the fact that most of us work in the service sector can be directly linked to the higher productivity of agriculture and manufacturing. But, high productivity is not limited to agriculture and manufacturing. Some service businesses exhibit a productivity that outshines their competitors and has been instrumental to their growth.[3] The push for greater and greater productivity is a constant business theme.

Only for a few selected services is productivity increase more a fond wish than a relentless mandate. It is an unfortunate, but inescapable, fact that some services will always be at the bottom of the productivity ladder. The costs of these services will not benefit much from productivity gains and thus their prices will stay high for consumers. For such services, it is hard for labor to be any more productive than it has been. The price of symphony tickets and Broadway and West End plays, for example, will continue to climb. After all, it will always take a full orchestra to play Beethoven and a significant cast to stage Shakespeare. And, the Minute Waltz won't get any shorter. Happily, these are the exceptions and not the rule.

The recent recession has underscored the importance of productivity for all of us. Countless companies whose productivity had slipped could not weather the prolonged downturn. Major companies across the globe, many of them banks, had to be bailed out by government. Some of their operations were divided into "good" and "bad," and they were forced to jettison assets and people in order to be saved. Those companies that had paid attention to their operations fared much better, and it is those companies that have been best positioned to reap the rewards of economic expansion, at whatever rate it comes.

Productivity – getting more output from a given set of inputs – is a noble calling.* Yet, for something so important, productivity is not as well understood as it needs to be. Of course, we know that the quantity of output, and thus the productivity of any process, depends on a host of things, many related to the engineering of the process: the technology used, how much capital equipment is applied to the task, the quality of materials used, the quality of the process itself, the product design, the efficient allocation/scheduling of resources, the education and training of the workforce, worker effort, and … management. However, the precise impacts of these factors are not well known. They are not well known because disentangling the various impacts is very difficult to do. For this reason, economists have traditionally treated productivity as a residual. That is, when the growth of output is stripped of the growth due to the factors of production, typically labor and capital, what is left is assumed to be the growth of productivity. Treating productivity as a residual, however,

---

* The most common measure of productivity is labor productivity, defined as output per worker-hour. It is the easiest measure to gather data for and the most consistent. It is the measure that governments usually report. One could also consider machine productivity (output per machine-hour), which is a measure that makes sense for processes with little labor input and considerable machine input. Likewise, one can think of material productivity (output per unit of material input). A summary measure of productivity, total factor productivity (output per unit of a composite input of labor, capital, materials, and energy), can be calculated, although typically with some difficulty. Although it has theoretical appeal, it is not routinely calculated and does not lend itself well to managerial interpretation.

is fraught with problems of measurement, and heroic assumptions are typically needed in order to interpret the results cleanly.[4]

Of course, managers – and orthopedic surgeons – cannot treat productivity as a residual. Managers are under constant pressure to unlock the secrets to productivity growth at their companies and to keep productivity growing year in and year out. It is for these harried managers, searching for any way to boost productivity, and those who sympathize with them, that this book was written. It is devoted to explaining how managers can fulfill their obligations to get the most out of company processes of all kinds, from the processes that fabricate and deliver a company's products and services to the processes that create new products or keep track of the company's cash. Getting the most out of a set of resources is not easy. With uninspired management, even a well-conceived engineering of the process can fall well short of expectations. Unfortunately, companies fall victim to uninspired management more frequently than they should. And, to make matters worse, the path to enhanced productivity contains many traps and pitfalls into which managers over the years have inadvertently fallen.

TRAPS AND PITFALLS

Before we can move on to what really matters for productivity, it makes sense to confront these traps and pitfalls. For me, they make up my list of the "usual suspects." They describe plausible policies for productivity gain, but in the end, they are not the sure, satisfying steps to take to keep productivity growing. They can work sometimes, but they do not provide the most fruitful ways to think about productivity.

No. 1. Chopping heads

When costs are deemed too high, the frequent management reaction is that "heads have to roll." It's a seductive notion. People's wages and salaries are certainly a highly visible cost. And, it's relatively easy to order an across-the-board cut of 10 percent to a company's departmental budgets. Managers at lower levels, closer to the real action, can figure out who is "excess" and how the work can be reapportioned.

It can work, but chopping heads is certainly a blunt instrument. It does not ensure that a process is accomplished any differently. The same inefficiencies that got the company into trouble could still persist. And, after a while in many companies, the people let go months ago come creeping back, perhaps as consultants, perhaps in new jobs that get approved once sales start to climb again. Nothing really gets "fixed" and morale within the company can take a hit.[5]

There are variations on this theme. Organization charts get examined carefully and are redrawn. Spans of control are widened. Some functions are centralized. But, too often, not much is done that removes cost for the long term.

And, what is our orthopedic surgeon to do? Which heads roll? Nurses and staff in the operating room? Office staff? It's not at all clear.

No. 2. Automation

Automation, or, more generally, capital-for-labor substitution, is a classic means of seeking productivity gain. Equipment, often of the latest vintage, is installed and various workers, typically direct labor wage earners, are eliminated as a result. The engineering justifications can be persuasive, as presumably high-cost direct labor and the overhead that applies to that direct labor are removed.

Automation surely can improve productivity, but it is not a surefire way to do so. The traps with automation can be subtle. First, of course, the direct labor that was targeted in the capital appropriation request may not be removed but may instead simply be shifted elsewhere. The advertised capital-for-labor substitution thus may not actually occur. Even if the direct labor itself is removed, however, the overhead attached to it may not be. In many companies, overhead is allocated to a product via its direct labor component, and the overhead allocated may be easily 300 percent or more of the direct labor cost. What does such an overhead allocation consist of? A lot of it is engineering of various types – product design, industrial and process engineering, quality control and testing – plus supervision, space, logistics, and utilities, among other things. Do the expenditures for these things really tie to the quantity of direct labor used in the process? Certainly not now, if they ever did. Much of the engineering in a company is completely divorced from the labor content found in its products. It is far-fetched to think that reducing direct labor via automation will, at the same time, reduce this overhead expense. New equipment is simply not going to reduce many other costs, particularly the personnel component of overhead. What is more, automation can itself be more costly and more inflexible than anticipated. And, automation may, in fact, trigger expense elsewhere, expense that was ignored by the capital appropriation request that ushered the automation into the company.

These foregoing arguments act to diminish the impact that capital-for-labor substitution may have on the company's cost saving. An even more damning criticism is that, in some instances, capital-for-labor substitution, and even automation, may not have much impact on productivity itself. I have too often heard plant managers lamenting the purchase of some new piece of equipment – "I don't know why they made me purchase this thing," or words to that effect. More often than not, the new equipment was not integrated well with the rest of the production process, and it showed with increased levels of inventory.

We have all seen instances where automation was regarded as the company's silver bullet for cost reduction and/or quality improvement but where the reality was painfully short of that vision. The best known example is probably the $40–45 billion that General Motors spent in the 1980s, under Chairman Roger Smith, to catch up with the Japanese, much of it devoted to robotics and other factory automation. The catch-up never happened, expenses only grew, and there were a myriad of better uses for the money. In fact, GM's former CFO noted in the mid-1980s that the money the company poured into automation could have purchased both Toyota and Nissan at the then prevailing stock prices.[6]

But, mistakes with automation occur all the time. It is hard to be disciplined when it comes to something new and shiny. And, here again, what is our orthopedic surgeon to do? There are new medical instruments developed all the time, but a knee replacement operation is not going to be automated any time soon.

No. 3. Efficiency measures

For many companies, the daily measure used to proxy productivity – the metric that is managed – is an efficiency measure. Labor efficiency, the ratio of actual labor input to some preset standard labor input, is common. If a worker's actual time beats the standard, labor efficiency tops 100 percent. An allied metric is machine or capacity utilization that looks at actual time in use as a fraction of the total time available. The presumption is that higher levels of efficiency, either of labor or of equipment, aids productivity.

Let's examine machine utilization. The trouble with such a measure is that the company does not get paid when any one machine is used. Rather, the company gets paid when the service is delivered or when the factory ships its products. What happens with a single machine, no matter what its cost, is irrelevant, unless that machine is the bottleneck for the entire operation. If it is, then, we need to lavish attention on it. Tracking machine or capacity utilization does not help us for productivity; it only helps us if we are interested in adding new capacity or, perhaps, shedding old capacity. Indeed, for many types of production process, machine utilization should be low. Job shops, for example, typically run low machine utilization rates on many machines as a matter of course. Indeed, it is only for the high-volume, continuous flow operation that, in essence, operates as one big machine, that machine utilization makes much sense as a measure of the factory's performance.

Similarly, the labor efficiency measure is a flawed one, if productivity is the goal. Whether a labor efficiency measure is high or low depends critically on the preset labor standard. If the standard is set looser than it should be, labor efficiency is artificially high. Whatever the labor efficiency measure is, however, it need not be related to the ratio of output to input (productivity). Labor efficiency does not tell us if the task being measured is well designed and adds true value to the product. For some people such a measure does not make much sense at all. Should our orthopedic surgeon be subject to a labor efficiency measure? What would it really tell us?

Consider the following evidence from one of my past studies. Over a 30-month time period, labor efficiency data were gathered for five factories of the same company by its accounting department. Also gathered were the factories' plant-wide productivity measures (good, classic output per unit of labor input measures). Of the 29 month-to-month changes during that 30-month period, the times when the labor efficiency measure and the productivity measure moved together were counted, as were the times when the two measures moved in opposite directions, that is, when labor efficiency went up and productivity went down or vice versa. If labor efficiency were really a good way to get at productivity gains and to lower costs, then one should expect that whenever labor efficiency went up, productivity would follow and that when it went down, productivity would drop. In reality, for much of the time, that wasn't the case for the five factories. The percentage of time when there were mismatches in the direction of change varied from 28% of the time, at the low end, to 62% of the time, at the high end. Specifically, for the five factories, mismatch percentages of 28%, 31%, 38%, 45%, and 62% occurred. Labor efficiency and productivity are not highly correlated.[7]

Related to the issue of labor efficiency is time and motion study, the creation of Frederick Taylor (the time study portion) and Frank Gilbreth (the motion study portion) from roughly a century ago.[8] Time and motion study is one of the tools of industrial engineering and a principal means by which a labor standard can get set. While there is nothing inherently wrong with the careful (or, as Taylor would have put it, the "scientific") study of a worker's job to determine the time standard that should be attached to it, in practice, doing this well is anything but easy. Having a job "rated" is not something that workers relish and securing worker cooperation for something that might end up cutting a worker's pay can be difficult. Trying to compensate for any "dogging it" that a worker engages in can be very subjective. Moreover, unless the job has been well studied to eliminate any non-value-added movement, setting a time standard may enshrine waste in the process. Time and motion study can also lead to a concentration on the "trees" (i.e., individual jobs) and a neglect of the "forest" (i.e., whether the entire process, as conceived, is the best way to operate). Time and motion study itself is thus no panacea for productivity woes.

Efficiency measures are but the most visible of the host of problems stemming from reliance on traditional accounting systems for productivity improvement. If costs are to be reduced, pulling out the income statement or the balance sheet is almost an instinctive reaction for so many managers. Perusal of labor cost, or materials purchased, or overhead can lead to actions such as investment in automation or beating up on vendors. These won't get a company very far. Accounting is always after-the-fact. What is needed is real-time assessment of what to do and how to do it. Resist the urge to look at the accounting numbers as a source of inspiration; the answer doesn't lie there.

No. 4. Economies of scale

It is so tempting for managers in larger companies to think that their costs are low, and thus their productivity high, simply because they are large and thereby enjoy economies of scale. The fact that there are diseconomies of scale that rival the better-known economies of scale eludes them. These managers look to the fixed costs that can be spread across the significant volume of their production, like so much butter, to render their unit costs low. But, is this advantage long lasting? If, for any reason, the high volumes melt away, the unit costs of the company become as high, if not higher, than anyone else's. The advantage is simply an accounting artifact; it is not rooted in any fundamental, long-enduring difference in how the service is delivered or how the product is manufactured.

Scale can come in "lumps" and those lumps can be expensive to duplicate. Adding more capacity can thus be tough for larger companies and put them at a disadvantage. Furthermore, these "lumps" of capacity can be inflexible and can leave the larger company less able to meet product variety and delivery demands from customers.

Enduring economies of scale are, in fact, scarce. Some operations have geometries that help them. For example, processes that use vats and tanks (think brewing) are at an advantage because their capital costs are mainly tied to the two-dimensional surface areas of those vats and tanks, while their production output is tied to their three-dimensional volumes. These instances are not common, however. Scale does not mean much to most operations. It certainly doesn't mean anything to our orthopedic surgeon. He has to work one knee or one hip at a time. No real economies of scale for him.

For much of the 1970s, a variant of scale economies, the learning curve, was the rage. Texas Instruments became famous for its use. The learning curve, sometimes termed the experience curve, noted that costs in many industries seemed to go down in real terms in a very regular way as the cumulative volume of production increased. The mandate, then, was to push volume because costs would go down as a result. What was never so clear about the learning curve, however, was the mechanism for the reduction of those costs. What was it about volume, per se, that lowered costs? The answer, of course, is that volume itself was never the driver. Rather, it was all of the other levers that one could pull that led to the cost reduction. Not surprisingly, the learning curve as a management tool has faded from the scene.

Most differences in productivity that are in any way tied to production volumes involve the ability of larger producers to use technologies that are superior. However, for the most part, these distinctions are constantly changing and, more often than not, they are more related to the existing portfolio of technological possibilities than they are related to scale itself. Any company that thinks it has an advantage because of scale risks falling by the wayside as more clever companies figure out new technologies and better ways to produce that do not rely at all on scale.

No. 5. Systems

For decades, prognosticators have touted the influence of computers and how they were revolutionizing business. For many businesses, this has meant investment in ERP (Enterprise Resource Planning) systems, and before them, MRP (Material Requirements Planning) and MRP II (Manufacturing Resource Planning) software. The investments made in such systems have been significant, and companies such as SAP and PeopleSoft have made their names with such software.

The allure of such investments is strong, especially when they are replacing ancient, patched systems that cannot easily talk to one another and for which amendment is difficult because few people, if any, are familiar with the original code. Yet, the cost of new systems is often much more than companies originally estimated and the time it takes to implement them much longer. Sometimes, too, the new system enshrines past waste in the process. And, for some operations, systems mean relatively little. They do not mean much to our orthopedic surgeon.

To boot, the impact of computers and computer systems on productivity has been elusive. In fact, it is sometimes referred to as the Solow "productivity paradox," after MIT economist and Nobel laureate, Robert Solow, who quipped, "You can see the computer age everywhere but in the productivity statistics."[9] More recent evidence has found some positive impact on productivity from the introduction of computers, but it has been with a significant lag.[10]

"THE USUAL SUSPECTS" ARE SUSPECT

These are the traps and pitfalls that managers often succumb to. If one were looking for productivity, trotting out a lineup of these "usual suspects" is not the way to find it. What's wrong with this thinking? In short, the "usual suspects" all focus on the factors of production. They go after labor cost, thinking that the way forward is to lighten, or remove entirely, the expense that labor represents. They go after capital cost, thinking that capital equipment has to be humming all the time in order to pay for itself. They go after materials costs, thinking that the problem lies elsewhere, with their suppliers, and not with them. If only these factors of production could be used more efficiently, so the thinking goes, then productivity would increase. It's an approach that relies on the company's accounts to show the way to improvement. If costs are high, it is reasoned, then labor costs or materials costs or overhead costs need to come down. It's as plain as the numbers on the income statement or the balance sheet.

The result, unfortunately, is suboptimization. Only when the process completes its product or service – only when things "ship" – does the process reap any rewards. One worker at one workstation doesn't pay for himself, and one piece of equipment working by itself doesn't pay for itself either. Only when the operation "ships" its output to the marketplace does the money come in. Focusing on the factors of production or on what the accounts can show limits us. We need to dismiss this lineup of the usual suspects. Productivity is not about the busyness of the factors of production. Busyness does not help the surgeon position the knee or hip implant and fix it in place. We need to abandon such ideas and think about productivity in a different and novel way.

This book divides into two parts. The first part, the first three chapters, is devoted to an alternative to the usual suspects. It examines a fresher way to think about productivity and makes the case for why this new way is the best way for doing so, using both contemporary and historical data. The second part of this book, the subsequent six chapters, introduces a wide range of situations – real cases – that scream for productivity improvement, and then it uses this fresher way of thinking to help the managers involved to get out of the muck they are mired in. These cases involve operations in a variety of settings: the manufacturing and service sectors, the supply chain, new product development, outsourcing, and strategy. My goal is unvarying – to spur you to think differently about processes and their productivity and thus to help your companies get and stay more productive.

2   Swift, even flow

Productivity has long been studied. What can possibly be a different and novel way of thinking about it? What alternative is there other than making the factors of production more efficient? How else can or should you think of things? Here is the alternative that I hope by the end of this book will become second nature to you: concentrate on the flow of materials or information through the process. Abandon a focus on whom or what does the work and how busy they might be. Instead, redirect your focus to what gets worked on. Specifically, *become* the items being worked on and think about making the flow of those items – materials or information – as quick as it can be and with as little variation as possible. *Throughput time* and *variation* capture the things that matter for productivity; the only things that matter. You want swift, even flow.

There, I've said it. Swift, even flow. The remainder of this book is devoted to explaining and expanding on the implications of these three words.[1]

It may seem strange to abandon a focus on the labor doing the work when labor productivity – output per worker-hour – is the typical measure used, but that is exactly what I am advocating. By reducing throughput time and variation, labor productivity (or any other definition of productivity) will increase. Moreover, output per worker-hour will not increase if either throughput time or variation is not also reduced. This may appear incongruous now, but I hope that, by the end of this book, this approach will seem perfectly reasonable.

Let's begin by laying some groundwork. First, let's think about the "even" portion of swift, even flow. "Even" refers to the reduction of variation, of all kinds: quality, quantities, and timing.

VARIATION IN QUALITY

Quality in operations is, thanks to generations of contributors, one of the aspects of processes that we know the most about. We stand on the shoulders of quality giants from Walter Shewhart, who created the process control chart at Bell Labs in the 1920s and 1930s, to his disciples, W. Edwards Deming and Joseph Juran, who led the evolution of quality management in the years after World War II and provided the early teaching to Japanese business, to the raft of major Japanese contributors such as Kaoru Ishikawa, Genichi Taguchi, and Shigeo Shingo. It has been proven to all of us that the payoff for quality – defined best, for me, as "conformance to specifications, as valued by customers" – is great. It may even be "free," in Philip Crosby's sense, namely, that quality pays for itself. Invest in lowering defects and you save the many costs of failure (e.g., rework, scrap, warranties, after-sales service, poor product reputation) and of inspection.[2]

This book is not the place to expound on, or even summarize, what we now know about quality management. Much is readily available and it is well ingrained in many businesses. The widespread impact of programs such as Six Sigma is testament to the power of the tools that the quality gurus have given us. Not that all of business applies these tools diligently. There is still much to do. However, the path ahead for many companies has been staked out, and it can be followed by those who understand its power.

The important thing, for our purposes, is that variation in quality – instances of rework, scrap, warranty costs, and more – saps capacity from any process and adds expense. If quality is "free," then variable quality is expensive. When the product or service is not produced in conformance with specifications, the process bogs down and capacity suffers. The recovery from poor quality can be costly. Productivity suffers. When processes are not foolproofed – what many regard as the low cost way to great quality – then cost can build up. Variation in quality is to be avoided and, fortunately, we have the tools to make it so. Questioning what can be done to improve quality is always fair game for managers at every level.

The American Productivity Center, created in 1977 by C. Jackson Grayson, a businessman, academic, and former price control commissioner within the Nixon Administration, began its work by measuring productivity and taking a lead in studying what the Japanese were doing. Grayson became a cochair in the establishment of the Malcolm Baldrige National Quality Award, and the American Productivity Center then began including more quality management in its training. In 1988, the Center changed its name to the American Productivity and Quality Center. It did so, to quote its website, "because it is almost impossible to improve productivity without improving quality." Amen.

VARIATION IN QUANTITIES AND TIMING

Less well known to many is variation in either quantities or timing. This kind of variation can occur either with the demand on the process – what the order says about how much of what needs to be produced and when – or with the process itself – when the individual steps of the process are accomplished, how long it takes to do them, and how much of what is produced. Such variability can result from the equipment or the labor input for the process or from the materials and other resources employed. There can be variation as well in the mix of what gets produced (how much of what) and when that mix gets produced. Thus, variation can affect both the demand and the supply sides of the process.

For me, the best way to understand these sources of variation is to explore the queuing phenomenon. Figure 2.1 captures the essence of the issue.[3]

This figure captures the truism that the time a customer spends waiting for a product or service increases as the capacity utilization of the process increases. Moreover, as the capacity utilization approaches 100 percent, the wait time soars at a faster and faster pace. This phenomenon is inescapable; it can be considered a law of nature.

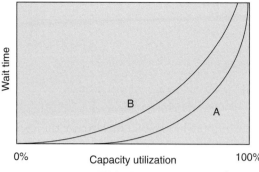

FIGURE 2.1 Wait time vs. capacity utilization

This relationship can describe a wide variety of situations, some writ small and some writ large. We all observe it when we drive on major, limited access highways. The flow of traffic can be moving smoothly and well ... until relatively few additional cars enter and then traffic starts to slow dramatically and the spacing between cars becomes erratic. In some cities, there are stop lights at the entrance ramps simply to slow the addition of new vehicles so that the highway does not come to a crawl. We observe this phenomenon at the fast food restaurant which is humming along, providing meals to customers quickly ... until the bus carrying the touring old age pensioners arrives and the capacity utilization of the restaurant is severely taxed. Wait times explode.

We even see this phenomenon at the level of the national economy. Periodically we hear about the capacity utilization of the US economy. A typical figure is about 80 percent. And, when the figure rises to 85 percent or more, you hear that economists become worried. Why? Economists get worried about inflation when capacity utilization rises that high. How are capacity utilization and inflation related? When wait times for products and services rise, some customers are willing to bid higher in order to jump the queue and receive them sooner. Inflation can result. Wait time and capacity utilization pervade our economy.

If the relationship between wait time and capacity utilization really is a "law of nature" then how should managers react? Is there

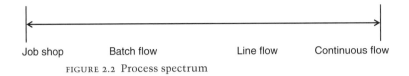

FIGURE 2.2 Process spectrum

anything that can be done? Consider that in Figure 2.1, there are two lines, one marked A and one marked B. Which one describes the better scenario? Line A is clearly superior to Line B in the sense that the wait times described by Line A are always less than the wait times described by Line B for the same level of capacity utilization. Any customer would prefer to be served by A rather than B.

Suppose that A and B represent different processes. In fact, for the sake of clarity, let us say that they are different manufacturing processes. What constitutes the difference between them? Let's take a step back and reflect on the major types of manufacturing process.

COPING WITH VARIATION: DIFFERENT MANUFACTURING PROCESSES

It is fairly standard practice to think about four major categories of manufacturing process to describe how products are made in repeated fashion. (Ignore, at least for the time being, the project that typically produces a unique, large-scale product.) The four process types are: job shop, batch operation, assembly line (or line flow), and continuous flow. They can be arrayed on a spectrum, as in Figure 2.2.

1. The job shop. At one end of the process spectrum is the job shop. It is the most flexible process for creating a wide variety of products in significant quantities. Machine shops, tool and die shops, and many plastic molding operations are job shops, working to fulfill particular customer orders that can vary greatly in the quantities demanded and when those quantities are due.

The job shop layout groups similar equipment together, primarily because no single product generates enough sales volume to justify the creation of a product-specific array of equipment.[4] Often a job shop has a diverse array of equipment and capabilities to choose from.

The flow of material in a job shop can be complex and far from straight line in character. Materials can be routed in many directions and can loop back to the same equipment later in the processing cycle. With each order (job) capable of such complexity, it is absolutely essential that information on how the order is to be routed through the factory, what is to be done to it at each step of the way, and how much time and effort is actually spent on it, follow the job. The job shop lives by its information flows. This information is vital, because job shops typically bid for work. Without good information on costs, times (run times, setup times, labor content times), routings, and process steps, a job shop would be seriously disadvantaged. Thus, a job shop can be characterized by great variation in its materials flows (i.e., what can be produced, the quantities that are produced, the timing of orders, and the time to complete those orders) but rigidity in the flow of its information.

Job shops can be very profitable, however, as customers are typically willing to pay for the flexibility and customization that the job shop offers.

2. The continuous flow process. At the other extreme of the process spectrum lies the continuous flow process. Many high-volume consumer goods and commodities are made by continuous flow processes – oil refining, food processing, papermaking. The continuous flow process's most significant characteristic is how materials move through it – hardly ever stopping, moving constantly from one process operation to another. With a continuous flow process, one can estimate realistically how long it takes to transform raw materials into a specific product, and that time is often staggeringly short. Work-in-process inventories exist at well-defined levels and are low relative to the value of output the continuous flow process generates. Capital investments and automation, on the other hand, are often higher than those of other processes, especially when contrasted with the workforce employed. Layouts are frequently product-specific, typically with a straight-line character to them, as the products in the making go from one operation to another. The range of products that a continuous flow process can make, on the other hand, is narrow. It can only produce what its process is designed to produce.

Continuous flow processes can be very productive and very profitable, assuming normal sales levels. Only when sales levels plunge is the profitability of the continuous flow process in jeopardy.

3. The batch flow process. One step toward the continuous flow process from the job shop is the batch flow process. The job shop and the batch flow process have a good deal in common. Their layouts are similar, with equipment grouped by function rather than by product.[5] The product is regarded as moving from department to department within the factory. A batch flow operation depends on information such as routings and process steps, and tracks costs and times spent. However, batch flow processes typically have a set menu of products that they produce, frequently, in set quantities (lot sizes). The batch flow operation is thus somewhat more standardized than the job shop, particularly as it relates to routings and costs.

While the job shop usually operates to fulfill an outside customer's order by an agreed upon due date and in whatever quantity is ordered, the batch flow operation usually produces in established lot sizes that move into an inventory from which further production or final customer orders are filled. Batch flow processes are commonplace, especially when one considers all the times "fabrication" must be done. Examples of batch flow processes include much of the chemical industry, semiconductor fabrication, apparel, much of the steel industry, and huge chunks of the metal bending, metal forming, and metal machining industries.

4. The line flow process. Between the batch flow and continuous flow processes, along the process spectrum, lies the line flow process. In reality it lies closer to the continuous flow process because it presents some substantive distinctions from the batch flow. The line flow process is most popularly exemplified by the moving assembly line that one finds in the auto industry, but it is also found in a host of other assembly industries such as consumer electronics and computers. In contrast to the batch flow process, the line flow process exhibits the following characteristics:

- A product-specific layout with different pieces of equipment placed in sequence ready to perform operations on the product. There are, of course, mixed model lines that can produce distinctly different models of the basic product, but the more diverse the products made, the less satisfactory the line becomes at producing them.
- The product moves readily from one operation to another so that there is little work-in-process inventory, nor is there a stockroom in the product's path. This also means that there is a great need to examine the "balance" of the process so that the different tasks to be accomplished take roughly the same amount of time to perform and have the same capacities, not just over weeks of time, but over minutes of time.
- The paperwork needs of the line flow process are less demanding than the batch flow and much less than the job shop. Routings are not needed and operations sheets can frequently be simplified, if not eliminated altogether. The need for tracking labor and machine inputs to particular products/parts also fades away.
- In contrast to the continuous flow operation, the line flow is somewhat more flexible, and generally less automated and more labor intensive.

As one proceeds across the spectrum from job shop to continuous flow, one tends to move from a highly individualized, flexible process to one that is much more inflexible in the products it can make but, at the same time, much more productive and efficient in how it makes them.

BACK TO VARIATION IN QUANTITIES AND TIMING

With this background of different manufacturing processes, let us return to considering the distinctions between Lines A and B within Figure 2.1. Assume that Lines A and B represent equally well-managed processes. Why are they different?

Variation makes them different. Line A could well represent a continuous flow operation or a line flow operation, whereas Line B could represent a job shop or a batch flow operation. The job shop, in particular, inherently suffers from more variation. Orders for jobs can come in at any time and for widely varying quantities with widely varying due dates. The steps that must be accomplished to fulfill the order can also vary dramatically so that the routings of materials throughout the job shop can be vastly different and the times spent on each job at each workstation can vary greatly, too. Thus, the variation in quantities and timing for the job shop involve both the orders coming to it and the equipment and processes within it.[6]

Such is much less the case with the continuous flow operation. There is very little variation to it. It is geared to create nearly identical products in high volumes.

Thus, it is perfectly natural for us to expect that wait times for job shops and batch flow operations will be much longer than wait times for continuous flow or line flow operations, for any level of capacity utilization. Alternatively, for any level of wait time for customers, one should expect that the capacity utilization of the job shop or batch operation should be less than the capacity utilization of the continuous or line flow operation. Put another way, when you enter a job shop, you should expect to see idle equipment. If you don't, you know for sure that wait times are high. You can't have both high utilization and low wait times, especially not in a job shop or batch operation.

This is hard for many managers. Akin to nature abhorring a vacuum, managers abhor idle capacity. The reflex is to squeeze in just one more job. But, like gravity, the relationship between wait time and capacity utilization is a law of nature. The only thing that you can do to improve things is to try to reduce the variation in quantities and timing so that you look more like Line A and less like Line B. In either case, however, the most effective way to reduce wait time is to reduce capacity utilization, to come back down the curve, perhaps by adding capacity or perhaps by withdrawing work from the queue of work-in-process.[7] Reducing variation will help, but it can be costly and it doesn't have nearly the impact that reducing capacity utilization can have, especially if that capacity utilization is high to begin with (that is, when capacity utilization is close to 100 percent).

The continuous flow operation is the paragon of productivity in the manufacturing world. Its productivity can be remarkable. When, years ago, Japan was the feared competitor that was going to take over, the United States did not have to fear that Japan would put continuous flow operations out of business. Rather it was the batch/line flow hybrid operations (e.g., parts fabrication followed by an assembly line) such as are found in the auto industry that suffered. And, even today, with China known as the manufacturing workshop of the world, continuous flow operations have little to fear. Low wages are relatively insignificant to the continuous flow process; China cannot make up with low wages what it would lose in extra logistics costs delivering the products of high-volume continuous flow operations. The low variation in the quantities produced and in the timing of production helps to make the continuous flow operation as productive as it is.

VARIATION FOR SERVICES

The discussion above has referred to variation in quantities and timing in manufacturing. Of course, the same phenomenon exists for service operations. Indeed, variation in services is common because, for many, the distinguishing characteristic for services is customer interaction with the process. Customers, apart from being demanding, can be disruptive, erratic, and ill-informed. If services are to be well managed, service processes need to cope effectively with their customers.

Services may not be able to remove as much variation in quantities and timing as can occur in manufacturing. The splendid isolation of the factory has its advantages. Nevertheless, service customers can be managed in ways to reduce variation – think reservation systems, pricing to shift activity away from peak times, rewards for behavior that helps the service operation cope, and disincentives for behavior that does not. However, these tactics do not always work, and the service operation may have to increase capacity or redesign its services or target particularly attractive customers if it is not to suffer too much from the deleterious features of variation.[8]

"EVEN" IS THE GOAL

Reducing unwanted, uncompensated-for variation – in quality, quantities, and timing – should be a goal of any process seeking to become more productive. Japanese operations, first, and then operations everywhere, have convinced us that the pursuit of quality is essential to good productivity. The very best factories and service operations across the world are those that practice great quality management. The link between quality and productivity is something that experience has shown us.

The link between variation in either quantities or timing and productivity is easier to prove. Indeed, mathematical models can show how the variation in either the timing of orders or in the timing of process steps saps capacity from the process and thus reduces productivity. Similarly, variation in quantities moving through a process can do the same. Process simulation models can show how tinkering with timing or quantities, or making the variation of that timing or quantities greater, can lower productivity. Such models can show how introducing buffers (typically buffer inventories) can help to lessen the impact of the variation and how changing the statistical distribution that characterizes the variation (lowering the standard deviation of the distribution so as to bunch the distribution closer to its center) can improve productivity. Still, we cannot remove all variation in quantities or timing from a process, even if we can well understand the nature of that variation and its distribution.[9]

Such an insight can also be intuitive. We all have experienced situations where we were working on something – and feeling productive about it – when we were interrupted by someone or something, be it in person or by phone call or whatever. Getting back to work, and at the same level of productivity, was then hard to do. We all perform tasks better when we are not interrupted and when what we are working on is more consistent, with only small changes in character or quantities. Reducing variation, then, should have some real appeal to us as a mechanism for improving productivity.

More examples of variation in quality, quantities, and timing, and how to cope with them, will come later in this book.

SWIFT FLOW

The other key element to productivity is swift flow. The assertion, here, is that the faster materials or information flow through a process, the more productive that process is. The goal is to reduce the throughput time – the "clock" time that tracks the time the materials (or information) are in the process, from start to finish. Throughput time measures how long it takes, by the clock or by the calendar, to produce the good or service from scratch.

Throughput time differs from the commonly used term, lead time. Lead time can mean a lot of things – the time to respond to a customer order, the time it takes suppliers to get materials to the operation, the time that is planned for in any MRP (or ERP) system used, among other things. Throughput time, by contrast, deals solely with the clock time that it takes to produce the product or service, starting from scratch. It's a measure of all of the value that has to be added to the product or service and all of the wasted time that gets associated with that added value. It is often a big figure, longer by far than any lead time quoted by the company. It's that way because there is so much non-value-added, wasted time when materials (or information) simply sit. Often, especially for job shops and batch operations, 95 percent or more of a product's throughput time is spent waiting for something to happen. And, as we shall see, that waiting time can be very costly.

And, throughput time is not the time that the process could get an expedited order through, either. That "rush" time isn't at all standard and expected. It is not a true measure of the process. After

all, you want to improve the throughput time of the standard process so that you do not even need to contemplate expediting, for any
order.

SWIFT FLOW AND WASTE

If materials (or information) travel through a process quickly, with
little or no stopping, then it is clear that value is being added. Waste
is much less likely. But, what is waste anyway? Shigeo Shingo's classic list of seven types of waste[10] is a good place to start:

- **Overproduction** – produce only what's needed and not any more than is
  needed.
- **Waiting** – everything is coordinated so that neither materials nor labor
  nor equipment waits long.
- **Transportation** – layouts are rational and effective so that materials do
  not have to travel far between process steps.
- **Unnecessary processing steps** – good manufacturing engineering
  eliminates superfluous steps in the process or unneeded moves into and
  out of a storeroom.
- **Inventories** – lower inventories mean less carrying cost and less
  obsolescence.
- **Motion** – good industrial engineering limits difficult motions by the
  workforce.
- **Defects** – good quality management means lower rework and scrap.

When waste prevails, defects and inventories accumulate and
it is costly to track down and remedy defects and to carry inventory.
The throughput time lengthens when inventory mounts and as time
is taken to find each defect and rework it or to produce a new unit
after a bad unit has been scrapped.

Reducing throughput time does not mean working faster or
running machines faster. Such work tempts bad quality, and, if
throughput time is measured properly, with rework time or time
to make up for scrapped product factored in, then bad quality will
always lengthen throughput time. Rather, throughput time comes
down when wait time is removed and when the flow is rationalized

so that it takes minimum time to move from one value-added step of the process to another. Inefficient layouts, unneeded transportation and storage, overengineered systems, and unnecessary processing or decision-making steps add to throughput time. Improve on the layout or remove the unnecessary step and throughput time will drop and productivity will increase. When bad quality is discovered and remedied, then throughput time will be reduced as well, and productivity will gain.

A reduction in throughput time also means that bottlenecks have to be identified and dealt with. Bottlenecks can be fixed in location and encountered every time the product is produced. In that case, attention to a bottleneck typically results in a capital investment to break it, either with add-ons to existing equipment or with new equipment and labor. If an investment cannot easily be made, then the bottleneck step needs to be showered with preventive maintenance and scheduled fully. After all, the bottleneck determines how much the entire process produces and everything needs to be done to make sure that it is not "down" any longer than can be helped.

However, bottlenecks can also be movable. That is, for different production schedules, with widely different demands on equipment or people, the bottleneck may shift from one part of the operation to another. Given this, attention needs to be paid to the schedule of production so that it can be smoothed out to the extent that demand permits. Production plans that are "level," with little variation in quantities and timing, are to be prized. And, interruptions due to expediting or engineering changes only serve to augment the effect of the bottleneck.

All of this is easier said than done, of course, but the goal is clear. Throughput times need to be reduced, and eliminating variation can be helpful to that goal.

Quicker throughput times have some other, very distinct advantages.

- Reaction time to the market can be quick. If demands are highly changeable, then the shorter the throughput time, the more likely that they can be met. Customers often value speed to market and they are frequently willing to pay a premium for fast response. Those processes that can be quick are at an advantage over those that rely solely on finished goods inventory.

- Overheads can be lower. Why? What does overhead do, anyway? Lots of overhead is devoted to the problems that can occur in a process. Much engineering talent that actually touches the process is devoted to remedying something wrong. The product may need attention (e.g., quality engineering). Or, the process may need fixing (e.g., process and industrial engineering). Schedules may need to be adjusted (e.g., production planning, production control) or inventory tracked down (e.g., inventory control), or, worse yet, expediting done as the way to save an order or a customer. What is the clearest indication that the process is under stress and overhead is being expended? When its throughput time grows. The faster the materials routinely move through the process, the more likely that all is well and the process is working smoothly. The more that materials bog down and throughput time grows, the more likely that the workforce that is classified as overhead is slaving away to fix things that are not working as they should. Improve a process permanently, then, and watch its overhead shrink. There is less for it to do. This is where costs can really be cut.

SWIFT FLOW AND INVENTORIES

The buildup of inventories[*] is an important symptom of something impeding the swift flow of materials through a process, but swift flow and inventories are not inexorably linked. The ties between inventories and throughput time are captured in what is now known as Little's law:

Inventory = Processing rate * Throughput time

Little's law tells us, for example, that the work-in-process inventory within an operation is determined by the processing rate

[*] Throughout this book, whenever I speak about inventories, I am speaking about work-in-process inventories and not either raw materials inventories or finished goods inventories. All of these types of inventory have their place and they all cost money to carry, but the decisions on how much of which type to carry are different. The work-in-process inventory is the one that most affects productivity and it is the one that is under the control of the process. It is the focus for discussion in this book.

of the operation and the throughput time for the materials being worked on. It is an intuitively appealing notion that is independent of the variability of the process.

Little's law assumes that the averages used in the calculation are long-term averages from a stable system. The processing rate is essentially what makes a system stable. If the processing rate stayed the same, then throughput time and work-in-process inventory would be linked directly. Measure inventory and you would also measure throughput time.

But, the processing rate is not something that those wishing to improve productivity want to keep the same. Productivity is enhanced when the processing rate increases. For a given level of inventory, the higher the processing rate, the lower the throughput time. The goal of swift flow, then, is a goal for increasing the processing rate of the operation while keeping inventories low. That rate may or may not depend on the speed of any equipment. It could just as well relate to the elimination of waste within the operation. Consider the tortoise and the hare.

THE TORTOISE AND THE HARE

I find it useful to think in terms of the fable of the tortoise and the hare. In that fable, the hare brags about its speed and ridicules the slow-moving tortoise. The tortoise is provoked to challenge the hare to a race. The hare quickly takes the lead, but, well ahead, pauses to nap. Meanwhile, the slow but steady tortoise keeps moving to the finish line, and crosses it before the hare wakes from its nap.

In my industrial interpretation of the fable, the hare's factory is filled with fast equipment but it is not well maintained. Quality can be compromised. Machine setups and changeovers are lengthy. Materials wait in long queues before they are worked on. The layout is scattered, with much movement into and out of the storeroom. The production schedule is stop-and-start, with lots of interruptions for expediting and change. Rework is common. Work-in-process inventory is piled up everywhere. Communication among the workforce is minimal.

The tortoise's factory is totally different. It is slow but steady, always in motion. Value is added all the time and every aspect of the process is able to perform perfectly when called on. Great quality is an integral part of the process. The equipment is run at slower than its rated capacity and it is well maintained, always able to run. Setups and changeovers are studied and improved so that they can be made faster. Materials do not wait long to be worked on. Layouts are compact and rational, and materials move economically between operations. The production schedule is smooth, with few interruptions. Little, if any, rework is required. Work-in-process inventory is low. And, everyone gets involved in studying and improving the operation. Aesop would have made a fantastic plant manager.

The hare scampers all over the place. There appears to be lots to do, and certainly lots of troubleshooting to engage in. The tortoise, on the other hand, is all about swift, even flow. The tortoise's operation is productive because the non-value-added steps have been eliminated. Everything is rational and thought through. In essence, the tortoise gets to run a much shorter race than the hare.

What is more, the faster the flow of the process, the more productive the process is. Managing the flow of goods or materials is the one best way to earn money throughout any supply chain (see Figure 2.3). The faster the flow, the more money can be made, both by cutting costs and by increasing revenues. However, managing the flow of materials or goods through a process requires managing the backward flow of information that starts at the customer and comes back up the supply chain, eventually coming back up to the suppliers. The tortoise cannot operate independently. The customers at the finish line must always be in view so that the tortoise's factory can adapt to their needs.

SOME EXAMPLES

At this point, it makes sense to start talking about some familiar examples, to anchor our understanding of swift, even flow and how it leads to productivity.

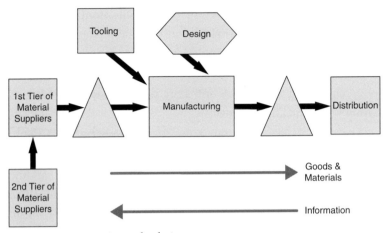

FIGURE 2.3 A supply chain

1   Southwest Airlines and easyJet

The pioneer in low-cost air travel in the United States has long been Southwest Airlines. Its newer imitator in Europe is easyJet. (One could pick Ryanair as well.) Both Southwest and easyJet have historically followed much the same innovative business model. Here are its chief components:

- *One type of aircraft (the Boeing 737 for Southwest and the early years of easyJet and the A320 for the later years of easyJet).* Having only one type of aircraft makes it much easier to do maintenance and the inventory of replacement parts is lower. Planes and crews can substitute for one another without concern for the number of seats or the certification of the crew to a particular aircraft.
- *Fly from less-congested airports.* Not only do less-congested airports have cheaper fees, but the airplanes are less likely to waste time on the ground in long queues of taxiing flights.
- *Point-to-point network (no hubs).* The flights are on their own and do not have to wait for other aircraft. Schedules can be better kept that way and more time can be spent in the air.
- *Aircraft turnarounds in 30 minutes or less.* The ground crew is trained for quick turnarounds. Lots of people pitch in. This means that the aircraft is in the air, earning revenue, for a greater fraction of the day.

Both Southwest and easyJet have been consistently profitable, even with reduced fares. Their planes cost the same as those of other airlines, and the cabin crew is paid comparable wages to the other airlines. Yet, their profits are greater as a result of their higher productivity and lower costs. How did they do it? They reduced both variation and throughput time.

The single type of aircraft reduced variation, particularly in quality and quantities, for maintenance and repair, and for the training and scheduling of crews. The less-congested airports and the point-to-point network helped to reduce variation in timing. The quick turnarounds reduced the throughput time of the service, measured say as the time between touchdowns at destination airports. Southwest and easyJet planes spent a greater fraction of their days in the air, earning revenue. In short, the original business models of Southwest and easyJet followed the precepts of swift, even flow.

Over time, the purity of the business model for Southwest and easyJet, and thus the impact of swift, even flow, has been somewhat compromised. Continued growth in both airlines has meant that they have sought landing rights at more-congested airports. (The variation that an airport such as New York's LaGuardia or Paris' Charles de Gaulle can introduce to the network can be substantial, although, of course, those airports promise lots of customers and the revenues from them can justify the reduced productivity of the aircraft serving them.) Different types of jets have joined the easyJet fleet, making substitutions more difficult. The stresses of high utilization of aircraft and crews have had an effect as well. On-time performance has suffered, particularly for easyJet. In short, there has been some "backsliding" at both carriers, and it has hurt performance, if not profits. When swift, even flow is neglected, the consequences can be substantial.

2 Dell

Dell Computer Corporation has been a modern manufacturing success story forged by Michael Dell's unwavering devotion to collapsing throughput time, from order to delivery. Although Dell's manufacturing might has ebbed somewhat recently, at least relative to the competition, a lot of the early success of the company was directly attributable to its ability to deliver computers to customers quickly. Indeed, if Dell were to ship computers to match the specifications of individual customers – and this was the initial competitive advantage of the company – then it had to streamline its supply chain.

The company started its existence by assembling computers to order from stock components. Other makers at the time were delivering quantities of the same computer configuration in large batches. Dell quickly realized that collapsing the throughput time for manufacturing was not only attractive to the customer, but it was also economical. If the company could speed components through its supply chain, it would not be subject to obsolescence or to the problem of falling components prices. Customers could be charged a then-prevailing price and the company would not have to eat any component price changes in the period between the purchase of those components and their inclusion in a completed product that was paid for. The company could make money on the float between the receipt of its customers' money and the payment of its suppliers. Dell could then also concentrate its marketing on finding out what customers wanted in a computer, and it was not forced to think about how to sell an existing design that had taken months to assemble.

Keeping inventory low has been a mantra at Dell. In the early days of the company, this meant assembling close to the customers, and Dell established several US factories to do so. As computers have become more and more a commodity, Dell has shifted more of its assembly to lower-cost countries. Still, a streamlined supply chain remains a focus. And, although anyone can configure the computer he wants, Dell does try to steer its customers, via better pricing, to choose specific configurations that, in the end, reduce the variation that it has to deal with. Despite some backsliding, swift, even flow has generally prevailed at Dell and does much to explain the current wealth of its founder.

3 Zara

One of the strongest competitors in the retail fashion business is
Zara, part of Inditex, owned by Amancio Ortega Gaona, reputed to
be Spain's wealthiest man. Zara is famed for its "fast fashion." It
can design, manufacture, and distribute a new clothing item in 4–5
weeks (vs. six months in some competitors), and it can modify an
existing item in as little as two weeks. It does this by:

- Grouping the "commercial team" (designers, market specialists, and
  buyers) together so that they can do quick designs and appraisals.
- Making its most fashion-sensitive items in northwest Spain (Galicia) and
  northern Portugal in a system that combines company-owned operations
  and subcontractors that typically do the sewing. (The company owns
  the factories that cut the fabric and receive and check the quality of the
  sewn clothes from those subcontractors, and it has substantial interests
  in fabric and dye producers.)
- Fabricating only the basic, less-fashion-sensitive products elsewhere,
  chiefly, Asia.
- Producing some of its items without dyes, so that mid-season color
  changes can be accommodated easily.
- Connecting its factories via monorails to its vast distribution complex in
  Spain.
- Owning the bulk of its stores worldwide and being in constant touch
  with them to find out what is selling and what is not.
- Shipping directly, and routinely, to those stores from its massive complex
  of distribution centers in Spain.

This system can produce roughly 11,000 distinct items each
year, considerably more than competitors. If items do not sell well,
they are immediately withdrawn and sent to places where they are
selling, or back to the distribution center in Spain. With an integrated design, production, and distribution system like this, Zara
can enter the selling season with only 15–20 percent of the production "committed" and wait for orders to materialize. Its speed can
then provide 40–50 percent of production within the sales season
itself, an unusually high percentage. This way, Zara can make only
the items that are selling well and it does not have the burden of

trying to guess what the sales would be, like so many other fashion retailers. It even tolerates stockouts, knowing that customers will want to return to the store frequently to find out what is new and fashionable. In this way, inventories can be kept down and Zara can realize a greater fraction of the full price of an item than its competition. It can often collect from its customers before it has to pay its suppliers. The company does next to no advertising. Inditex owns most of the roughly 5,000 stores it operates across the world.

Zara's entire supply chain, from design to the retail store, is geared to swift flow, and the repetitiveness and routine of the process is all very standard. It can offer a lot of variety in the fashion that it produces, but its process is cleverly designed to cope with that variability so that it can produce and sell productively.

4 Nucor

The Nucor Corporation, now one of the world's largest steel companies, did not even start out in the industry. Its turbulent roots are in automobiles and nuclear products. Only after it got into the fabrication of steel joists and became unhappy with the steel it was supplied, did it contemplate a move into steel-making. When it did make the move, it made it with fresh ideas that stood the traditional notions of the integrated steel producers on their heads.

Nucor was the pioneer of the mini-mill. Instead of producing steel from iron ore and the conventional blast furnace, Nucor produces its steel from steel scrap using an electric arc furnace. Steel scrap, typically in the form of old automobiles, is abundant, and it is found everywhere, permitting Nucor to locate its mini-mills in unconventional, often rural places.

More than this, Nucor has been a trendsetter with ideas about how to make steel. From its beginnings in the late 1960s and 1970s, it has tried to make steel in a continuous flow, marrying the electric arc furnace, state-of-the art chemistry on the resulting molten steel in the ladle, sliding gate valves into the tundish for faster and more precise flow of the steel into a continuous caster, specially designed reheat furnaces, and the then-latest roughing and finishing mills. It pioneered thin-slab casting in the 1990s and ultra-thin strip casting in the early years of this century, which compete favorably with traditional hot- or cold-rolled steel. These technologies have quickened the time it takes to turn molten steel into useable products.

In its early years, the quality of steel produced was only good for bar steel (e.g., joists). The improved technical features of the steel Nucor is currently capable of making has greatly widened the product line it offers the marketplace, now including bars, beams, sheet, and plate. It has eaten into more and more of the markets of the integrated steel-makers. And, the company has done so with personnel policies that have been as innovative as its steel-making technology has been (e.g., hiring "farm" labor with no previous steel experience, using an unconventional incentive pay scheme).

Nucor, over the years, has become better and better at producing steel products quickly and directly from furnace to finishing, from slab casting to thin-slab casting to strip casting. It has prided itself in casting continuous heats of steel without stop. Its vision has clearly been swift, even flow.

5 Joint implant surgery

Let's return to our orthopedic surgeon. One of the fastest growing corners of medicine is the replacement of knees and hips. And, with the aging of the baby boomers, this is likely to continue to be a growth industry. Many orthopedic surgeons are specializing in knee and hip replacement and are doing quite well at it.

Here's an example.[11] A specialized surgeon can perform 750 to 1,000 operations a year. Typically, that means performing between 15 and 20 a week. And, those operations are often done on Mondays and Tuesdays, so that patients can, after two or three nights in the hospital, return home for the weekend. (This is, of course, advantageous to the attending doctors and nurses.) If a surgeon is to perform eight to ten knee or hip operations a day, then, the typical operation has to

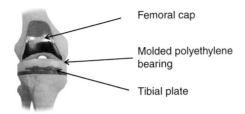

Femoral cap

Molded polyethylene
bearing

Tibial plate

The Vanguard® knee consisted of four distinct pieces: a metal end (called
the "femoral") for the base of the femur (thigh bone), a metal plate (called
the "tibial plate") for the tibia (shin bone) on top of which sat a high-
density molded polyethylene surface (called the "bearing") that took the
place of cartilage, and a patella "button"(for the back of the knee cap)
that rode in the groove of the femoral metal cap. The surgeon removed
slices of bone from the femur to create five facets to position the femoral,
which was then cemented or press fit into place. Then, the surgeon sliced
off the top of the tibia and drilled a hole in it, into which the metal plate
with the polyethylene surface was fitted and cemented. Finally, a portion
of the back part of the patella was removed and a "button" placed there
so that the patella could ride easily over the groove of the metal femoral
cap.

FIGURE 2.4 A Biomet Vanguard® complete knee replacement
Reproduced with permission of Biomet Inc.

be done in less than an hour.[12] Figure 2.4 shows a knee replacement
from Biomet and describes what the surgeon has to do to install it.

How can an operation of this type be accomplished in less than
an hour? One way is to equip two identical operating rooms and staff
them with two teams that stay together. Each member of the team
does the same thing for every operation, in standardized fashion. The
surgeon, the bottleneck in this process, shuttles between operating
rooms. One operating room is always treating a patient and the other
is being readied for the next patient. The operation itself resembles
a choreographed dance. This requires that the surgeon does everything the same way every time. The surgeon's actions have to be
anticipated by the others on the surgical team. The surgeon does not
rush anything that he does, but the amount of wasted or idle time is
drastically reduced as the surgical team keeps everything "in step."
What can be a stressful situation is reduced to an almost stress-free
one. The added benefit is that the wound itself is open for just a short
time, and that helps to limit infection.

This move to reduce variation and throughput times carries
over to more than simply the operating room. The entire patient

experience can be coordinated and standardized, from preoperative tests and informational sessions to postoperative physical therapy. A Friday planning meeting for next week's surgeries can assess what may be problem issues and deal with them in advance, so that expediting, and its disruption, is reduced as much as it can be. This builds up even more communication and trust for the teams surrounding the patient.

Some patients may complain that they are on an assembly line, but, I'd argue, that is exactly where you want to be; assembly lines are wonderful ways to produce consistent quality. Indeed, it is more helpful to think of the surgeon as an assembly line worker than as a project coordinator or as the ringmaster in the operating room. Here again the theme is swift, even flow. The surgical and support teams are designed to eliminate as much variation as possible, and the throughput time for the patient is impressively short.

REVISITING THE USUAL SUSPECTS

With this understanding of swift, even flow under our belts, it is time to revisit the usual suspects to explore again why they are deficient.

- *Chopping heads*: chopping heads only looks to labor cost, be it direct or overhead labor. While that cost may be significant, there are so many other costs that could be reduced. The goal is to discover where there is waste and to remove it. Cutting heads does nothing to identify waste and thus it cannot readily show us the way to a new, more productive definition of the process. It is much too one-dimensional.
- *Automation*: automation, too, looks primarily to remove direct labor. It ignores most of the other potential sources of waste that can exist with a process. Indeed, one risks automating waste, completely missing a better way to produce the good or service. Automation, too, can tempt managers into embracing more complexity and variation – under the guise of more flexibility – than may be warranted by the business. It may cause managers to stray from the task of hunting down variation in quantities and timing and taking steps to limit that variation. For some managers, it may seem that automation is the silver bullet, providing both flexibility and low cost, effortlessly, simply

by purchasing the right piece of equipment. Of such thinking, white elephants are born.

New equipment is conventionally justified by labor savings and by savings on other costs such as inventory. Unfortunately, such savings can be manipulated, drawing into question whether the new equipment purchase is truly economic. If, on the other hand, the calculation of the cost savings were augmented in the capital appropriation request with a compelling story of how throughput time and/or variation would be reduced with the addition of the new equipment, the new investment would be more thoroughly justified. Automation, or, indeed, any capital-for-labor substitution only increases productivity to the extent that it reduces variation or throughput time.

- *Labor efficiency and machine utilization*: these metrics look to the factors of production themselves – labor and capital equipment – and not to the materials (or information) that the process adds value to. Yet, measuring what gets worked on is a much better indicator of productivity than measuring how something is worked on. Labor or machines can be busy, but they may not be adding all of the value that they should be, and the measures on them are piecemeal measures to boot. Unfortunately, the time and motion study lying behind the setting of efficiency metrics may not be able to ferret out the non-value-added aspects of any job or of the broader, and more important, process itself. Much of the time that materials (or information) spend in the process is time divorced from either equipment or labor. Focusing on labor efficiency or machine utilization ignores this nonproductive, wasteful time. And, there is always inadvertent waste in the process. Throughput time is thus a more natural, total process metric that can capture both where value is added and where waste lies.
- *Scale*: labor efficiency and machine utilization do not affect either throughput times or variation, and neither does scale. Only when scale leads to the definition and design of a different way to make the product could it be said to offer some hope for increased productivity. Just like automation, scale only serves to increase productivity when it acts to reduce variation or throughput time.
- Consider the example of making steel. The major integrated steelmakers' facilities are at a scale much larger than that of Nucor Steel. The chemistry of an integrated maker also permits it to produce any kind of steel, including the most complex alloys. Yet, Nucor, a mini-mill

producer, has been steadily eroding the market share of the major integrated producers. This has been a classic attack from below, in the jargon of the literature on disruptive technology.[13] What has negated the alleged cost advantage of scale? Speed. As noted above, Nucor's embrace of continuous casting, now including thin-slab and strip casting, wastes less energy and permits the final product to be produced quicker than by the standard technology used by the integrated producers. Nucor has also been innovative in the chemistry of the electric arc furnace and of the ladle that shuttles steel from furnace to caster. Time after time, speed trumps scale.

- *Systems*: systems, like automation, can suppress managerial drive to rid a process of variation and/or to find ways to reduce its throughput time. Systems can conceal waste rather than making it visible. For example, many ERP systems have modules that will automatically calculate lot sizes for production using variants of the long-recognized economic order quantity formula. Yet, as will be discussed later, lot sizes calculated in this way are fraught with problems and are at odds with lean manufacturing principles. Complacent companies that unwittingly permit their systems to generate lot sizes for production risk doing themselves and their productivity a great disservice.

UNDERSTANDING PRODUCTION PROCESSES IN A NEW LIGHT

The realization that surgical operations can be assembly lines suggests that we take a closer look at processes. Earlier, the four archetypal categories of production process – job shop, batch operation, line flow (or assembly line), and continuous flow – were introduced as a spectrum, with the job shop at one end and the continuous flow process at the other. With the notion of swift, even flow behind us, we can take another look at these processes, from a different angle.

Suppose instead of a simple spectrum, we examined a matrix, one where the elements of swift, even flow were represented on the axes. Thus, we can look at variability along one axis and the speed of flow along the other. Then we can array the different kinds of production processes along a diagonal. Figure 2.5 captures the idea.

This diagonal makes sense. The job shop is clearly the process subject to and designed to cope best with variability. The continuous flow process, on the other hand, is least able to cope with variability. Likewise, the continuous flow process is the one with the shortest throughput times, with the job shop having the longest. The batch and assembly line (line flow) processes fall in between. As one moves down the diagonal, productivity increases. As processes shed variability and pick up speed of flow, productivity increases and the characters of the processes change.

Moreover, there are forces that act to define the diagonal cleanly. Suppose that a process occupied Area 1, with low variability but yet a low speed of flow. The pressure to reduce costs would be such that a process like that would look to invest in equipment and technology to speed up its flow. It would be unlikely to add variability; it would be pushed, rather, to reduce costs by increasing its capacity and productivity with higher speed equipment or processes.

Likewise, suppose that a process occupied Area 2, with a technology capable of producing at high speed, but with constraints from the market or elsewhere that subjected the process to high variability. The pressures in this instance would push the process and its products to become much more standardized so as to reduce its variability. The pressure would not likely be to abandon its high-speed processes.

Some careful readers will note that Figure 2.5 looks very much like the product–process matrix, advanced by Hayes and Wheelwright in two articles in back-to-back issues of the 1979 *Harvard Business Review*.[14] The product–process matrix has been, for years, a very appealing depiction of product volume and mix – what Hayes and Wheelwright called "product life cycle stage" – on the one hand, and the character of the production process stretching along a spectrum from job shop to continuous flow process – what Hayes and Wheelwright called "process life cycle stage" – on the other hand. The arguments behind the product–process matrix assert that the diagonal offers the best match of product volume/mix and process

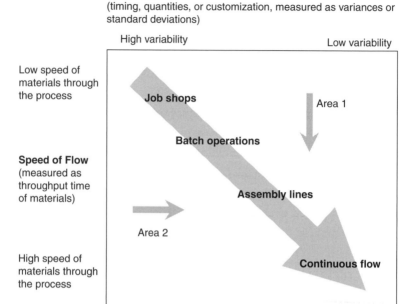

Variability
(timing, quantities, or customization, measured as variances or standard deviations)

High variability   Low variability

Low speed of materials through the process

Job shops   Area 1

Batch operations

Speed of Flow (measured as throughput time of materials)

Assembly lines

Area 2

High speed of materials through the process

Continuous flow

FIGURE 2.5 Swift, even flow and processes

character, but the authors did not dismiss the possibility for operations to exist off the diagonal.

It is my contention that Figure 2.5 and the concept of swift, even flow "tidies up" the loose ends in the Hayes–Wheelwright product–process matrix. For example, in their articles, Hayes and Wheelwright do not propose a particular measure for either their "product life cycle stages" or for their "process life cycle stages." In fact, in their second article, they superimpose the learning curve on the matrix, together with its altogether differently labeled axes. Figure 2.5 is much more precise about the definition and measurement of the axes. The product-process matrix is obviously more suggestive and representative than theoretically precise. Hayes and Wheelwright see that the lower right portion is the most cost-effective area of the matrix. Swift, even flow explains more clearly why their intuition is correct.

In addition, the product–process matrix does not offer many predictions. While Hayes and Wheelwright see the diagonal as home to the best "patches" of space within the matrix, they do not necessarily predict ill fates for off-diagonal operations, although they do counsel caution in such situations. The mechanisms by which off-diagonal operations either die or change is not spelled out in detail, although it is recognized that firms are unlikely to coordinate product life cycle stage changes with process life cycle stage changes and so must linger in off-diagonal situations from time to time. Swift, even flow, on the other hand, offers an explanation for why operations not on the diagonal are likely to be pushed toward the diagonal. Swift, even flow provides an adjustment mechanism that is not present in the product–process matrix as it was first envisioned.

PRODUCTIVITY AND VARIATION, PROFIT AND UNCERTAINTY

We can use this process matrix to explore two other distinctions related to processes. One concerns uncertainty and the other profitability.

As we noted when discussing the queuing phenomenon, job shops and, to a lesser extent, batch operations, exhibit more variation than either line flow or continuous flow operations. The demands placed on them and the process steps needed to produce those demands are simply more variable. Projects, which can be viewed as lying above and to the left of job shops in Figure 2.5, are even more subject to variation.

The more we understand about the distribution of variation, the more effectively we can cope with it. When we know little about the distribution of variation that affects a process, we enter the realm of uncertainty. When we are uncertain about the nature of the variation affecting a process, we are in more need of various buffers of inventory or of time in order to cope. There is more of this uncertainty in the upper left of the diagram.

Swift, even flow is about productivity, and productivity needs to be kept distinct from profitability. There are economics to profitability – sales price and the probability of achieving the sale – that do not come into play when considering productivity. Yet, one can say with some confidence that the profitability of line flow and continuous flow processes are, in general, tied more to productivity than is the profitability of job shop and batch operations. One does not invest in line flow and continuous flow operations without being confident that demands on those processes are fairly steady, that the distribution of variation of sales is reasonably well known. The risks – the uncertainty – associated with orders on those processes are less, in general, than the risks associated with job shops and batch operations, and much less than the risks associated with projects.

These distinctions are captured in Figure 2.6. It shows that the lower right portion of the matrix is characterized by variation that is likely to be better understood and thus less uncertain than that prevailing in the upper left of the matrix. And, the profitability of the lower right of the matrix is more likely to come from high productivity than the upper left, where the increased variation and the uncertainty surrounding that variation are more likely to mean that profitability is less tied to productivity and more tied to pricing.

These distinctions will be important when we consider the merits of swift, even flow in dealing with new product development, for example.

IT'S THE SAME FOR SERVICES

Lest we think that swift, even flow only matters for manufacturing operations, let's consider services. In the past several decades, a number of service operations have transformed their industries. Think of Southwest Airlines (discussed above), Wal-Mart, McDonald's, IKEA, FedEx, and many others. They have been game changers. McDonald's

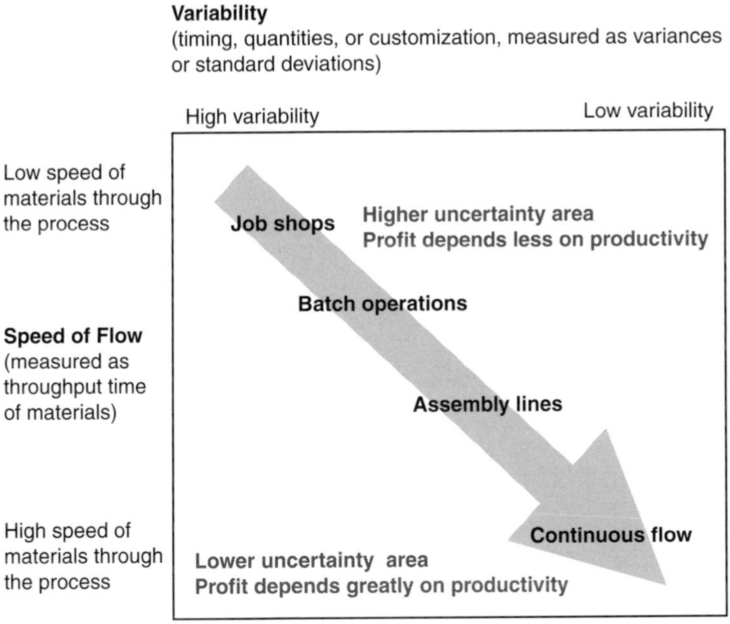

Variability
(timing, quantities, or customization, measured as variances
or standard deviations)

High variability   Low variability

Low speed of
materials through   Job shops   Higher uncertainty area
the process   Profit depends less on productivity

                                    Batch operations

Speed of Flow
(measured as
throughput time   **Assembly lines**
of materials)

High speed of   **Continuous flow**
materials through   Lower uncertainty area
the process   Profit depends greatly on productivity

FIGURE 2.6 Profit and uncertainty within the process matrix

more or less invented the fast food restaurant and we now look at eat-
ing out in a whole new way. IKEA has revolutionized how furniture
shopping is done, especially in Europe, and FedEx has brought us a
previously unheard of service, next-day delivery. We can tell similar
tales about a number of other companies.

It is my contention that this transformation is a transformation powered by productivity. The new business models that companies such as McDonald's, IKEA, or H&R Block have developed are
business models that have productivity improvement at their heart.
And, if one is to believe the thesis of this book, then swift, even flow
is at the center of things.

These kinds of transformations can be captured in a diagram
much like that of Figure 2.7.

In this diagram, we see the evolution of some of the services
we have talked about. To help the discussion, the quadrants have
been named. There is a rough correspondence between these service

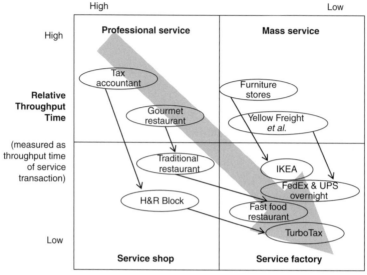

Degree of Variation
(customization for and interaction with customers)

FIGURE 2.7 Swift, even flow in services

designations – professional service, mass service, service shop, and service factory – and the labels that we use to discuss manufacturing. For example, professional service shares much with the job shop. What is asked of professional services is highly variable, even idiosyncratic, and the steps to accomplish the task can be many and long. A tax accountant working on an uncommon business situation provides a model for the professional service, but we could also include doctors working on medical diagnoses and treatments, or architects designing some new structure, or attorneys either prosecuting or defending an interesting case.

Mass service shares some characteristics with the batch operation. Here, low variability is paired with high relative throughput time. Think of the furniture store. The sales interaction with the customer at a furniture store is somewhat more complex than that of other retail operations (think choice of wood and of upholstery), but it is a fairly standard interaction. The choices available can be significant, of course, and that can draw out the interaction, but it is an interaction that is much less complex than those a doctor or lawyer would be faced with. The result of the customer interaction at the furniture store is typically the placement of an order. Afterward, the customer must wait weeks, or longer, for the order to be fulfilled. The full-service, less-than-truckload (LTL) trucking company such as Yellow Freight is another example of a mass service. It can deliver almost any kind of shipment, although it may take some days for the shipment to work its way through Yellow Freight's series of terminals and break-bulks. The transaction that arranges such a shipment is a standard one.

The service shop, on the other hand, routinely offers the service more quickly and with greater customization/interaction. Think of a traditional restaurant. You can order exactly what you want, often asking for something to be substituted for something else. The item ordered can be cooked to specification and the server is around, ready to provide something else to make the meal experience a good one. A service such as H&R Block is another example, and it offers a good contrast with professional service. H&R Block can typically help its customers to do their US tax returns quickly, although it cannot easily research and complete the highly technical tax returns that people go to a tax accountant for. It is not designed for that high degree of customization and/or interaction. Yet, it can provide the tax client with a comfort that the purely software solution of TurboTax cannot provide.

The paragon of productivity in services, however, is the service factory, where variation is low and so too is the relative throughput time. Here is where services can be offered on a massive scale. Fast food is a classic example. The interaction and choice are both limited but the speed of the service transaction can be remarkable. A number of services over the past 50 years or so have evolved service factory options that have defined new niches within their industries. Think of Wal-Mart or Southwest Airlines or Toys R Us. FedEx is an especially interesting case of a then totally novel service that now feels natural. The range of what it transports cannot match the range for a ground hauler such as Yellow Freight and the cost of the service, given the form of transportation, is higher, but the speed is breathtaking and the productivity great. Even with retail furniture there has been the development of IKEA, where many items are immediately available, although they may have to be assembled from flat packs. Yet, the assembly is frequently fairly easy to accomplish with the special assembly system that IKEA has devised and which is designed into its product offerings.

The point, however, is that the service factory, much as the continuous flow operation for manufacturing, is where productivity reaches its zenith. It has been designed with swift, even flow in mind, and, often, it can be replicated and brought to consumers far and wide. In many service industries, it has been the service factories that have pushed change. They have been the ones that have lowered prices and/or speeded up delivery, and they are the respected, indeed sometimes feared, competitors in their industries.

SHOULD PRODUCTIVITY ALWAYS BE THE GOAL?

This book is about productivity. Increased productivity can lead to increased profit. Cutting costs and getting the most out of resources are often worthy goals. But, productivity and profit do not always go hand in hand. There can be times when the pursuit of productivity and what it means for variation, in particular, are not in accord with the best strategy for the business.

When the company strategy calls for flexibility – new product models, lots of customization, wild swings in the product mix, considerable fluctuation in the quantities and timing of orders, clouds of uncertainty – a fixation on productivity can be exceedingly inappropriate. As was noted above, the drive to productivity is a drive down the diagonal of Figure 2.5. But, profit may well reside in the upper left of the matrix. Customers are often willing to pay a lot for customization or novelty or the latest thing. In such a case, what is at stake is the capability of the process to produce and not so much the cost to produce.

This is not to say that the job shop or the batch operation cannot squeeze waste out of what they do. There may be unwanted variation that can be removed. However, offering variety to the marketplace is critical and a slavish pursuit of variation reduction or throughput time reduction can defeat that.

Think about the examples above. Zara offers roughly 11,000 new items to the marketplace every year. Its fashion may be fast, but its purpose is to provide distinctive fashion. Could Zara be even more productive if it reduced its portfolio of fashion items? Absolutely. Is that wise? Definitely not.

Dell, too, offers its customers considerable choice in specifying the features of its computers. Yes, it typically tries to steer its customers to particular models, and customers who want something different have to pay somewhat more for the nonstandard item. Nevertheless, Dell will still assemble the custom order and happily pocket the extra revenue for it.

It was noted above that Southwest Airlines now offers flights to LaGuardia Airport in New York City, one of the most congested airports in the United States. This is at odds with Southwest's original business model and at odds with what swift, even flow would argue is the most productive way to operate. Nevertheless, having a foothold in New York City could be lucrative and enhance the profit of the entire airline, given the prices charged and the potential to increase the traffic on the Southwest flights that feed into and out of LaGuardia.

This distinction between productivity and the profitability that can be derived from flexibility needs to be kept in mind. Swift, even flow does not argue for a blind pursuit of productivity; it is merely the mechanism by which greater productivity is achieved. The search for productivity must be tempered by the profit that should guide such a search.

HOW DOES SWIFT, EVEN FLOW FIT WITH CURRENT THINKING?

In the past several decades, operations have benefitted from a number of initiatives:

- The quality movement: first Total Quality Management (TQM), then Six Sigma.
- The Toyota Production System and its various interpretations: first Just-in-Time Manufacturing, then Lean Manufacturing, and the lesser-known but well-regarded Quick Response Manufacturing (QRM).
- The use of cells to reengineer processes.
- Goldratt's Theory of Constraints.

Let's take a closer look at these.

Quality: the constants within the quality movement have been the tools that can be applied to study quality problems and to foolproof processes and thereby assure good quality. These tools are the tools that reduce variation in the production of goods and services and are clearly part of the "even" of swift, even flow. They are the legacies of the quality gurus. Six Sigma differs from TQM in several ways, but those differences are generally differences in implementation and not in the use of the superb tools that have been developed over the years. Swift, even flow can accommodate either TQM or Six Sigma; it's the use of the variation-reducing tools (e.g., statistical, logic-enhancing) common to both of them that is powerful and enduring.

Toyota Production System: the Toyota Production System and its interpretations and extensions as Just-in-Time, Lean, Lean Six Sigma, QRM, and others speak to both the "swift flow" and the "even" portions of the concept. These ways of thinking about operations go straight to throughput time reduction by slashing inventories and focusing on the flows of materials. One can also argue that, at base, these "philosophies," if you will, have quality improvement in mind and the reduction of variation of all sorts. Toyota does not use Six Sigma at all, but it does routinely employ the tools of quality management to improve product and process. The concentrations on flows that stem from lean-related programs have led to significant investments in reducing setup/changeover times, so that small lot sizes can be easily run and throughput times slashed. Thus, to pursue swift, even flow is to pursue the elements of the Toyota Production System and its offshoots. As Taiichi Ohno, the father of the Toyota Production System, is reported to have said: "All we are doing is looking at the time line, from the moment the customer gives us an order to the point when we collect the cash. And we are reducing the time line by reducing the non-value adding wastes."[15]

These wastes are sometimes referred to by a Japanese term, *muda*. Indeed, there are three Japanese terms of relevance here: *muda*, *mura*, and *muri*. *Muda* is often characterized by Shingo's seven wastes, which were mentioned earlier. It is the easiest concept to grasp. *Mura* refers to variation in timing and quantities, and is generally translated as unevenness. It argues for gradual changes in the quantities produced and when they are produced. The goal is for every day's production to look pretty much like every other day's production, with few dramatic fluctuations. After all, every day the market buys a little bit of all that the company produces, so it stands to reason that every day the operation should produce a little bit of all that the company offers for sale. *Muri* is not as straightforwardly understood. It refers to standardization in the work and regularity in how it is accomplished. The notion of standard work, where what is to be done is documented and known thoroughly by the workforce, is central to this concept. The regularity in the pace of the work is dictated by the needs of the marketplace, often characterized as the takt time, the pace at which sales occur.

These Japanese concepts capture key elements of what swift, even flow is about. On the other hand, they miss the focus on *being* the materials that is central to swift, even flow and the perspective that comes with that. Enough said for the moment. Chapter 4 will spend considerable time discussing lean production and its tie to swift, even flow.

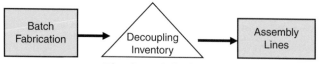

FIGURE 2.8 The classic hybrid process

Cells and process reengineering: for me, one of the points of great genius in the Japanese contributions to our thinking about operations – and the Toyota Production System is only the most prominent of their contributions – has been the way that they have changed our thinking about the common batch–line flow hybrid process. Much of manufacturing that involves assembly is actually done by a hybrid process whereby parts are fabricated in large batches, those batches are placed into a stockroom, and the assembly operation pulls what it needs from the stockroom.

Diagrammatically, this classic hybrid operation can be seen in Figure 2.8.

The inventory in the stockroom can be termed a "decoupling" inventory because the production plans for the assembly line and the batch fabrication are different. The assembly line is typically planned to meet the market requirements that the company foresees. The fabrication operation, on the other hand, is not seen as flexible enough to be scheduled the same way. Rather, the batches produced are large, to lower the setup/changeover time, and, while, over the long run, the quantities produced and consumed are matched, over the short run, they are not.

By focusing on the establishment of cells for families of parts and on setup reduction so that small lot sizes, sometimes even one at a time, can be run easily, the Japanese have shown us how the decoupling inventory can be removed, entirely, from the process. The demands of the marketplace can then trigger both the assembly line schedule and the part fabrication schedule. The cells can be married directly to the assembly line. See Figure 2.9 which displays the cells as U-lines, although the cells could just as easily be straight lines.

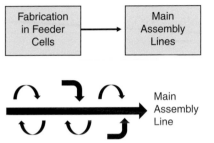

FIGURE 2.9 Cells feeding an assembly line

Each cell has a mix of equipment in it, all of the equipment needed to produce the family of parts or subassemblies. Some equipment will be used more than others; that is only natural. As we've seen, however, the utilization of any one piece of equipment is irrelevant to the productivity of the cell. What is important is that the cell, as a unit, produces, and keeps up with the speed of the main assembly line. The creation of the cell and its reengineering of the process remove the mismatch of quantities and timing for the family of parts that existed before and thus greatly reduce the impact of those sources of variation.

The implications of this change in thinking on the throughput time of materials in the classic hybrid process are dramatic. Automobiles, for example, have been produced with hybrid processes for years, and waste intruded into the process. What Toyota did was to squeeze a lot of the waste out of the process, and that both reduced cost and improved quality. The throughput times for a company such as Toyota, from the production of basic engine components and body parts through to final assembly, have been much less than the typical auto manufacturer in North America or Europe. The final assembly lines moved at similar speeds, but the throughput times of the major parts and subassemblies for a car have been vastly different. It was this change that struck fear into the hearts of Western manufacturers during the 1980s, as many did not understand how the Japanese could produce high quality products so cheaply without subsidies or other distortions to a "level playing field." All of us now know better.

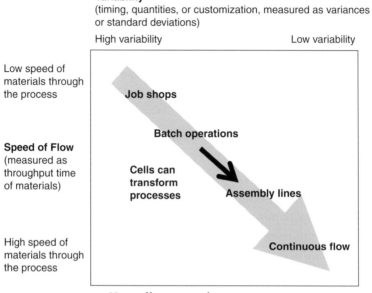

FIGURE 2.10 How cells can transform a process

Figure 2.10 captures what cells have meant to process change. Cells have helped to shift what was once a strictly batch process into a process that is much more assembly line in character. That move down the diagonal is a move to greater productivity, and it has been a powerful one.

Theory of Constraints: Eli Goldratt's widely read book, *The Goal*, introduced many to the need to concentrate on the bottleneck operation and to ignore, in essential ways, the non-bottleneck operations. This important insight, too, is captured by the concept of swift, even flow. If one is to reduce throughput time for a product or service, one must address the bottlenecks in the process and either break them or work to cope effectively with them. To do otherwise simply adds time to the materials flowing through the process.

SWIFT, EVEN FLOW CAN BE MORE

In important ways, then, the concept of swift, even flow can help to unify the initiatives that have been the focus of operational thinking over the past several decades. These initiatives – such as Six Sigma, Lean Manufacturing, cellular manufacturing and process reengineering, and the Theory of Constraints – can all be seen as facets of swift, even flow. Indeed, swift, even flow is, for me, the underlying and unifying concept that stands behind these initiatives. Understand swift, even flow and you understand why these other initiatives work as they do.

But, swift, even flow is more than this. Swift, even flow is more than a convenient way to re-title the concepts that have helped so many companies in the last couple of decades. Six Sigma and Lean Manufacturing, for example, are typically implemented with a recognized process in mind. That is necessarily limiting. They become tools to "fix" an existing process that has been identified as "broken." In their typical use, they do not become tools for envisioning what the process should be, or, even more broadly, what the business itself should be. Swift, even flow can be used to examine business situations and not simply underperforming processes. Its sweep can be strategic and grand or tactical and very particular. Swift, even flow is a powerful addition to the initiatives of Six Sigma, Lean Manufacturing, cellular manufacturing and process reengineering, and the Theory of Constraints. It is a concept that can unify these approaches to operations improvement and show us why they work as they do, but it can go beyond them to provide strategic vision that they would be hard-pressed to demonstrate themselves. (The business history recounted in the next chapter is replete with example after example.)

In this sense, swift, even flow operates as a theory, and according to a famous quotation, "There is nothing so practical as a good theory."[16] Part II of this book, beginning with Chapter 4, is all about the application of swift, even flow to a variety of business problems and situations. Some of those situations are situations about which Six Sigma and Lean Manufacturing are mute. It is my contention that swift, even flow can mean more to the manager. In the pages ahead, I invite you to judge its practicality.

3   The old-fashioned way to make money

The several examples of companies whose operations model swift, even flow, mentioned in the previous chapter, may be enough to convince some people to follow these precepts, but others will certainly need more convincing. This chapter provides more evidence – of different kinds – for the worth of swift, even flow, and it shows how it is, in fact, the way big money has been made for centuries.

SWIFT, EVEN FLOW IN THE DATA

My own quest for the truth about productivity stems from the late 1970s and early 1980s. At the time the Japanese were riding high. Japanese cars and Japanese consumer electronics were making substantial inroads into the American economy, on their way to making substantial inroads into the world's economy. US quality was under attack. W. Edwards Deming and Joseph Juran had been rediscovered by American business but the lessons they were teaching were not embraced by all. Excuses were being made about the performance of US companies. There was much talk about the lack of level playing fields. Various antidotes to the Japanese were being touted, chief among them my list of "the usual suspects," from Chapter 1.

Surely, I thought to myself, not all of these remedies for the American manufacturing malaise of the time would be effective. Some would naturally be better than others, and some may be the equivalent of management snake oil. But which ones? What was the truth underlying the concerns of those years?

Resolving these confusions set me off on a series of research projects to ascertain what it was that distinguishes high-performing, productivity-gaining manufacturing plants from their less well-performing brethren. The series of projects took me to an array of North Carolina factories, then a group of national factories in a variety of industries, and then to some international factories, including significant data gathered from a collaborator in South Korea. In all, detailed information from 561 factories was collected and analyzed, and time-series data from five factories of a major automaker were also studied.[1]

This research did throw cold water on a number of the remedies that were being offered to business at the time. For example, neither economies of scale nor efficiency measures (e.g., labor efficiency, machine utilization) were supported by the results. Investments in IT systems were also unimportant to the results. And, importantly, the factory's particular location in the world played no role in explaining the rate of growth of productivity; factories can be good, productivity-gaining factories anywhere.

Other themes, however, did arise from the analysis as important. Here were the themes that came through consistently as statistically significant to productivity gain:

1. throughput time reduction;
2. inventory reduction;
3. process technology advance (which is not the same thing as automation);
4. strengths in the areas of quality and purchasing;
5. the level of involvement of all of the workforce in productivity advance;
6. clarity about how the plant competes.

These deserve more comment. The research asked plant managers to look at their productivity gain (or loss) over the previous year, using a labor productivity measure. (The data components for a more general measure, total factor productivity, were also asked for, but most factories have a much better grasp on their labor productivity measure than they have on any more general measure. Other measures of the perceived rank of the plant within the industry and within its company were also asked for. The themes above also played out in those results.) The single most consistent finding was that those factories whose percentage reductions in throughput time were greater did better on productivity gain. (Throughput time was defined as the time from the release of an order to the factory floor until shipment – an easy definition for the plant manager to understand.) Similarly, those plants with greater increases in inventory turns over the past five years tended to have greater gains in labor productivity.

The finding about process technology advance was more subtle. The two variables that showed themselves as important were the average age of the equipment in the plant (the lower the average age the better) and the level of involvement that the plant showed in pursuing process hardware advance (the greater the involvement the better). These variables suggest more than simple automation – and there were questions that asked about automation. Rather, the results suggest commitment to the process itself, modernizing where appropriate.

The other influences on productivity also reflected commitment – perceived strength of the quality function and of the purchasing function, and, the level of involvement in seeking worker participation (e.g., teams) and in involving staff in the generation of productivity-enhancing ideas. Those plants that were more committed in a variety of ways had greater productivity gains than the others.

It was also found that those plants that compete on product performance, as opposed to cost, customization, delivery, flexibility, or new product introduction, do better. And, those plants that acknowledge product lines that compete differently from one another also do better. This latter finding is suggestive of the focused factory idea where plants that manage competitively different product lines in distinct ways do better.

In short, the statistical results are very compatible with swift, even flow. Throughput time reduction, higher inventory turns, and commitment to process technology smack of "swift flow." And, the attention to quality and how the plant competes support "even-ness."

Thus, while the anecdotal stories that one can tell about swift, even flow can help one to envision what the concept is all about, these statistical tests provide some convincing contemporary evidence.

THE OLD-FASHIONED WAY TO MAKE MONEY

The experience of contemporary companies underscores the usefulness of swift, even flow. But, if the concept is to be both true and far-reaching, should it not also be able to explain what has occurred in the past? If swift, even flow can explain productivity gains both past and present, then it stands to reason that its prescriptions for the future should be more credible. Happily, swift, even flow does unlock a number of insights about business history.

THE ARSENAL

One of the most celebrated stories of productivity is that of the Arsenal in Venice (Arsenale, in Italian, from whence we get the English word), where the galleys of the Venetian navy were built and outfitted.[2] (See Figure 3.1 for a model replica.) Venice, and its galleys, controlled the Mediterranean Sea for many years.

The Arsenal was for centuries Europe's largest industrial site, built in 1104 and only dismantled with Napoleon's defeat of Venice in 1797. The Arsenal was a state-run enterprise, responsible for the navy's warships and not for Venice's commercial fleet. It reached its heyday in the fifteenth and sixteenth centuries when it was famed for the speed in which a ship could be outfitted.

The Arsenal built a single design of ship, the galley – a long, low, narrow ship powered by both sail and oars, with guns mounted fore and aft, but not along the sides. The galley was effective in the often-calm waters of the Mediterranean. The Arsenal was a vertically integrated manufacturing site. It made all aspects of the ship, from hulls to oars to rigging. The hulls were fabricated and then planked in the lagoon at the heart of the Arsenal. They were then

FIGURE 3.1 A model of a Venetian galley
Reproduced with permission of Dr. Akira Sasano who carefully
researched and painstakingly constructed this model of a 16th century
Venetian galley.

floated in a channel that led to the Adriatic. The other parts were
manufactured in dedicated warehouses located along the channel
within the Arsenal's walls. Parts such as masts, sails, and benches
were fabricated in batches and kept in inventories of up to 50 or 100
ship-equivalents. When it was determined that the navy needed
more ships, the hulls, caulked and planked, began a trip through
the channel where they were outfitted in assembly-line fashion with
rudders, masts, benches, spars, sails, cordage, ironwork, arms, and
all the other things needed for the sea. This outfitting of the galley –
the first documented assembly line in history – was what stunned
the people of the time; it could be done in under an hour. A story
is told of a visit to the Arsenal in 1574 by Henri III, king of France.
At that time he saw a hull started in the lagoon, went to lunch, and
returned to see the finished galley. Of course, not all galleys were

outfitted in so short a time, but the Arsenal could turn out two ships a day with relative ease.

Given this speed, one can understand why Venice could hold its warships as work-in-process inventory on land rather than as floating inventory of finished goods in continual need of maintenance and repair. Unfortunately for the Arsenal and Venice, much of the power of the swift, even flow of galley construction was lost in the late sixteenth century when ship design turned toward the much larger ships-of-the-line and frigates. The old assembly line could not cope and it fell by the wayside.

THE ROBBER BARONS

Let us jump ahead 300 years. The late 1800s and early 1900s witnessed tremendous economic growth and the development of some formidable companies that are still with us today. This was the era of the "robber barons." Great fortunes were created. However, these titans of industry did not start out that way. Their beginnings were much more modest. Consider some of the most prominent.

John D. Rockefeller

John D. Rockefeller (1839–1937) made his fortune with Standard Oil, the forerunner of nearly all of the American petroleum companies that we know today. The Standard Oil trust was a huge monopoly that was split up by order of the US Supreme Court in 1911, the culmination of the anti-trust movement that had passed the Sherman Anti-Trust Act of 1890. But Standard Oil did not start out as a fully integrated company. It began as a refinery in Cleveland, west of the Pennsylvania oil fields that had been discovered by Col. Edwin Drake in 1859. Rockefeller and his partners ran the fastest refinery around and, although theirs was not initially larger than other refineries, they could refine more barrels of oil a day than their competitors.

Here is what the great business historian, Alfred Chandler, wrote about Rockefeller and the industry in *The Visible Hand*, his Pulitzer Prize winning book:[3]

The refiners initially increased output per facility by applying heat more intensively. They developed the use of superheated steam distillation, which they borrowed from recent innovations in the refining of sugar. Next they devised the "cracking" process, a technique of applying higher temperatures to higher boiling points to reshape the molecular structure of crude oil. Such cracking permitted as much as a 20 percent increase in yield from a single still. The output of stills was further expanded by the use of seamless, wrought iron and steel bottoms; by improving cooling as well as heating operations; and by changing the fundamental design of stills so as to increase further the temperature used.

As the individual units were enlarged and made more fuel-intensive, the operation of the units within a single refinery was more closely integrated. Steam power was increasingly used to move the flow of oil through the plant from one refining process to another. In the late 1860s and early 1870s P. H. Van der Weyde and Henry Rogers began to develop and then Samuel Van Sickle perfected continuous-process, multiple stage distillation. This innovation permitted petroleum to flow through the refinery at a steady rate and separate products to be distilled out at different stages ...

Increased size of still, intensified use of energy, and improved design of plant brought rapid increase in throughput. Early in the decade, normal output was 900 barrels a week; it reached 500 barrels a day by 1870. Large refineries already had a charging capacity of 800 to 1,000 barrels a day and even more. At the same time, unit costs fell from an average of 6¢ to 3¢ a barrel, and cost of building a refinery rose from $30,000–$40,000 to $60,000–$90,000. The size of the establishment was still small, in terms of capital invested, costing no more than two miles of well-laid railroad track. But the economies of speed were of critical importance. And one does not need to be an economic historian to identify the senior partner of the fastest refinery in the west in 1869. The high speed of throughput and the resulting lowered unit cost gave John D. Rockefeller his initial advantage in the competitive battles in the American petroleum industry during the 1870s.[4]

Scale did not define in 1869 the refineries that Rockefeller and his partners operated, speed did. Samuel Andrews, a chemist who was a partner with Rockefeller in his initial refinery, was the inventor of fractional distillation, a technological breakthrough that speeded up the refining of petroleum and was critical to the company's success. With refining speed as a lever, Rockefeller and his partners were able to negotiate lower freight costs from the big business of the time, the railroads. That advantage was enough to bring to heel many of his fellow refiners and consolidate them into what became Standard Oil. It took nearly 20 years for Standard Oil to become the vertically integrated behemoth that the Supreme Court later broke up. But, the initial, and crucial, story is one of speed and not scale.

Henry Ford

Henry Ford (1863–1947) has been alternately praised and vilified. What we do know is that in the relatively short time period from 1914 through 1926 or so, Ford accumulated a fortune that rivaled Rockefeller. How did he do it? The key, of course, was Ford's decision to abandon the production of the company's other models to concentrate on the Model T and to create a moving assembly line to do so. The Model T dominated the market for a bit more than a decade and put the United States on wheels.[5] Indeed, by 1921, Ford was producing over half of the passenger cars produced in the United States.

The moving assembly line and the components production to supply it were able to slash the time and the cost of assembling a car.[6] Shortly after the spread of the moving assembly line to all of the manufacturing at the Highland Park works during the torrent of activity that was the period of 1913–1914, the labor content in the production of the Model T dropped from 12.5 hours to 1.5 hours. The throughput time for the Model T, from iron ore to finished car, became as short as 33 hours.

Everything at Ford was geared to reducing variation and throughput time. Indeed, Ford's prescription for mass production, stemming from well before the advent of the moving assembly line but guiding the experimentation that went on prior to the development of that innovation, focused on the "principles of power, accuracy, economy, system, continuity, and speed."[7] Prior to the development of the assembly line, Ford's ever-experimenting lieutenants had developed machine tools better than any others to produce interchangeable parts, sequenced those machines to match the assembly process, and positioned them close to one another to lessen the amount of handling that had to be done. Even the fixtures and gauges were designed by Ford's engineers for speed and accuracy. Famously, you could have a Model T in any color as long as it was black. But why did Ford insist on black? Why not some other color? The answer lies with physics. Radiation-absorbing black is the fastest drying paint.

Unfortunately, after attracting talented engineers and managers and giving them the freedom to experiment with the elements of mass production, Henry Ford became a victim of his management style. Disaster ensued. Many of his most competent managers either quit or were fired. Some jumped ship to General Motors, which was backed by the du Ponts.[8] Alfred Sloan of General Motors and his lieutenant William Knudsen, a former Ford protégé, also cleverly exploited Ford's inflexibility and began changing models regularly. The now richer consumers of the day valued this variety. Ford, the initial innovator of the moving assembly line, had not created that assembly line with model change in mind and thus could not match GM's flexibility. Ford soon lost its lead in the automotive market.

But its run, while it lasted, was fantastic, and testament to what swift, even flow can do.

Impressively, the glorious final act for the Ford managers who created the moving assembly line was the manufacture and assembly of the B-24 Liberator bomber in World War II. Those managers, operating out of the Willow Run factory outside Detroit, completely rethought the assembly process for airplanes and they were able, at the height of the war, to produce a bomber an hour, where, before, a bomber a day was the best that anyone had been able to do. It is no wonder that Taiichi Ohno, the creator of the Toyota Production System, studied Ford and all that he and his team did.

Andrew Carnegie and the sorry case of US Steel

The rise of US Steel is an excellent example of the power of swift, even flow. Its fall is an even better example of what neglect of this concept can mean to a company's competitiveness. Consider Chandler:

> Andrew Carnegie, like John D. Rockefeller and Henry Ford, acquired industrial power and a vast personal fortune by understanding the significance of throughput. "Hard driving" was Carnegie's term for it.
>
> The story of steel differs from that of oil, however, in that the most effective first mover sold out. Senior executives of Carnegie's successor company, the United States Steel Corporation – those who were lawyers and financiers – failed to appreciate the value of operating "steady and full." They dissipated Carnegie's first-mover advantages and thus permitted the rapid growth of challengers.[9]

What had been the first-mover advantages that Chandler refers to? As the economist Peter Temin tells it, it was speed: "The speed at which steel was made was continually rising, and the new innovations were constantly being introduced to speed it further."[10] The time it took to make steel was steadily dropping with the introduction of better sources of power and a variety of other innovations.[11]

Carnegie, in particular, had recognized the talent of Alexander Holley. Holley designed his steel mills, most prominently the Edgar Thompson Works in Pittsburgh, with materials handling in mind. And, Carnegie's lieutenants loved running the company's mills flat out, what they and Carnegie termed "hard driving" and "steady and full." Unfortunately, all that Carnegie and his men had done to improve the process of making steel and to drive down its cost was dissipated by Elbert H. Gary, a lawyer who became the first chairman of the board of US Steel, placed there by J. P. Morgan who had bought out Carnegie in 1901. Gary eschewed price competition. His policy was to maintain price, even if it meant running at half capacity. Such policies squandered the power of swift, even flow. These decisions drove those of Carnegie's old lieutenants who remained at US Steel crazy.[12]

By turning its back on swift, even flow, the steel industry's giant became an also-ran. Elbert Gary's management of US Steel permitted Bethlehem Steel and others to thrive and to take market share away from what was initially the industry's overwhelming leader. It was backsliding on a huge scale. During the decade from 1901 to 1911, US Steel's market share fell drastically from over two-thirds of the market to half. The upshot of such a disaster was that US Steel was spared as a target of the era's trust-busters. The US Supreme Court did not break it up in 1911 as it did Rockefeller's Standard Oil Company; it didn't need to.

What about the other companies that were targeted as monopolies in the early 1900s? All of them had swift, even flow at their centers. James Buchanan (Buck) Duke and the American Tobacco Company controlled the Bonsack cigarette-making machine that could produce cigarettes faster, better, and far cheaper than others could. That speed created a vast market that Duke's interests monopolized. The company's devotion to swift, even flow led to its breakup in 1911 by the US Supreme Court.

The other successful trusts – cottonseed oil, linseed oil, lead processing (focused on the chemical processing of lead required for paint production, among other things), sugar refining, and whiskey – were similar. Continuous flow operations were their critical advantage in the marketplace.

EXPLAINING THE INDUSTRIAL REVOLUTION

So much for the stories of the "robber barons" and their era. Their ties to swift, even flow seem clear enough. But what about the grander issues of industrial development? Can appeal to swift, even flow help to explain these big, broad questions? With some trepidation, then, let us wade into the grand realm of economic development and see whether swift, even flow has anything to contribute to the biggest issue of all, why and how the Industrial Revolution came to be.

Consider the key facts about countries and industrialization, facts that cannot be ignored if the Industrial Revolution is to be properly explained. Permit me to cite them.

- Britain was the engine of the Industrial Revolution, and, within Britain, it was cotton textiles that first industrialized.
- China, India, and other countries of Europe were not the ones to lead the Industrial Revolution.
- Japan, a set of islands with substantially fewer natural resources than found in either China or India, industrialized much sooner than any of the other countries in Asia.
- Portugal, Spain, the Netherlands, and France were, at least for a time, wealthier countries than Britain before the Industrial Revolution. Yet, their wealth was quickly overtaken by Britain and its industrialization.
- The United States rather quickly overtook Britain as the leader of what has come to be known as the Second Industrial Revolution, when industrialization spread to a variety of industries other than textiles.

The Industrial Revolution has, of course, been much studied. Several important works on the subject have recently been published, notably those by David Landes, Robert Allen, and Joel Mokyr.[13] There are a variety of forces that people can persuasively argue caused the Industrial Revolution and explaining those forces in detail can take up entire books. My aims are more modest. Given that the Industrial Revolution is about factories and their creation, it seems to me that the field of operations management ought to have something to say about it. How operations management fits into the Industrial Revolution is my focus, and whether swift, even flow can help to explain what happened.

What was the Industrial Revolution? Landes defines it in terms of the "factory system" that combined newly invented machines ("rapid, regular, precise, tireless," with some of them deemed macro inventions by some historians and some deemed micro inventions), inanimate sources of power (e.g., the water wheel, and later, the steam engine), and the use of new, abundant, and typically mineral (as opposed to animal or vegetable) raw materials. The factory was where workers were brought together under supervision, using a central source of power.[14] This innovation led to a rapid and sustained rise in productivity and, in turn, income per head, although, it should be noted, the increase in income per head was not immediate, and, in fact, took some decades to occur.

The Industrial Revolution first involved cotton textiles. This was the lead industry. In Britain at the time, wool was the fiber of choice, as it provided warmth. Yet wool manufacture was not easily converted to machinery. Cotton was a much better fiber to work, and it was much cheaper than silk, the other fiber that could have been mechanized. With cotton, one had the marriage of huge demand (undergarments, shirts, etc.) to increasingly effective manufacture. A succession of scientifically based inventions created a production process that became increasingly fast and capable. First came the spinning jenny and the water frame. Later came Crompton's mule, the power loom, and allied gains in steam engines, metallurgy, and machine tools. Scale was not important, especially at the start.[15]

Gradually, too, processes became integrated. Cotton preparation and carding were combined with spinning. And, later, spinning was combined with weaving. As these advances were made and as the factory system grew, inventories were reduced, especially as compared with the "putting-out" system that prevailed before the creation of factories. In the putting-out system, the individual steps of the process, such as carding, spinning, and weaving, were subcontracted, typically to individuals in homes, and simply coordinated by an agent. Such coordination, naturally, took time, and "shrinkage" was common in each step. Inventories were substantial. In factories, these process steps were joined and balanced, and skills passed from artisans to machines.[16] The water frame and, later, the mule could make better cotton yarn than those available in India, and for far cheaper a cost. Variations in quality, quantities, and timing were all reduced, and throughput times plunged. The Industrial Revolution, centered as it was with cotton textiles, is where we first see swift, even flow played out on a grand scale. More on the nature of the factory later.

WHY BRITAIN?

Why Britain? Why not China or India or the other countries of Europe? China and India were the most populous countries and they were prosperous. Both enjoyed abundant raw materials and skilled workforces. They were rich by comparison. The Mogul emperor Aurangzeb of India, for example, had an income in the late 1600s that was ten times that of his contemporary, Louis XIV of France, the creator of Versailles.[17] China was a center of invention. The Chinese invented the wheelbarrow, the stirrup, the compass, paper, printing, gunpowder, and porcelain. They built huge ships and made iron. Yet, Britain soon passed both China and India.

Before Britain launched the Industrial Revolution, other countries in Europe had taken turns as the region's wealth leaders. Portugal was the first great seafaring nation. It led the way around the Cape of Good Hope to the riches of the Spice Islands. Spain overtook Portugal with the gold of the New World and then the Netherlands muscled in on Portugal's spice trade. France, too, was richer than Great Britain. Nevertheless, once the Industrial Revolution got rolling, Britain began to create wealth at a rate far in excess of what any of these countries could do.

There are a number of explanations as the works by Allen, Landes, and Mokyr make plain. Allen argues persuasively that Britain was a high-wage country and that such high wages encouraged labor-saving invention. What, in turn, contributed to Britain's high wages? Trade. We know from David Ricardo that comparative advantage can benefit a country, but it takes trade, and Britain had become a trading nation. The Netherlands was also a trading nation with high wages, but unlike the Netherlands, Britain had streams for water power and cheap coal that could encourage energy-intensive invention such as the initial steam engines.

It helped, too, that Britain was a nation with a common identity and characterized by relative equality.[18] As the cotton textile industry developed, products were made for a "large national and international market and focused on standardized goods of modest price – just the kind that lent themselves to machine production."[19] Such a large and standardized market meant a steady demand for cotton textiles (read "even flow"). This was definitely not the case in India, the former industry leader.[20] Britain's was the first market geared to the common man.

Economic historians all also point to the mind-set of the British. Science, literacy, and numeracy were pursued widely, as Mokyr and Allen document. The Royal Society, with noted early members such as Robert Hooke, Robert Boyle, and Christopher Wren, was founded in 1660. Sir Isaac Newton was its president from 1703 until his death in 1727. Invention took hold and a patent system developed.

After a fast, early start, science in southern Europe faltered. The case in point is Galileo, the father of experimentation. After pathbreaking work, Galileo (and other scientists in southern Europe) ran afoul of the powerful Catholic Church. The Church was not about to grant Galileo and others the freedom of thought that we associate with breakthrough science. Galileo's open belief in the Copernican system led the Church to pressure him to recant. Northern, Protestant Europe accepted Copernicus, but not southern, Catholic Europe. Even Descartes, the leader of French science, hemmed and hawed about it. It was a devastating blow to science in all of Europe under the sway of the Catholic Church. It was years before science in Italy, Spain, and Portugal could recover. France fell behind too. Protestant Europe accepted science and was able to apply scientific principles to a range of endeavors. Catholic Europe, China, and India did not. Without science, forging an industrial revolution was essentially impossible. The inventions and advances made during the Industrial Revolution were nearly all anchored in science.

IT'S ALSO ABOUT TIME

Landes also takes pains to document the cultural factors that he argues contributed mightily to Europe's and Britain's rapid industrial growth. Of particular interest to him is the attitude toward time itself. For example, prior to the last quarter of the thirteenth century in Europe, time was the province of the Church. People's lives were dictated by the bells of the church, indicating when to pray (e.g., matins) and when to engage in a variety of other tasks. Day and night were divided into equal hours, but, of course, the length of those hours varied with the seasons of the year. The newly developing towns of the era had need for more consistency. To help bring about this consistency, what happened in the last quarter of the thirteenth century, roughly simultaneously in England and Italy, was the invention of the clock. Having a tower clock, in the center of town, spread like wildfire, and it changed the way people in Europe thought about their lives. The Church initially fought the equal hours of the mechanical clock, but it eventually came around to accepting them.[21]

Britain became particularly enamored by the clock and what it meant for people. The British became the leaders in designing and producing clocks and watches of all types.[22] Importantly, the clock was a device that spawned other inventions and industries. From its earliest years, the goals soon became to make clocks that were smaller and more accurate. This demanded great craftsmanship, but also new devices for inclusion in clocks and watches (e.g., escapements, springs), new tools and materials for making them (e.g., gear-making equipment, better metallurgy), and new advances in mechanical engineering, particularly for the increasing miniaturization of the works. There was a constant pressure to improve. It was not the wheelbarrow, the stirrup, or the compass; it was not a one-off type of invention. The clock screamed for continuous improvement, and in Britain, more than any other place, continuous improvement happened.

Landes presses the point that northern Europe, and particularly Britain, created a time-valuing culture that was conducive to the development of industry. He is sympathetic to Max Weber's provocative explanation for the faster industrial development of northern over southern Europe. Weber's thesis was that Protestantism defined and sanctioned "an ethic of everyday behavior that conduced to business success," one that stressed "hard work, honesty, seriousness, the thrifty use of money and time."[23] Landes makes a particular point of the attitude toward time.

> Even in Catholic areas such as France and Bavaria, most
> clockmakers were Protestant; and the use of these
> instruments of time measurement and their diffusion to rural
> areas was far more advanced in Britain and Holland than in
> Catholic countries. Nothing testifies so much as time sensibility
> to the "urbanization" of rural society, with all that that implies
> for rapid diffusion of values and tastes.[24]

Such preoccupation with time, especially time as a linear progression, and the saving of time was not evident elsewhere in the world. Indians did not think like the British. Clocks and progressive time were not important to them. In China, time was the province of the emperor. The mechanical clocks brought by the early Europeans were viewed as interesting curiosities, but the Chinese never sought to learn how to make them, let alone live by them. Only the Japanese were swept up with clocks and mechanical time. They copied what the Europeans brought and they sought to miniaturize these clocks and to put their own stamp on their design. Thus, lest one think that the Protestant ethic is about religion per se, we need only look at the clock-loving Japanese and how they developed very much the same kind of ethic.[25]

Track where time became important and, to a large extent, one tracks where industrial revolutions began.

The problem of longitude is an apt example of Britain's interests and mastery. While the Portuguese had solved the problem of latitude centuries earlier and had beaten everyone around the Cape of Good Hope to the East Indies, the major navigational problem lay with determining longitude. It was left to John Harrison, an Englishman, to create a marine clock (chronometer) that won the prize for solving the longitude problem. The consequence: the world is compelled to anchor time to a British location and to call it by a British name, Greenwich Mean Time.

The British, more than any of the others at the time, appreciated swift, even flow. Reducing throughput time and reducing variation became part of the fabric of British life. And, this appreciation has easy parallels with the creation of the factory system that lies at the heart of the Industrial Revolution. We can appreciate this most acutely by examining Richard Arkwright and the invention and implementation of the water frame.

ARKWRIGHT, THE WATER FRAME, AND THE FACTORY

Sir Richard Arkwright (1732–1792) was not the inventor of the water frame (1769) so much as the driving force in its invention. Others had input into it, but it was clear that his was the entrepreneurial hand behind it. He was also behind the invention of a carding machine (1775).

The water frame (initially called the spinning frame) was a step forward from Hargreaves' spinning jenny (mid-1760s), which was itself a step forward from the ubiquitous spinning wheel, which

FIGURE 3.2 Arkwright's water frame, circa 1775
Reproduced with permission of the Science Museum, London / Science
and Society Picture Library, London.

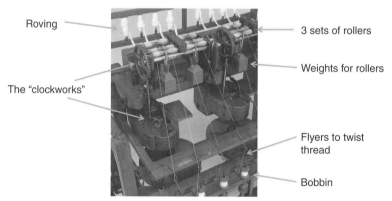

FIGURE 3.3 A close-up of Arkwright's water frame, showing the
"clockworks"
Reproduced with permission of the Science Museum, London / Science
and Society Picture Library, London.

dated from the early 1500s. The water frame, so called because it
used water power to do its spinning, took cotton rovings that had
been carded and directed them through three pairs of rollers (see
Figures 3.2 and 3.3). What was new about this arrangement was that

the second pair of rollers spun at twice the speed of the first pair, and the third pair of rollers spun at twice the speed of the second. These increasing speeds pulled at the cotton and stretched it out progressively. Flyers located lower on the machine took the stretched cotton and twisted it and then coiled it onto bobbins. The water frame became the first powered textile machine to spin cotton thread successfully and continuously.

Arkwright's contribution was a determined program of what, today, we would call "research and development." Arkwright, together with John Kay, a clock-maker, spent five years perfecting the design – speed and spacing of the rollers, composition of the rollers (grooved metal, wood, leather), pressure on the top roller, and how the gearing was designed. From the accompanying photos, one can easily see why the guts of the water frame were termed the "clockworks," depending as they did on the gears that only clock-makers knew how to engineer and make.

Arkwright was more than simply an inventor. He had a vision that was bolder. He took the water frame and his carding machine, located them together in specially constructed buildings next to streams where he could take advantage of water power, and hired workers to operate and oversee these machines. Thus were born the first true factories. Arkwright's initial efforts at factory design started in 1769, but it was Arkwright's mill no. 2 at Cromford, built in 1776, that became the prototype, the dominant design, for many others in Britain and elsewhere. In Cromford no. 2, Arkwright worked out a good solution to issues such as how the water power would be distributed, how the machines would be spaced throughout the factory, and how materials would flow.[26] It employed 450 workers and ran both day and night. For me, Cromford no. 2 is the epicenter of the Industrial Revolution.

Arkwright went on to build a number of other factories. To do so, he employed many clock-makers to produce his water frames and the "clockworks" that made them work. Problems with his patent meant that he never earned much money from it, but his development of the factory and his construction of many of them more than compensated for that disappointment. Arkwright died hugely wealthy, arguably the richest man of the Industrial Revolution.

His is a story of swift, even flow. Arkwright invented two machines that could operate on water power continuously. He integrated the two processes of carding and spinning and greatly reduced the inventories, and the calendar time, that had existed with those two processes in the putting-out system. The output of his machines was a consistent product of good quality. It did not produce as fine a cotton thread as Crompton's mule would soon produce, but it was more than adequate for most needs, being used chiefly as the warp (the longer, stronger thread) for weaving. The power of Arkwright's vision of manufacturing was quickly recognized. Arkwright himself invested in many mills, and others copied his ideas. At one time, it is estimated that there were 150 Arkwright-type mills in England and Scotland and over 800 clock-makers employed in them.[27] And, not only England and Scotland. Samuel Slater, sometimes known as the Father of the American Industrial Revolution, had worked at Cromford and brought its design to Rhode Island to begin the first successful cotton textile factory in the United States.

Much has been made of the fact that many of the early mills were staffed with children. I am far from an apologist for child labor, especially in so rigid an environment as existed with the early mills. However, I find it noteworthy that the skill of spinning, which in the putting-out system had largely been an activity for the adult women of the household, migrated from human hands to a machine. More than that, the skill now rested in a machine that could be tended by children.

It is fitting, too, that the key portion of the water frame owed its design and production to clock-makers. Not only did the newly established factory demand on-time performance from its workforce, but it was founded on technology that only clock-makers possessed. Other countries may well not have been able to provide so many clock-makers and so much technical support to the task as Britain could.

It is hard to underestimate the importance of clock-making to industrial progress. The historian, Daniel Boorstin, the Librarian of Congress Emeritus, writing in his book, *The Discoverers*, notes the following:[28]

> Precisely because the clock did not start as a practical tool
> shaped for a single purpose, it was destined to be the mother
> of machines. The clock broke down the wall between kinds of
> knowledge, ingenuity, and skill, and clockmakers were the first
> consciously to apply the theories of mechanics and physics to
> the making of machines. Progress came from the collaboration
> of scientists – Galileo, Huygens, Hooke, and others – with
> craftsmen and mechanics.
>
> Since clocks were the first modern measuring machines,
> clockmakers became the pioneer scientific-instrument makers.
> The enduring legacy of the pioneer clockmakers, though
> nothing could have been further from their minds, was the basic
> technology of machine tools. The two prime examples are the
> gear (or toothed wheel) and the screw.[29]

The upshot of this review is to establish that, in Britain, a host of factors combined to ignite what became the Industrial Revolution. Other places in the world lacked one or another of these factors. Trade helped to make Britain a high-wage country, and that encouraged labor-saving invention. Cheap coal encouraged energy-intensive invention, particularly important for the steam engine and all that it meant to industry, especially in the first half of the nineteenth century. Britain enjoyed a mass market and its people were literate and numerate and embraced science. And, they had the mentality, not only for invention, but also for appreciating time and the saving of time, and the clock-making that supported that mentality. Cotton textiles became the perfect industry in which these factors could combine and thus launch Britain on its way to an Industrial Revolution. Its hallmark was the factory system, and the swift, even flow of the factory outpaced all other means of production.

THE AMERICAN CONTRIBUTION

Even as Britain led the world to the Industrial Revolution, it was soon overtaken by two other countries: the United States and Germany. Let us concentrate on the Americans. US labor productivity in manufacturing was higher than Britain's by the early years of the nineteenth century, if not before.[30] Such a high level of labor productivity was not the result of a higher capital-to-labor ratio; Britain had more capital relative to labor than the US for most of the nineteenth century.[31] This is an important fact because a high capital-to-labor ratio, which economics would typically look to first, cannot be invoked to explain why American labor productivity was higher than Britain's so early. Rather, the innovation that was new was what the British began to call "the American system of manufactures." This innovation highlighted standardized designs, interchangeable parts, and attention to the flow of work that enabled materials in the factory to move more quickly, and with less variability, than was the case in Britain.[32] The prowess of American industry was no more evident than at the Crystal Palace Exhibition in London in 1851. There, the American manufacturer Robbins & Lawrence stunned the British with a display of rifles that could be disassembled, their parts swapped, and the rifles reassembled perfectly.[33] The "fitting" that characterized the final steps in a typical rifle factory (as elsewhere in industry) was not needed and its elimination caused such a stir that the British Government commenced a study of the American system, much as Americans 130 years later would study what the Japanese had done.

As noted, the archetypal product for the American system of manufactures was the rifle, and specifically the military rifle that was in constant and high demand by the American Government. The rifle that first met the test of part interchangeability was the M1819 Hall rifle (see Figure 3.4). This rifle, designed by John Hall and produced by him at the Harpers Ferry Armory, was a breech-loaded rifle, the first military rifle of that design, and one that could be fired more rapidly than the muzzle-loaded rifles that preceded it. To make

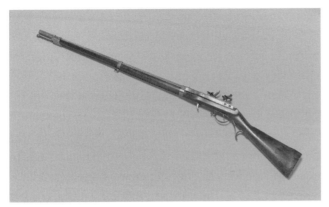

FIGURE 3.4 The M1819 Hall rifle
Reproduced with permission of the North Carolina Museum of History

his rifle, though, John Hall spent years developing the machine tools
(e.g., lathes, drilling machines, drop-hammers, balanced pulleys, the
forerunner of the milling machine) and techniques that could hold
the tight tolerances that permitted manufacturing to free itself from
the "fitting" (with its files and other ways to tweak the manufactured
product) that had characterized manufacturing beforehand. Hall's
work led to much bigger and more sophisticated machines than had
existed before, machines that could produce identical parts, plus the
fixtures for holding parts in those machines, the gauging to make
sure that the tolerances were kept, and the sequencing of the operations that enabled higher volume production than had been possible
before. This was new ground, and Hall's techniques swept through
the gun-making industry, especially that of the Connecticut River
valley.[34] From there, the lessons learned in gun-making dispersed to
other industries. Gone was the fitting of prior production and in its
stead was the reduced variation of the new system and the new ability to produce things in much more of an assembly-line fashion.

The managers who were well versed in the American system
of manufactures became those that were in constant demand. The
dispersion of the techniques really came from the dispersion of the
managers and engineers who cut their teeth in the firearms industry.
For example, the McCormick Harvesting Machine Company did not

really become good at manufacturing until it hired a manager who had learned his trade at the Colt factory in Hartford.[35]

The importance of swift, even flow as an explanation of American productivity gain during the nineteenth century is bolstered by the histories of the companies and industries that led US industrial development then. As Alfred Chandler saw it, the factory system that spread so quickly in the middle decades of the 1800s was characterized by a drive for high-speed throughput. The pinnacle of such a movement was for him the development of the continuous process factory, exemplified by the "the automatic all-roller, gradual reduction mill" with its automatic materials handling equipment used to process wheat and other grains. Such equipment was an inspiration to Ford's pioneering engineers.[36]

Productivity in this era was growing by leaps and bounds. Swift, even flow even came to services in that era.[37] Fred Harvey, beginning in 1876, created a string of 65 restaurants along the Atchison, Topeka and Santa Fe Railroad line in the southwestern United States that were famed for consistent quality and the ability to feed a train's worth of passengers within 30 minutes, the time it took the trains themselves to be serviced. Harvey's system incorporated telegraphed information about passenger menu orders, standard operating procedures, and a well-rehearsed choreography of service once the passengers arrived at the stop.

Harvey grew wealthy from designing and managing, over a broad geography, a standardized service. And, he did it in the late 1800s, well before the world knew about McDonald's. It was the era of the robber barons. We may call them robber barons, but, for my money, their major exploitation was of the productivity gains from swift, even flow.

PRODUCTIVITY RATES DURING THE INDUSTRIAL REVOLUTION

Recent scholarship has observed that the productivity rates of the Industrial Revolution were really not that high.[38] Productivity rates did not really show dramatic progress until the middle of the 1800s, and certainly not before about 1830. One explanation for this seems to lie in the fact that the cotton textile industry did not comprise that large a fraction of the economy so that its productivity advances could not sway the overall productivity numbers.

But, this is not the only explanation. Importantly, the full integration of different processes (in cotton textiles, think carding, spinning, and weaving) was not widespread until the 1830s or later. And, here again, it was the United States that was quicker to integrate. Francis Cabot Lowell first integrated carding, spinning, and weaving in 1814 with his Boston Manufacturing Company.[39] The resulting profits were dramatically good, but, as could be expected, it took some time for this innovation to be copied. The British cotton textile industry did not integrate spinning and weaving either as early or as completely. Thus, quick throughput times were either delayed or forgone entirely.

We can see then that the workings of swift, even flow throughout the supply chain of even the first industry of the Industrial Revolution does not become evident until the 1830s and afterward. Cotton textiles led the way, but, even there, it took decades to lower throughput times substantially. Such results did not occur in other industries until later. The invention of various machines does not affect productivity right away, and that includes the steam engine and its history. The key is the reduction of variation and throughput time, and it can take years for that reduction to occur, mainly because the elements of the process need to be integrated and refined so that materials can flow easily and in a balanced way from one portion of the process to another.

SWIFT, EVEN FLOW AND CLOCK-MAKING

The foregoing discussion has focused on the impact of clocks and timekeeping on the mentality of the British, and later others such as the Americans, and how it helped to foster an appreciation for swift, even flow. The history of British timekeeping has been a parade of successively smaller and more accurate timepieces of lower and lower cost. And, great was the demand for them as the British, in both town and countryside, used clocks and watches to regulate their lives. Understandably, then, the history of mechanical clocks and watches has also been a search for greater and greater productivity. With this in mind, we can reverse things and speak to the impact that swift, even flow, itself, has had on clock-making.

The clocks of the Middle Ages, beginning in the latter half of the thirteenth century, were the large clocks that were mounted in towers that overlooked the center of town. Initially these clocks had only hour hands. Constructing such clocks took much customization and they were themselves one-of-a-kind projects.

Over the years, of course, there was increasing demand for clocks that could be used in the home. This was a significantly larger market and the table clock began to appear in the 1400s. Watches soon followed, but the costs were high. It was not until the 1700s that we got watches in quantity, and by then, the center of clock-making and watch-making had shifted to Great Britain. The Swiss followed the lead of the British. It was the Americans, however, beginning in the mid-1800s, who really started to make quality clocks and then watches in great numbers and with high accuracy. This was the era when the American system of manufactures shone and interchangeable parts took over. The Swiss copied this and the British slowly lose their former position as the center of clock- and watch-making. The culmination of high-volume manufacture of accurate but inexpensive mechanical watches occurred just after World War II with the American brand, Timex.

Shortly thereafter, the quartz movement began to take over the mechanical watch market so that today, only high-end brands make mechanical movements and for consumers who value the workmanship and who do not demand, as much, the precision of the quartz movement.

We can capture the history of mechanical clock- and watch-making in Figure 3.5.

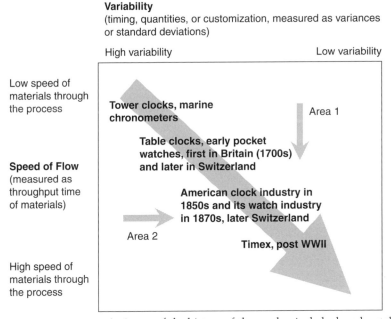

Variability
(timing, quantities, or customization, measured as variances or standard deviations)

High variability   Low variability

Low speed of materials through the process

Tower clocks, marine chronometers   Area 1

Table clocks, early pocket watches, first in Britain (1700s) and later in Switzerland

Speed of Flow (measured as throughput time of materials)

American clock industry in 1850s and its watch industry in 1870s, later Switzerland

Area 2

Timex, post WWII

High speed of materials through the process

FIGURE 3.5 A picture of the history of the mechanical clock and watch

Here we can see how the march of history and the relentless push for smaller and smaller clocks and watches of greater and greater accuracy traces the diagonal of swift, even flow. The tower clocks of the Middle Ages and the marine chronometers that were designed and built to solve the problem of longitude (e.g., John Harrison's work) could be labeled as job shops, if not projects. Output was very low and very customized.

The early table clocks and early pocket watches that were made in Britain in the 1700s were done in small batches. There was considerable division of labor in the small shops that produced these items. The apprentices would do the easiest, roughest work, saving the more delicate tasks for the master. This division of labor spilled over to Switzerland as that country's workers caught up with the British. As the industry progressed, designs improved, the metals used improved, and the tolerances for gears and other components improved.

However, it was only with the application of the elements of the American system of manufactures to the production of first clocks and later watches that we see the beginnings of what standard designs and interchangeable parts could really do to lower costs. The Waltham Watch Company, in Massachusetts, led the way. At Waltham, new, heavy machines were designed and built that could hold small tolerances. These machines were designed to do particular jobs and the materials, such as brass, were passed from one special-purpose machine to another. Although true interchangeability was not perfected until the 1900s (Timex being the exemplar), the watches initially made at Waltham were good enough. What in Britain and Switzerland was done by highly skilled fitters was done at Waltham by sorting through what was produced by machine and then, using the fruits of statistical distribution, matching companion pieces. The volumes produced of these standard designs were significant, their costs were very low, and the industry continued to develop cheaper models of good quality up until the time of the quartz movement.[40]

Thus, we can observe that the history of mechanical clock- and watch-making is a history of relentlessly pushing down the diagonal of swift, even flow. Variability was continually reduced, throughput times were cut, and volumes rocketed ever higher. Clock-making helped to foster the factories where swift, even flow first flowered, and swift, even flow helped clock-making itself to evolve more productive operations.

MASS PRODUCTION VERSUS MASS CUSTOMIZATION

This march through industrial history has, among other things, highlighted Henry Ford and what he did to create what has been termed mass production. Ford and the others underscore how important greater and greater speed of flow has been for any number of goods that can now be termed "mass-produced." If we follow the diagonal of Figure 2.5, however, we see that the move toward greater speed of flow is matched by a move toward less variation. There are some people, however, who do not see speed and variation linked in the same way. They do not see speed of flow and variation as necessarily linked at all. In the past couple of decades, the term "mass customization" has been much touted and has attracted a following.[41] It has been defined as

> the use of flexible computer-aided manufacturing systems to produce custom output. Those systems combine the low unit costs of mass production processes with the flexibility of individual customization. Mass customization is the new frontier in business competition for both manufacturing and service industries. At its core is a tremendous increase in variety and customization without a corresponding increase in costs.[42]

Can one enjoy a customized product for the mass production price? Are speed and variation really not linked? What does the concept of swift, even flow have to say about mass customization? In short, it's a snare and a delusion. Customization necessarily introduces variation into a process. There is no other way. That increase in variation means that a customized product cannot be produced as cheaply as a product without that variation and with a similar throughput time.

This is not to say that technology advances have not been able to provide a wide variety of product options fairly easily. It is true that the costs of customization are lower now than they have ever been. This is especially true for electronic products but this flexibility exists for all kinds of goods and services. Nevertheless, mass customization and wide product variety are not the same thing. True customization costs more.

Given the hype that mass customization has enjoyed over the past couple of decades, one might think it easy to identify those firms that are its exemplars. On the contrary, discovering exactly which companies have implemented mass customization is not easy. Dell is often mentioned, but Dell does not literally customize its computers for the mass production price. Rather, it provides customers with a large array of product options from which they can choose, for a price. The low-cost deals that it offers customers are on combinations of options that it selects. Customers who wish to customize, or "personalize," their computers in any other way have to pay more for the options that they choose. Even a different color computer – and the choice of different colors is not great – costs more money. Dell has done a great job of providing the customer with extensive choice, but it is not a mass customizer.

Here is what the Wikipedia entry on mass customization says about implementation:

> Many implementations of mass customization are operational today, such as software-based product configurators which make it possible to add and/or change functionalities of a core product or to build fully custom enclosures from scratch. This degree of mass customization has only seen limited adoption, however. If an enterprise's marketing department offers individual products (atomic market fragmentation) it doesn't often mean that a product is produced individually, but rather that similar variants of the same mass-produced item are available.
>
> Companies which have succeeded with mass-customization business models tend to supply purely electronic products. However, these are not true "mass customizers" in the original sense, since they do not offer an alternative to mass production of material goods.[43]

This certainly is not very reassuring, especially after 20 years. It makes one wonder why the term still has adherents. Mass customization is a myth.

THE PLACE OF SWIFT, EVEN FLOW IN THIS HISTORY

This exploration of business history has stretched centuries, from the Arsenal to Henry Ford. I have taken you through it not only because I find it fascinating, but because it shows how entrepreneurs and managers who have stamped their mark on business history have intuitively appreciated the power of swift, even flow. Whether they happened upon it by trial and error or by flash of insight, these pioneers have demonstrated how the reduction of variation of all kinds and the collapsing of throughput times yielded dramatic increases in productivity.

No Six Sigma black belts were around. No lean manufacturing consultants were choreographing the action. Eli Goldratt hadn't been born. Frederick Taylor was a voice in the wilderness; Ford's lieutenants were unaware of him.[44] These guys did it on their own. They didn't make their millions by chopping heads or by being concerned with labor efficiencies or machine utilizations. They were all about swift, even flow.

These men of history persuade me that the concept of swift, even flow is something more than the re-branding of the business innovations of the past several decades – lean production, Six Sigma, cells, process reengineering, and the others. It is more far-reaching. Those who embraced swift, even flow changed history. Their understanding of the concept, however conscious or unconscious it may have been, led them to take grand and strategic actions that altered the landscape of business. And, when they neglected swift, even flow, as US Steel did, productivity and profit suffered.

Importantly, swift, even flow is not simply the felicitous, accidental result of good decisions and technological breakthroughs that led to highly productive factories. Swift, even flow is not a "symptom" or an "outcome" of something else. It is what Arkwright and the robber barons sought to achieve. It was the driving force in their thinking and actions. Arkwright *became* the cotton fiber and saw how it could flow from raw state to thread on a bobbin. Arkwright's vision was a huge conceptual leap from the piecemeal, scattered, individual contracting of the putting-out system that pre-dated his creation of the factory. Rockefeller and his partners *became* the crude oil and saw how it could be turned into kerosene quickly with the application of new technology such as fractional distillation. Ford and his lieutenants *became* the metal and the parts and saw how it could all come together as a car on a radical new innovation, the moving assembly line. Carnegie and his "hard driving," "steady and full" colleagues *became* the iron and steel that traveled around Holly's design for the integrated mill. After these men led the way, others in the industry immediately followed suit; they recognized the importance of the production innovations that these pioneers championed.

Swift, even flow did not just happen. As Landes observes, "In big things, history abhors accident."[45]

In the chapters ahead we will see how the concept of swift, even flow can continue to work for managers in this day and time.

PART II Application

4   Vision

The true power of swift, even flow can only come by demonstrating how it can help managers solve important, and perplexing, problems. Here begins the second part of this book where swift, even flow gets applied to a variety of situations.

In this chapter, we deal with how swift, even flow can provide managers with expansive visions about their processes. First, three diverse settings are investigated: two in service industries and one in manufacturing. All three companies involved have been very successful, with clear, distinctive visions as to what operations can do to enhance productivity and profit. In each case, swift, even flow is at the root of their visions. Lastly, a different type of vision is explored, that of using swift, even flow to alter how cost accounting is done.

A FRATERNITY OF HERNIA SUFFERERS

Here is a famous but revealing example that is still going strong.[1] Around the time of World War II, Dr. Earle Shouldice, a Canadian doctor, developed a surgical procedure for repairing hernias that proved to be very effective. He combined that with his belief that activity, chiefly walking, after surgery promoted quick recovery. With the surgical procedure and the immediate exercise afterward, Shouldice could have patients up and out of a hospital in three days where typical procedures of the time would take a week or more.

Some information about hernias is in order. Hernias are protrusions of the intestines through holes or slits in the abdominal wall. The most common are external abdominal wall hernias, frequently inguinal hernias in the groin, caused primarily by slight weaknesses in the muscle layers there brought about by the dropping of the testes in male babies. This explains why hernias are an overwhelmingly masculine problem. The Shouldice method of hernia repair works best on these external abdominal wall hernias. Hernias usually are nagging problems for people. Many go in for surgery only when they have suffered for years. It is definitely an elective type of surgery.

The managerial issue that Shouldice faced was how to design a hospital so that it could make money. Productivity would be critical because the cost of the procedure would have to be very competitive to attract patients from far outside the Toronto area. What to do?

The first big decision that Shouldice made was to limit the hospital to hernias. Nothing else would be done. And, more than that, only external abdominal wall hernias would be treated, the easiest to treat with the Shouldice method. Just like a manufacturing cell that only produces parts within a particular family, the Shouldice Hospital would only treat such hernias, leaving the more involved types of hernias for other hospitals. This may remind people of quick-change oil places, such as Jiffy Lube, that leave more difficult car repairs to dealers and others, but such a decision to limit the scope of the operation is critical. It goes a long way in reducing the variation that would otherwise afflict the process.

If one is to restrict the hospital's scope in this way, then one has to control admissions, especially if patients come from a wide area. This meant developing a screening mechanism to identify the low-risk patients from the higher-risk ones. Shouldice created a questionnaire that quizzed prospective patients about their hernias and also about their general state of health. Patients who were too heavy or who exhibited other sources of risk were informed that they did not qualify. (If patients lied about their medical condition, they would be found out on entry to the hospital and politely told to leave.)

Limiting the scope of the hospital to low-risk hernias had a profound impact on the design of the hospital itself and on the capital investment it required. It did not need the huge investments of the typical hospital. A lot of diagnostic equipment could be forgone and even the operating rooms could be simplified. Intensive care rooms and lots of monitoring equipment were not needed.

More interesting are the design decisions the hospital made when it wanted to stimulate the recently operated-upon patients to walk and exercise as much as they could, important for their swift flow through the hospital. Consider the following:

- a hospital design that was more ranch-style and sprawling than is the usual case – all the hallways were carpeted;
- the hospital grounds invited walks when the weather permitted;
- no room service was provided unless absolutely required – all patients had to walk to a central place for meals and snacks;
- no televisions or telephones in the rooms – nothing is in the room that would keep the patient there rather than roaming the halls and spending time in the games rooms and other congregating places.

Shouldice also wanted to promote camaraderie, so that the patients could enjoy their time recuperating from the surgery and thus promote their own swift flow through the Shouldice method. More than that, patients who had recently been operated on could help to calm the nerves of those just arriving. This is reminiscent of upperclassmen and freshmen in college; there is a mentoring that can occur. Indeed, the more the hospital becomes a fraternity, the better for all concerned. With this is mind, Shouldice decided:

- to have double rooms, so that new patients could enter a room where the other patient had already been recovering;
- to match the patients for each room so that they had some common interests to share, in the same way as college roommates are matched;
- that the patients could be self-sufficient, feeding and entertaining them-selves – they could even shave themselves prior to surgery;
- there would be common times for meals and snacks; again, like college.

The decision to limit the hospital to inguinal hernias had some fundamental implications for the doctors and nurses, too. The doctors were not general surgeons. They were rather specialists, doing a standardized operation that is not that difficult once the technique has been learned. While some research and development could be engaged in, this was not a teaching hospital and the rewards to the doctors needed to be different. Such an environment may thus have been more conducive to the doctor who wanted a more traditional lifestyle, with time for family and friends. The pay could have been attractive, but it may not have been especially high. Rather, the regular hours and the family nature of the hospital became important features.

The doctor's day became one of surgeries in the morning, a communal time at lunch, and an afternoon spent examining the newly entering "class" and looking in on the recently operated-upon "class."

Likewise for nurses, the daily tasks were not the usual fare of the big hospital with a diverse assembly of patients. No need for the constant monitoring of intensive care. In fact, no need for the traditional bedpan. The requirement was much more social, keeping the patients up and moving around, encouraging them, and seeing to it that the atmosphere was warm and inviting. Nurses also provided an orientation for the new class of patients.

Shouldice's success has, over the years, fostered a huge word-of-mouth reputation that has been invaluable in attracting new patients. What was a worrisome, nagging problem for men has, with the Shouldice Hospital, become an almost pleasant respite from the world. The fraternity of patients has become a huge asset. It even reached the point where Shouldice was able to hold annual reunions of the patients who were eager to check up on their fellow "fraternity brothers" and the people who cared for them.

The vision of Shouldice is a vision of swift, even flow. The materials handled are, of course, humans, but the cleverly designed and all-encompassing process continues to yield uniformly excellent results for a low cost, year after year.

THE CIRCUS IS COMING TO TOWN

The era was the turn of the twentieth century.[2] The United States was a land of small towns stretching along railroad tracks crisscrossing the country. And, nothing could bring those towns to a complete standstill like the traveling circus. The circus was the one attraction that could pack an entire town into its seats. Everything stopped for the circus. Only for the largest cities, however, could the circus afford to stay a week or two. For 150 days of a seven-month season, the circus had to move from one town to another for one-day-only shows (2 p.m. matinees and 8 p.m. evening shows of two-and-a-half hours each). That meant that the circus had to arrive in a town in the early morning, "unload, deploy, perform, pack, load, and move on" during the night to the next town, where everything would be repeated.[3] The schedule was relentless but it was the only way that the circus could make money. The "Greatest Show on Earth" depended crucially on the processes that got it from town to town, on time, and with no hiccups. As Vince Mabert and Mike Showalter in their wonderful article relate:

> The following statement by John Ringling [of the Ringling Bros. and Barnum & Bailey Circus, the largest circus in the US] (1919, p. 183) highlights the recognition a century ago that a swift flow was a key element of the circus's logistics: "Our business is in constant motion. But beyond saving time, our object is to avoid mistakes."[4]

How did they do it? How did the circuses of the United States manage the recurrent "tasks of procurement, stowage, and transportation of personnel, animals, material, and equipment/facilities to support daily circus performances"?[5] Mabert and Showalter list a number of principles, with examples from the Ringling Bros. and Barnum & Bailey Circus of the era. All of them illustrate the power of reducing variation and throughput time.

- *Utilize an order lot size of one to minimize inventory.* The circus could not afford to carry extra inventory. Advance men were responsible for procuring and managing contracts for food and supplies for the 700 people who moved with the circus (400 workers and 300 performers) and for the performing animals and the draft horses that were also part of the circus.

- *Track procurement and point of use delivery.* The contracts that were entered into specified that the vendors would deliver precise amounts to precise locations. That meant that those vendors would deliver to a specific tent (e.g., cookhouse tent, dressing tent, horse tent, the big top itself) exactly what that tent needed.
- *Position operational equipment to minimize flows and waste.* The positioning of tents/facilities and the people, animals, and equipment that went with them was carefully laid out so that movements could be economically accomplished. Spectators were kept to one side of the layout while the circus's "back office" was kept to the other side. The layout remained the same each day, even to assigned seating in the dining tents. Everything was loaded and unloaded in the same order and stowed in the same way.
- *Design equipment to minimize setup and task times.* Circus wagons and the containers that went inside them were all custom-designed and built. Even the rail cars that the circus used were of custom designs and were owned by the circus itself. The designs were such that loading and unloading was as easy as possible. Care was taken, even, that the stock car for the horses was designed so that the horses would not stumble during the train ride and that they could feed while in the stock car. The horses wore harnesses so that they could be quickly deployed but there were special hooks so that the weight of the harnesses could be supported from above and would not weigh down the horses themselves while in transit. The procedures for setting up and taking down the circus were all standardized, often leaving no discretion to the worker.
- *Reduce/eliminate transit bottlenecks through lot splitting.* The circus traveled in separate trains so that those items needed first at a new location would be the first to leave the previous day's location and the first to arrive at the new location.
- *Minimize transit costs.* The circus train was routed from town to town to minimize transfers across different railroads and was of a size that assured favorable rates from the railroads.
- *Employ flexible materials handling resources.* The circus wagons and other equipment could be handled in different ways. For example, if bad weather made for sloppy conditions, more horses could easily be used to pull wagons out of the muck.
- *Maintain continuous communication.* The advance men for the circus used the latest technology, telegraph, and kept all concerned abreast of

the latest information about what was happening at locations next on the schedule. Expediting, if necessary, was done.

The Greatest Show on Earth was itself a model of logistics and of process design. Moving the circus was as much a rehearsed event as the show under the big top was. (Indeed, it was a show in itself. Many people got up early in the morning to watch the circus unload and for the performers and animals to parade through town to the show grounds.) Variation was reduced in nearly every way possible and throughput times were remarkably short. The very existence of the circus depended on the swift, even flow of all its elements.

A POWERFUL PHILOSOPHY

The resounding worldwide success of Toyota may be attributed to many things, but its manufacturing prowess is certainly at or near the top of the list. The Toyota Production System has spawned many similar versions that have been adopted in companies around the globe. It provides a powerful vision for many companies.

What follows, at some length, is my own interpretation of the Toyota Production System, generalized for multiple industries. As you will see, it is an interpretation grounded on the concept of swift, even flow. This interpretation contrasts what I'll call the "Lean Manufacturing Philosophy," based on Toyota, against what can best be described as the "Received Tradition" – the precepts under which at least some companies have implicitly operated. This Received Tradition is not a carefully constructed "philosophy" of manufacturing. Rather, it is a series of policies that have sprung up willy-nilly in response to the barrage of demands routinely made on manufacturing – demands particularly for quick delivery and for customization of the product. Also important to the development of this tradition has been the ascendancy of short-run financial measures by which to gauge the performance of business units. I hope that the Received Tradition's precepts smack, at least a little bit, of what you have heard or thought over the years, so that the innovation in thinking that is represented by this Lean Manufacturing Philosophy can stand in sharper relief.

Many people have viewed the Toyota Production System and Lean Manufacturing as a "bag of tricks" that, if used properly, will lower cost and improve competitiveness. Too many have not realized that the Toyota Production System is first and foremost a "people development system." That was certainly the intention of Taiichi Ohno, the Toyota executive who gave birth to this way of thinking about operations. For this reason, we should think of it as a "philosophy," an integrated, holistic way of thinking that can permeate individuals and color everything about how they see a process and what can be done to improve it. That is why the Toyota Production System is so hard to duplicate. A "bag of tricks" can be easily forgotten and it will not propel people to dive as deeply into the underlying causes of a problem as a philosophy, or theory, will.[6]

This analysis contrasts the Lean Manufacturing Philosophy with the Received Tradition via 15 precepts. Each contrasting pair of precepts will be presented, with a discussion first about the Received Tradition (designated RT) and then about the Lean Manufacturing Philosophy (designated Lean). By placing them all together here, I hope to encourage your understanding of how the pieces of lean manufacturing practice fit together. At times, the elements of this discussion will undoubtedly seem familiar. After all, lean manufacturing has been much studied. My goal, here, is to show how the various elements of lean manufacturing actually fit together into a philosophy and how that philosophy is grounded in swift, even flow. What follows is not an exercise in the components of lean manufacturing. Rather, it is an exercise in envisioning what a manufacturing process can be with the concept of swift, even flow as its intellectual underpinning and how markedly this thinking differs from conventional thinking.

1 Quality

RT: it costs money to make quality products
This precept states that conforming to the requirements is often difficult and thus costly. According to the Received Tradition,

there is a real, acknowledged trade-off between quality (defined as conformance to the product's specifications, as valued by customers) and cost. One cannot expect to be both the low-cost producer and the producer with the highest quality ratings. Quality, no matter what the degree of luxury in the product, comes at a cost. This precept contrasts starkly with the lean philosophy.

Lean: quality is free

From its own history of improving quality, Toyota has shown the world that, in the long run at least, working to improve quality can also lead to reduced costs. Doing things right the first time ensures not only quality products but also low-cost ones. Toyota has put meat on the bones of Philip Crosby's claim, mentioned in Chapter 2, that quality is free.

This notion of quality being free, or, indeed, a major source of potential profit, rests at the heart of the Lean Manufacturing Philosophy. Improving quality, eliminating waste, and reaping the profit rewards of so doing, are much of what the lean philosophy is all about. Many of the precepts that follow build upon, and support, what great quality can mean to a company, its operation, and its customers. The fundamental importance of quality and reducing that source of variation is what makes this set of precepts the first one.

2 Expertise

RT: engineers and managers are experts. Workers serve their desires

This Received Tradition acknowledges that charting the direction for the company is the responsibility of its management and engineering staff. These people are highly educated and are paid to be take-charge types. They are the ones with vision. Workers are the means by which the directions set by these managers and engineers are fulfilled. The jobs of these workers should be studied by industrial engineers, perhaps through time and motion study, so that they are well defined and can be done efficiently.

Lean: workers are experts. Managers and engineers serve them
According to the lean philosophy, if the company is to do things right the first time, it is the workers who have to do it. It is the workers who have to build quality in – workers on the line actually fabricating parts or assembling products, workers testing items, workers handling orders, workers handling materials. Under this philosophy, it is the workers who know the problems that are encountered in getting things done right the first time. They know what the problems are, although they may not know exactly how to solve them. Managers and engineers under this philosophy support the workers. They provide the wherewithal and skills to work on the quality problems identified by the workforce. These initiatives put the worker at the center of process improvement in the organization and view management and engineering as aids for the eyes, ears, and minds of the workers – not simply as the authorities from which orders come for directing the movements of their hands, feet, and backs.

This precept also serves as the basis for what is termed "standard work." Toyota is famed for having its workers write up formally what it is that they actually do at their jobs. This forms the baseline for improvement. No one knows better than the worker, at the point of value being added, what it takes to do the job properly. If a process is to be improved, then standard work is the springboard for improvement. (*Kaizen* is the Japanese term for this improvement process.)

This way of looking at things differs markedly from the attitude enshrined in the "scientific management" movement championed by Frederick Taylor. There, time and motion study is the management way to study a job and to dictate to the workforce how best to do it. With standard work, the responsibility shifts to the workforce itself.

3 Mistakes

RT: mistakes are inevitable and have to be inspected out

The Received Tradition recognizes the fact that all of us are imperfect and that we will make mistakes. If these mistakes are not to reach consumers, we have to inspect products to remove any that contain defects. The process should be designed therefore to make it fairly easy to identify products that have defects. Furthermore, the process should work to have those defects remedied (in a rework station) if possible and, if not, to have the defective products scrapped.

Lean: mistakes are treasures, the study of which
leads to improvement

Under the lean philosophy, mistakes are not inevitable. Recognizing that a defect exists is not enough, nor is purging any defects by some final inspection. This philosophy goes beyond the Received Tradition by espousing the view that every mistake is an opportunity to understand why the process is not foolproof. By tenaciously investigating every defect and its cause, one can gradually, bit by bit and project by project, improve the process so that it does not create defects. In this philosophy, zero defects is not simply a goal but a standard that can be obtained by diligent investigation of the errors created by the process.

To adhere to the standard of zero defects, the lean company tries to sustain a "habit of improvement," with all elements of the company engaged in continual efforts to improve product designs and process performance. Time is devoted to studying the work station and knowing exactly what tools and auxiliary materials are required to do each job. What is not needed can be removed. What is needed can be fussed over and codified. The five Ss can be followed (Sort, Set in order, Shine, Standardize, and Sustain). The work station and the standard work associated with it can then serve as the bedrock for sustained improvement.

Here, again, the workers are viewed as experts. Only they, once trained and equipped, can monitor all aspects of the process. To do such monitoring well, however, requires clear and compelling measures of product and process quality that are well communicated to all those associated with the process. (Charts and displays tracking quality measures are everywhere in lean factories.) Workers are often responsible for correcting their own errors. To make it easy to identify defects, considerable time, thought, and expense are devoted to developing foolproof devices and automatic defect checks (termed *pokayoke* in Japanese) that monitor product and/or process characteristics continuously.

Not only are workers expected to monitor quality and, if possible, to correct their mistakes (no rework stations on which to discard faulty work), but they are also frequently part of any study of process improvements. Workers are schooled in the tried and true statistical techniques of quality management and in cause-and-effect analysis (such as found in the "fishbone" chart). These tools are at the center of reducing variation.

4 Inventory

RT: inventory is useful – it keeps production rolling along
The Received Tradition recognizes that work-in-process inventory (WIP) can buffer a manufacturing process from defects and other problems (e.g., parts shortages, late vendor delivery) that could otherwise cause it to grind to a halt. Inventory is like grease for the process, enabling it to keep functioning despite adversities.

Lean: inventory is evil – it hides problems that should
be allowed to surface
According to the Lean Manufacturing Philosophy, not only does work-in-process inventory take up space and cost you money to carry, but it also lets you get away with things that are not perfect. If the process is to be studied and refined continually so that it turns out only perfect products, all the problems in the process must be identified and worked on. If excess inventory exists in the process, there is a temptation to avoid working to perfect it. Thus, problems that should be uncovered are not.

Toyota developed a useful idea, *jidoka*, that is apropos. *Jidoka* literally means "intelligent automation" that typically, in practice, is an add-on device that detects a fault in the process and may actually stop the process in its tracks. *Jidoka* makes problems with the process visible so that workers can take action to remedy them. It runs counter to the notion of inventory. What better way to focus everyone's attention on the need for quality than to have the process rigged so that there is no place for errors to hide? Banish inventory, adopt *jidoka*, and you expose non-quality work.

Japanese managers often refer to a flowing stream as a parable for production. Water does not always flow evenly and at the same pace everywhere along a stream. Water sometimes gets trapped in deep pools, blocked by rocks or by other obstacles that sometimes remain hidden under the surface. These rocks and obstacles impede the smooth, swift flow of the stream. In this parable, the flowing stream is the flow of materials in the process. The pools of water are inventories, and the rocks in the stream are the imperfections in the process such as quality problems – problems exacerbated by extra safety stock and poor maintenance. If the stream is to run fast and clear, the rocks and obstacles must be removed. To accomplish this, however, the water in the stream has to be lowered so that even the hidden rocks are exposed. The meaning of the parable is inescapable. To uncover the imperfections in the process, WIP inventories should be lowered. Otherwise, those imperfections are likely to remain hidden from view and the process will never be smooth flowing.

Lean companies recognize, of course, that some inventory is necessary and that circumstances (e.g., significant variability) could argue for more, and not less. No process can run without work-in-process inventory, but the quantity of inventory that is minimally required is generally much smaller than anyone thinks. (Indeed, process simulations can readily show that, while inventory buffers between workstations can reduce the impact of the capacity-sapping "blocking and starving" that is caused by mismatches in the processing times of those workstations, increases in those buffer inventories increase output at a diminishing rate. Work-in-process inventories demonstrate diminishing marginal returns.)

Running a process with little work-in-process inventory is no small task; keeping product moving through the system often is done by applying considerable pressure to the workforce to perform at the set rate so that other workstations are steadily supplied with product on which to work.

This pressure is sometimes deliberately applied either by removing inventory from the system or by shifting selected workers off the line and into other work. Such "experiments" to see how the operation copes are done to uncover the bottlenecks and quality problems in the process. In some operations, there are lights above each workstation that can be lit when a worker falls behind or when quality is jeopardized. The Japanese term is *andon*. Typically, a yellow light signals that a worker cannot keep up the pace without making errors; a red light signals that something fundamental is wrong and the process should be stopped; a green light signals that all is well. An operation with few, or no, yellow lights lit may indicate that too much labor or inventory is available, and management may react by removing workers from the line or tightening up on inventory until more yellow lights are lit. (Red lights, of course, are valued because under them treasures of mistakes are found.)

This important concept can be illuminated in yet another way. Product design engineers often push their designs to the limit, until the product fails. By understanding why the product failed, the engineers can begin to create another version that does not have that particular problem. The situation with the production process itself is analogous. You want to push it to its limits and discover what makes it fail. But how can you *break* a process? You break it by removing its inventory. That is a good way to expose the weaknesses of the process and indicate what needs to be improved. Here, the pursuit of swift flow works to aid the reduction in quality variation.

5   Lot sizes

RT: lot sizes should be economic
Good inventory management principles involve balancing the cost of carrying inventory against other costs involved in (1) setting up production, (2) granting price breaks for volume purchases, or (3) dealing with other variable costs associated with changing the order or production quantity. The simplest example of this balancing of costs is characterized by the celebrated economic order quantity equation, formulated 100 years ago and solved with calculus:

$$EOQ = \sqrt{2DS / iC}$$

In the Received Tradition, manufacturers should fill in the variables in the equation (i.e., demand for the period [D], setup cost [S], prevailing interest rate [i], and variable cost of the product [C]) to solve for the economic order quantity (EOQ). This is straightforward, impeccable logic.

Lean: lot sizes should be small
In contrast, according to the Lean Manufacturing Philosophy, the EOQ equation, although thoroughly logical, is not seen as an expression to solve for some economic order quantity. Rather, the formula is a mandate to lower setup costs, because if EOQ is to be low, the setup costs must decline. Lean companies have made tremendous investments in reducing the time required for each changeover in the factory and making sure that machine setups can be done quickly and routinely. The difference between the changeovers in many lean factories and those in conventional factories is like the difference between a typical motorist changing a flat tire and the pit crews operating at the Indianapolis 500. Whereas the typical motorist may take 15 minutes to do the job, the pit crews at Indianapolis typically take less than 15 seconds. The same order of magnitude reduction of time has occurred in many manufacturing companies, particularly metal working ones. What once took hours now takes minutes. Lean companies strive for "single setup" (i.e., single-digit

or less than 10 minutes setup) or even "one-touch setup" (less than one minute).

How do they accomplish this? Not too differently from the pit crews at Indianapolis, and usually, nothing fancy has to be done. Some precepts apply to setup reduction. Among them:

1. Approach setup reduction with the same techniques of industrial engineering and methods improvement that are routinely applied to operator tasks. This means documenting how the setup is done now (videotaping is popular) and then looking for ways to eliminate steps, improve the times of other steps, and make any adjustments either trivial or automatic. It means establishing a procedure and looking to improve it all the time.

2. Do as much of the setup as you can while the machine is still running. Have all materials ready for the setup so that the machine is down for as little time as possible. To foster this "external" setup reduction, workstations are often designed so that setup materials can be stored close by. Attention may also have to be paid to preparing for the next step carefully (e.g., cleaning, sharpening, adjusting) well before the next setup is required.

3. Modify the operating equipment to permit easy setup and little adjustment. This can mean designing cartridge-type connections, color coding, multiple connection pins or plugs, special clamps, and similar measures.

4. Know what you want the machine to be set up for. Do not make the machine any more general purpose than you need to. This means understanding what kinds of parts are going to be assigned to it and what kinds of tools and fixtures are to be used.

5. Let one person do as much of the setup as possible. This may mean designing special carts for storing tools/fixtures/attachments, perhaps at the same height as the machine, so that physical effort is reduced.

6. Practice doing the setup. Practice is as important for reducing setup times as it is for reducing operator process times.

With quick setups and small lot production, the level of inventory can be kept lower for two reasons: (1) inventory need not accumulate at workstations into large lots that have to be transported later to other workstations; and (2) with quick changeovers, the process becomes more flexible. Production can be scheduled to match, often precisely, the current mix of demand for product variations. No longer must orders be filled out of inventories that are kept solely because expensive setups dictate long production runs. Orders can be filled by a very responsive production process.

6 Queues

RT: queues of work in process are needed to be sure that machine utilization stays high
The Received Tradition recognizes that machines represent a substantial investment and it reasons that they can best earn a return on this investment if they are kept busy. Thus having a queue of work in process upstream of each machine is a way to make sure that the machine will stay busy, earning its keep.

Lean: once in motion, always in motion. Production should be just in time; there should be no queues of work in process
Under the Lean Manufacturing Philosophy, if inventory is evil and if lot sizes are to be small, all materials have to keep moving through the process continuously. For that to happen the process needs to be tightly coupled, with work done just in time, as it is needed. This may make it vulnerable to disruption, but only by such tight coupling can the performance of the process be made visible to all and the success or failure of segments of the process easily determined and traced.

In the lean philosophy, quality and just-in-time (tightly coupled) production are closely linked. Just-in-time production uncovers problems quickly, permits feedback to the workforce that is timely and meaningful, enhances the interdependence of workers and process segments, raises worker motivation and pride, and gives new meaning to cross-training. When these things happen, the quality of the product is worked on and improved; rework and scrap are reduced. The factory's systems created to cope with low quality or high inventories are no longer required and can be phased out. Productivity measures show great increases.

With improved quality, inventories can be reduced even more, space saved, and the process made even more tightly coupled. Thus quality consciousness and just-in-time production often feed one another, lowering costs even as quality conformance improves.

For some managers, unfortunately, the notion of just-in-time production is simply an excuse for berating suppliers. For these managers, going lean means forcing the supplier to hold all the inventory and blaming the supplier for any quality problems encountered. Just-in-time, for them, is not about production in the factory as much as it is about the incoming product of suppliers. This is a huge misunderstanding of what just-in-time really means. In reality, just-in-time (lean) production is less about supplier inventories than it is a prescription for linking together elements of the production process itself so that materials are seldom required to sit idle. To the extent that a factory can make its future materials needs highly visible to suppliers and that the suppliers themselves can improve their own process capabilities, just-in-time production can be applied to the entire manufacturing supply chain, and inventories for all firms in the supply chain can be reduced. Some managers inappropriately make procurement policy step one in their campaigns for lean production. In fact, procurement changes should follow, and not precede, a plant's conversion to lean operation. The conversion to lean production is more about process redesign, production control, quality management, and leveled, steady, and highly visible production plans than it is about just-in-time inventories from suppliers.

7 The value of automation

RT: automation is valued because it drives labor out of the product
In the Received Tradition, most capital appropriations requests are justified primarily by the labor savings that they generate. Automation is thus seen primarily as a capital-for-labor substitution.

Lean: automation is valued because it facilitates consistent quality
Under the Lean Manufacturing Philosophy, machines are seen as means to perform tasks the same way every time. Automation has a value that is over and above any labor savings that may occur; labor savings are secondary to the ability of automation to make the process perfect. This point of view also implies that automation does not have to be sophisticated to be valued. Many lean machine tools are simple, in-house creations of the company that are designed simply to perform a single task more perfectly.

If automation is valued because of quality, and not because of labor savings, then the justification for any investment in automation changes. One can still use the expected financials, but managers should, at the same time, be convinced that the automation will lead to either reduced variation (e.g., better quality, steadier quantities and timing) and/or swifter flow of the materials through the process. Financials alone are not enough; they are too easily manipulated.

8   Sources of cost reduction

RT: Cost reduction comes by driving labor out of the product and by having high machine utilization. High rates of production are valued
In the Received Tradition, the two most analyzed elements of manufacturing cost are labor's wages and capital equipment expense. Considerable engineering and management effort is devoted to assessing how the direct labor component of a product can be lowered or whether machines of various types will be utilized enough to justify their capital expenditure. Processes are seldom completely rethought. Rather, labor-intensive portions of the process are targeted for automation.

The inspiration for cost reduction comes from an examination of the factory's cost structure, not the dynamics of process improvement. Indeed, many companies fall victim to the following scenario: (1) cost pressure, from whatever source, strikes; (2) management examines the elements of the product's cost; and (3) questions are asked about how, and when, different components of cost can be reduced. Make versus buy is investigated, and the lure of shipping production offshore can be strong. A cost-reduction investigation that starts with the cost structure can often lead to chasing low-cost labor sites across the globe.

In such situations, the production process is evaluated highly if it can run large quantities of product through all the time, whether or not the output is needed by the marketplace. The more that can be manufactured, given the assets and people in place, the more productive the factory is thought to be and the more highly it is held in esteem. Little or no thought is given to the waste caused by overproduction.

Lean: cost reduction comes by speeding the product through the factory and reducing variation. Quick throughput times and reduced variation of all kinds are valued
In the lean philosophy, there is no particular focus on wages or capital expenditures or any other aspect of the cost structure. The focus, rather, is all about swift, even flow – on collapsing the time it takes for materials to run through the factory and reducing the variation in quality, quantity and timing. It involves making the flow of materials visible and understandable to all concerned so that any impediment to that flow can be identified, studied, remedied, and quality assured. This precept, which I see lying at the heart of the lean philosophy, is the essence of swift, even flow. The discussion in Chapter 2 details the reasoning. It's the difference between the tortoise's factory and the hare's. This is why I can claim that the concept of swift, even flow provides the intellectual underpinnings for lean manufacturing's philosophy.

9 Material flow

RT: materials should be coordinated and pushed out into the factory
Most conventional materials management systems try to coordinate the procurement and handling of materials according to a master

production schedule, with the goal that the factory's departments will have their materials just before they need them. This is the concept behind material requirement planning (MRP). This approach to production scheduling and control can be characterized as a "push," where materials are pushed out of material stockrooms or out of particular manufacturing departments according to a schedule that anticipates demand. In such a system, considerable time and effort are also spent making sure that any problems can be expedited efficiently if changes to the schedule have to be made on short notice. Extensive coordination is needed to be certain that the materials are made available even if the production schedule is changed. Buffer stocks, safety lead times, and other tactics are used to make sure that materials are there "just in case" they may be needed.

In practice, this often involves the accumulation of materials over time, be it a day or a week or so. The supervisors on the factory floor can then select which jobs will be first, employing the bundled materials available. Much of the shop floor control function revolves around the precise scheduling of work to be done and the determination of the status of all orders. In such a conventional system, the materials function drives the pace of production in the factory. To avoid idle worker and machinery time, the traditional outlook makes sure that there are queues of work upstream of each machine and that there are banks of parts awaiting work or assembly by the workforce.

Lean: materials should be pulled through the factory
Under the Lean Manufacturing Philosophy, to ensure that no work-in-process queues exist, the "downstream" operations must trigger the initiation of work in the "upstream" operations. Otherwise, there is a greater risk of accumulating work-in-process inventory ahead of any slow operations. By this philosophy, providing a unit more than is demanded is as bad as providing a unit less. Under such a philosophy, there can still be an MRP system that explodes requirements through bills of materials to ensure that materials arrive at

the factory in time to be used, but the MRP system must not be used to authorize the release of orders to the factory floor; only processes downstream can act to release such orders. Stockrooms are a nemesis in such a philosophy, as they can interrupt the signals between process steps that keep materials flowing smoothly. The ideal is for all of the inventory to be on the factory floor, visible to everyone.

The most famous example of this type of "pull" system is that operated by Toyota Motor Company, the *kanban* system. It should be remembered that the *kanban* system works well only when demands are fairly stable, when the production schedule is frozen for fairly long periods of time, and when few, if any, irregularities in product models have to be coped with.

The success of these lean production control techniques has been, at times, spectacular. Work-in-process inventory levels and space requirements typically drop sharply (often 50 percent or more) and the output produced typically increases, sometimes substantially. The use of *kanban* cards, of course, is not wholly responsible; there are the other important elements at work. Nevertheless, *kanban* cards have clearly demonstrated the potential that good production control has for improving operations.

Production planning is one of the toughest factors in a pull system. Planners must take care not to introduce too much change or to press production so much that there is no slack in capacity. (This point is about keeping variation in quantities and timing low.) Yet, on the other hand, the process needs to be kept reasonably flexible and free of sizable pockets of excess capacity. A master production schedule (and final assembly schedule) that meets these criteria is often a delicate thing to concoct.

10   *Flexibility*

RT: you get flexibility at a cost – excess capacity, general-purpose equipment, inventories, overhead, and so on
Under the Received Tradition, flexibility, like quality, is attained by sacrificing other things. It can be achieved, but only by specifically

planning for it and building up a stock of assets – space, machinery, people, materials – so that changes in the product mix, in product volumes, or in new product introductions do not cause havoc in the factory.

Lean: flexibility comes from contracting all times – factory throughput times, vendor lead times, new product development cycles, order entry and production planning cycles, engineering change order lead times, and other lead-times-to-change
With the lean philosophy, flexibility, while difficult to achieve, does not necessarily mean the imposition of additional costs. Rather, the strategy is to shrink all the times that affect the factory and its operations. If suppliers can react quickly, if orders can be handled quickly, if production can be planned and scheduled quickly, if engineering changes can be made quickly, if new products can be brought into production quickly, if all that the company does can be done without any wasted motion, then flexibility can be achieved along with low cost and high quality. Indeed, the more flexible the process can become, the fewer the restrictions that need to be placed on production planning. One can thus get closer and closer to the ideal of being able to schedule through the factory today what was ordered yesterday.

Times outside the factory – in the office, in engineering, etc. – are slashed in exactly the same ways that factory throughput times are slashed, by purging waste from them. It takes diligent investigation but operations can be modified to remove the non-value-added steps. No element of the job is too small to ignore. Removing waste from all the small operations and workstations of the company will remove waste from the big ones as well. This takes discipline to do effectively, but it can be done.

Here, again, the notion of reducing throughput time and/or variation is a useful way to identify where the waste is – be it the entry of an order or the handling of payables/receivables or the month-end accounting close or the processing of inquiries from the sales force.

When delays occur, there lies waste in the process. Diagramming the flow of the process and of information, and attaching times to it, is a proven technique for aiding the efficiency of the overhead activities of a company.

11   The role of overhead

RT: overhead functions are essential

At the same time that the Received Tradition advocates for lower direct labor cost and higher machine utilization, it often implicitly acknowledges the need for considerable overhead functions (such as purchasing, industrial engineering, production scheduling, inventory control, quality control, and materials handling). Much of this overhead is dedicated to either coordinating aspects of the process or studying it. Although manufacturers operating under the Received Tradition may grumble about overhead rates that in recent years have soared to hundreds of percent, or more, of direct labor, typically they do not take much action to arrest such growth in indirect labor.

Not only does the Received Tradition promote the growth of "staff" versus "line" management, but also the people picked for staff assignments are apt to be trained for their "specialty" and desire little, if any, rotation into other staff or line assignments. Their careers are often wholly within their discipline. Their allegiance as well may be more to the discipline itself than to the company.

Lean: any labor that does not directly add value to the product is waste

Lean manufacturers exhibit a fervor about ridding the process of extraneous labor, both direct labor and indirect labor. This may be done, for example, by implementing some simple materials handling schemes (e.g., one worker positioned close enough to another to hand over the product). More dramatically, by getting a process "clean" and by seeking to make the flows of materials and information swift and with reduced variation, overhead can melt away. There can be fewer inspectors, fewer rework stations, less scrap to be handled, simpler production schedules, and less paperwork.

Moreover, lean companies are much more committed to limiting the size of any staff and to rotating managers through many different kinds of jobs, rather than promoting specialization. Through lean production and the tight coupling of the process, many of the coordination tasks needed in job shop/batch flow processes are eliminated. Overhead can actually shrink as its waste and the process-related waste it supports are purged from the operation. Lean companies also require more thought and study from their line managers and workers than happens with many other companies. Lean companies can get away with adding such burdens to their line people, because the process itself is simplified and smoothed so that managers and line workers do not have to fight fires continually. Managerial time is viewed as better spent improving the process permanently rather than trying to get a "hot" order through.

12 The cost of labor

RT: labor is a variable cost

Under the Received Tradition, labor is one cost that can be forgone when demand drops. In many industries, layoffs are a hard fact of life. Although companies do not like to lay off their people, it is expected to occur when times are tough.

Lean: labor is a fixed cost

When Japanese manufacturing was in its ascendancy in the late 1970s and early 1980s, the notion of lifetime employment in Japan received much attention in the popular press. In fact, lifetime employment even then was a reality for only a quarter or so of the Japanese workforce, and only then in the very strongest companies. In such companies, during downturns in demand, workers would be put on special maintenance assignments or a considerable degree of subcontracting may have been brought in-house. Supplier firms that were less strong were made to suffer proportionately more than the larger companies that guaranteed employment for their workers and managers. Even today, lifetime employment remains a goal for even the weaker companies in Japan. The benefits of lifetime employment are clear both for society as a whole and for the companies involved. The dedication of the workforce is generally high, although this dedication is becoming less strong in today's Japan.

For lean companies everywhere, a no-layoff policy is a typical goal. This view of labor as a fixed cost reflects the attitude that the company holds toward its people. When workers are treated as if they were lifetime employees, the company is forced to take seriously its hiring, training, cross-training, management development, job rotation, and career path counseling. Personnel departments in lean companies are strong. Their work is not ignored and end runs are not made around them, as happens in so many other companies.

13 Machine speed

RT: machines are sprinters, and pulled hamstrings are to be expected

According to the Received Tradition, machines are expensive and if they are to return that expense (and more), they must run at capacity. Breakdowns may then be expected. They are accepted as an inevitable consequence. Moreover, in the Received Tradition, large, multipurpose machines are valued more than specialized, less flexible machines.

Lean: machines are marathon runners, slow but steady and always able to run

According to the Lean Manufacturing Philosophy, machines should be run only as fast as they can turn out perfect pieces consistently. Machine speeds in lean companies are often not set as high as they could be, and more importantly, preventive maintenance is performed religiously. Too often, the practice is to perform maintenance "when we can get to it," rather than at definite times that may be inconvenient for management's production goals. The best maintenance people are too frequently assigned to the false heroics of fixing equipment that has broken down, rather than devising and accomplishing better preventive maintenance procedures.

The freedom to perform religiously systematic preventive maintenance and daily machine checks in lean factories comes in large part from the practice of deliberately planning for less production than is theoretically possible. Rather than put pressure on the process to produce at capacity, lean companies provide for the slack required for maintenance, process improvement, and the like. What lean companies sacrifice in lost output, they more than make up for in reduced machine downtime, higher yields, less rework, and the like.

Lean companies also do not fear using specialized equipment, often of their own devising. Such equipment is frequently lower cost, slower, and more inflexible than is typically contemplated by other companies. Yet, for lean companies, such equipment is valued because it may help make the process more tightly coupled; throughput times can decline as a result of their use. Such home-grown equipment can actually result in a production system that is at once more flexible, quicker to respond, and less subject to breakdown than a production system that is built around a large, multipurpose, and expensive piece of equipment that can quickly become the bottleneck in the process.

14   Procurement

RT: procure from multiple vendors
According to the Received Tradition, the benefits of competition are legion. Vendors should compete vigorously for the company's business. Indeed, vendor should be set against vendor so that the resulting competition keeps prices low and service attractive.

Lean: procure from a single supplier
Lean companies view their suppliers as extensions of their companies. Indeed, they prefer to use the word "supplier" rather than

the word "vendor," which has a somewhat pejorative cast. They are part of the company, to be worked with to continually improve their quality and to assure that their delivery is "just in time." Price is not nearly as important as quality or delivery dependability. Why risk compromising quality and threatening just-in-time production for a minor break in price?

To lean companies, purchasing is a critical function. Much of management in lean companies, for example, can consist not so much of organizing people within the company as organizing other companies to do the work. The supply chain becomes the unit of competition within the industry. In such a world, the management of suppliers and subcontractors becomes a very important endeavor.

The activities of a lean company purchasing department have much less to do with the price negotiations and vendor qualifications engaged in by purchasing departments operating within the Received Tradition. Rather, the purchasing department's mandate is to support product quality and just-in-time production. This implies a number of changes:

- developing long-term contracts with suppliers for whom the company's business is significant;
- encouraging suppliers to produce and ship in small, frequent lots of exact quantities;
- enabling suppliers to react to "emergencies" (e.g., tool breakage, surprise demands) better;
- practicing "family-of-parts" sourcing so that the supplier provides a series of related parts so that product mix changes do not cause vast volume fluctuations for the supplier;
- encouraging suppliers to achieve a process quality sufficiently good as to eliminate incoming inspections;
- providing minimal part specifications to suppliers so that supplier talent and value engineering can be devoted to improving one's own product performance and cost even with new product introductions; and
- insisting on reliable transportation. Frequent deliveries are increasingly made by trucks modified for less-than-truckload shipments. These

trucks then enter a fixed-route cycle of pickups and deliveries, much like a bus route.

In essence, the time freed from seeking and evaluating quotes for work is devoted instead to working with suppliers so that they can truly meet the full needs of the customer company. If all goes well, inventories throughout the entire pipeline are reduced, not just those held by the customer company.

There is always concern that if a company goes to a single supplier, it will be too vulnerable to strikes and Acts of God. Such concerns are real – witness the industrial aftermath of the 2011 tsunami in northeast Japan – but they can be overdrawn. First, even though one supplier may supply the part or material, other suppliers can also be qualified to supply. This helps to diversify the risk, which in the case of a strike, is known with considerable lead time anyway. It is useful to distinguish between single sourcing and sole sourcing. The latter is what occurs when only one source can even be qualified. The former can usually be managed fairly easily.

15 Expediting

RT: expediting and "work around" are ways of life
If, as in the Received Tradition, delivery and customization are viewed as essential to one's competitive success, one must then be able to cope with the whims of consumers. Many of the factory's systems are developed with expediting in mind, and much of the time of the factory's managers is spent expediting material from suppliers, expediting orders through the factory, and scrambling to devise ways to work around the materials that are not yet there.

Lean: expediting and "work around" are sins
The surest way to destroy just-in-time production and quality is to change continually the production schedule or the engineering documentation on the product. In the lean philosophy, rush tags and

engineering change orders are inventions of the devil. Instead, production schedules are set well in advance. They are frozen for longer periods than is the case in other companies, and production is run with less chasing of demand and more of a level production strategy. If some product variety and customization have to be forgone, so be it. To do otherwise compromises quality too much.

This is not to say that lean companies cannot provide a wide range of products. Their concern for quick changeovers and small production lots permits greater product variety and flexibility than one might think. The configuration of production cells, the cross-training of the workforce, and concern for keeping the entire process tightly coupled argue for considerable changes in worker job assignments and enhanced flexibility in lean factories. Marketing whims are frequently less apt to disrupt lean companies than companies that accept the Received Tradition.

IT AIN'T EASY

These precepts from the Received Tradition and the Lean Manufacturing Philosophy are listed for comparison in Table 4.1. What should be evident from examining them is that their points of view about manufacturing are radically different from one another. The Received Tradition, although it often rings a familiar bell with managers, is just a collection of aphorisms born out of short-term or opportunistic thinking. The implications are not thought through very well and they do not hold together. The lean philosophy, on the other hand, is one that persistently seeks to reduce variation of all kinds and to reduce throughput time. Swift, even flow is at the heart of lean manufacturing, as it is with the service businesses of Shouldice Hospital and the circus.

It is not an easy philosophy to follow, however. As noted above, the Toyota Production System has people development at its heart. It has been much studied but never really duplicated. Why not? It is very difficult to learn completely and to sustain. It demands

Table 4.1. *Lean Manufacturing Philosophy versus the "Received Tradition": 15 precepts*

The Received Tradition
1. It costs money to make quality products.
2. Engineers and managers are experts. Workers serve their desires.
3. Mistakes are inevitable and have to be inspected out.
4. Inventory is useful – it keeps production rolling along.
5. Lot sizes should be economic.
6. Queues of work-in-process are needed to be sure that machine utilization stays high.
7. Automation is valued because it drives labor out of the product.
8. Cost reduction comes by driving labor out of the product and by having high machine utilization. High rates of production are valued.
9. Materials should be coordinated and pushed out into the factory.
10. You get flexibility at a cost – excess capacity, general-purpose equipment, inventories, overhead, etc.
11. Overhead functions are essential.
12. Labor is a variable cost.
13. Machines are sprinters, and pulled hamstrings are to be expected.
14. Procure from multiple suppliers.
15. Expediting and "work around" are ways of life.

Lean Manufacturing Philosophy
1. Quality is free.
2. Workers are experts. Managers and engineers serve them.
3. Mistakes are treasures, the study of which leads to process improvement.
4. Inventory is evil – it hides problems that should be allowed to surface.
5. Lot sizes should be small.
6. Once in motion, always in motion. Production should be just in time; there should be no queues of work-in-process.
7. Automation is valued because it facilitates consistent quality.
8. Cost reduction comes by speeding the product through the factory and reducing variation. Quick throughput times and reduced variation of all kinds are valued.
9. Materials should be pulled through the factory.

Table 4.1. (cont.)

10. Flexibility comes from contracting all lead times – factory throughput times, vendor lead times, new product development cycles, order entry and production planning cycles, engineering change order lead times, and other lead-times-to-change.
11. Any labor that does not directly add value to the product is waste.
12. Labor is a fixed cost.
13. Machines are marathon runners, slow but steady and always able to run.
14. Procure from a single supplier.
15. Expediting and "work around" are sins.

commitment and constant vigilance and continual learning, and that is never easy.

AN ALTERNATIVE VISION OF TYING COST TO A PRODUCT

One of the principal sources of friction within operations that have embraced lean thinking is the operations–accounting interface. In discussing the "usual suspects" in Chapter 1, cost accounting got knocked around, especially cost accounting that allocates overhead on the basis of direct labor (or, alternatively, for processes that are heavily automated, on the basis of machine hours). The notion that overhead expenses actually get saved when direct labor (or machine hours) is removed from the process strains credulity for many operations people. Some fine work by Jeff Miller and Tom Vollmann[7] has shown that overhead is better identified with transactions than with direct labor. Free the factory of transactions (order entry, inventory control, production control, quality control, purchasing, and the like) and you free it of overhead expenses.

How do you get out of the bind of allocating overhead on the basis of direct labor? What else can or should you use? One long-standing alternative is direct costing, which purposefully does not allocate overhead to product lines. Direct costing systems charge to products only those costs that are directly connected with their production (materials, direct labor) and they leave all other manufacturing costs as period expenses. Its adherents like that it avoids being arbitrary.

Many managers, however, want full costing and think that is the best way of making comparisons across products. But, then, how should you allocate the overhead expenses to product lines? Enter swift, even flow.[8]

The allocation that I advocate uses the throughput time of each product, rather than direct labor or machine hours. Throughput time is an apt proxy for the transactions that suck overhead resources to any product. Those products that speed through the process should be assessed less overhead than those products that languish, because the products that languish are the ones that cost the company most dearly. Products with longer throughput times are more likely to:

- Require many transactions (e.g., purchasing, inventory control, production control, quality control, supervision). As Miller and Vollmann argue, it is transactions that add to overhead.
- Take up relatively more inventory, space, materials handling and quality management time and also more general management time.
- Stifle the productivity of the operation, keeping the process from moving down the diagonal of Figure 2.5.

Any allocation scheme for overhead brings biases and incentives with it. A key advantage to throughput time as an allocating principle is that its implied incentives are preferable to those implied by other schemes. Throughput time reduction is precisely the incentive that managers should concentrate on. It is the incentive with the best chance of forcing the reduction of transactions of all kinds.

HOW WOULD IT WORK?

Some key aspects of the cost accounting system will change with a move to throughput time as the basis of overhead allocation. The system must be designed to keep track of the throughput times for orders. Even so, the gates for collecting the information (e.g., release to the factory floor, shipment or warehousing of the finished goods) are not likely to differ. The recording of throughput times themselves may well require new procedures, however. One must be careful to include in any order's throughput time the time any portion of the order spends in a rework station or some other side trip off the production path. A weighted average calculation would help to ensure attention to quality and reduce that source of variation.

How would the overhead actually be allocated? Under current systems, overhead is allocated via an overhead rate that is calculated essentially as overhead costs divided by total direct labor hours (or total machine hours). Thus, the rate is dollars of overhead per direct labor (or machine) hour. Under the proposed revision, overhead is allocated to a product line on the basis of its share of the total value of throughput time in the process. The value of throughput time is the multiplicative product of the value of production for a product line and the throughput time for an average order for that product line. The metric is dollar-days. The dollar-days would be greater for product lines that have high product prices, are produced in high volumes, or that take more time in the process. Such tendencies are both intuitively appealing and workable.

The overhead that would be allocated to any one product line would depend on that product line's share of the total dollar-days for all product lines produced. Multiplying the product line's calculated share of total dollar-days by the total overhead costs that could not otherwise be assigned to that product line yields the overhead assigned to the product line.

Here is an example of how this type of allocation works. Consider two product lines, A and B, that share essential elements of the process. Table 4.2 captures the relevant data.

Assume that the overhead costs that cannot be obviously allocated to either of the product lines total $43,500. The difference between factory sales revenue for the two product lines, $175,000, and the total of all costs is $29,000, the margin.

Under traditional cost accounting, assuming one overhead rate to be applied across both product lines, the calculation of that overhead rate is as follows:

Table 4.2. *Allocating costs with throughput time*

Items	Product Line A	Product Line B
Units sold	10,000	5,000
Factory sales price	$10/unit	$15/unit
Materials cost	$50,000	$37,500
Direct labor hours	500	1000
Direct labor expense at $10/hour	$5,000	$10,000
Throughput time per standard order	3 days	4 days

Overhead rate = Overhead costs / Direct hours

So, for the example, the computed overhead rate is

Overhead rate = $43,500 / (500+1000) = $29 per direct labor hour

Naturally, the application of the general overhead rate to Product Line B is disadvantageous to that product line, as it is the more labor-intensive. Of the total of $43,500 in overhead, Product Line B is allocated two-thirds of it, because its direct labor costs are twice those of Product Line A.

What does this mean for the unit costs of each product line? According to the cost accounting conventions in place (see Table 4.3), Product Line A is a winner and Product Line B is a loser, actually costing more to produce that its factory sales price.

With this traditional cost accounting, a favorable variance is enjoyed when direct labor is removed from the product. Removing 100 hours of direct labor from Product Line A, for instance, leads to an immediate reduction in total costs of $3,900 ($2,900 of it overhead). Even if the overhead rate is recalculated, total costs drop by $3,071 ($2,071 more than the drop in direct labor expense itself). In addition, if more units can be produced, other things being equal, then more than the standard overhead will be absorbed, and the overhead variance will be favorable.

Under the proposed revision that uses throughput time, the overhead allocation for each product line would be calculated as follows:

| Total overhead for any product line during period | = | Share of total value of throughput time attributable to that product line during the period | * | Overhead costs for the period |

Table 4.3. *Traditional direct labor cost allocation*

Item	Product Line A	Product Line B
Materials	$50,000	$37,500
Direct labor	$5,000	$10,000
Total direct costs	$55,000	$47,500
Overhead allocation	$14,500	$29,000
Total costs	$69,500	$76,500
Units	10,000	5,000
Unit cost	$6.95/unit	$15.30/unit
Sales price	$10.00/unit	$15.00/unit
Margin	$3.05/unit	−$0.30/unit
Margin as a percentage of product line sales price	30.5%	−1.96%

For, the method of determining the share of total value of throughput time attributable to a product, see Box 4.1.

Box 4.1

The share of the total value of throughput time is determined by the product line's sales and by its throughput time. This share is probably best defined in mathematical terms. The following is an expression for this share of the total value of throughput time:

$$\text{SVTT}_{it} = \frac{(U_{it} {}^{*} P_{it} {}^{*} TT_{it})}{\sum_{i=0}^{L} (U_{it} {}^{*} P_{it} {}^{*} TT_{it})}$$

Where $SVTT_{it}$ is the share of the total value of throughput time for product line i during time period t, U_{it} is the units of product line i produced during the period, P_{it} is the price of product line i during the period, and TT_{it} is the throughput time for product line i during the period. There are L product lines, so that $SVTT_{it}$ varies between 0 and 1.

For the example, the total value of the throughput time can be computed as follows:

Product Line A: 10,000 units * $10/unit * 3 days = 300,000 dollar-days

Product Line B: 5000 units * $15/unit * 4 days = 300,000 dollar-days

Product Lines A + B = 300,000 dollar-days + 300,000 dollar-days = 600,000 dollar-days

Product Line A accounts for 50 percent of the total and Product Line B accounts for 50 percent, so the overhead allocation to each product line is half of $43,500 or $21,750.

What does this mean for the unit costs of each product line? The results are in Table 4.4.

The contrast between the traditional cost accounting system's results and those of the system using throughput time is instructive. The labor intensity of Product Line B really affects its profitability if one uses the traditional system. It appears to lose money even with a significant contribution margin. Nevertheless, Product Line B moves through the factory in only one day more than Product Line A. One could reasonably conclude that it does not consume that much more in overhead cost as a result. Given this fact, it is quite reasonable to think of Product Line B as a profitable product line. Throughput time-based costing supports that intuition.[9]

This way of doing things has some real advantages:

Table 4.4. *Throughput time allocated costs*

Item	Product Line A	Product Line B
Materials	$50,000	$37,500
Direct labor	$5,000	$10,000
Total direct costs	$55,000	$47,500
Overhead allocation	$21,750	$21,750
Total costs	$76,750	$69,250
Units	10,000	5,000
Unit cost	$7.68/unit	$13.85/unit
Sales price	$10.00/unit	$15.00/unit
Margin	$2.32/unit	$1.15/unit
Margin as a percentage of product line sales price	23.20%	7.67%

- the overhead allocations made are arguably more representative of what the overhead personnel and expenses are devoted to during the work day (i.e., transactions of one sort or another);
- incentives for line managers lead to decisions that can aid the process's productivity and competitiveness; and
- the incentives can help to reduce overhead and not simply to allocate it.

5 Making a bad process better

Grand visions are fine, but, for the most part, managers are stuck in particular situations that they have to make better. They have to cope with some trying times, and if swift, even flow is worth its salt, it has to help these managers think through what keeps their processes less than fully productive and what can be done to remedy things. Featured in this and subsequent chapters are condensed versions of actual cases. I invite you, then, to read these short cases and think about what you would do if you were in the shoes of the manager involved.

A BACK-OFFICE NIGHTMARE

USA Services (originally, United Student Aid) is now owned by Sallie Mae, but this is a situation that they faced prior to their sale.[1]

> ### USA Services – Loan Disbursement Services
>
> USA Services provided a host of services to universities and to the banks that helped to finance the education of their students. Sometimes either the universities or the banks needed to change the terms or information in a loan and thus needed to contact USA Services. The Loan Disbursement Services department handled such requests. The requests came either by letter or by phone. Unfortunately, the average time to make any of the 36 kinds of requested changes was lengthening and customers were getting increasingly upset about the company's service. During peak months, the letters could be over 20,000 pieces per month, while letters in nonpeak times might only be 12,000 pieces per month.

The letters entering this department of USA Services were handled first by one of two correspondence processors who counted the letters and distributed them to five account representatives. The account reps and the mail that they received were matched to banks, and the banks typically served specific universities. Once the correspondence processors sorted and counted the letters, they did not see them again. Once the account reps finished their work, the letters were filed by separate file clerks.

The processing task involved a number of steps. Account reps read the letters carefully to determine exactly what was being requested. They could also receive direct telephone calls from the banks or the universities requesting a change, or, often, asking about the status of a request that they had previously sent in. The requests could be very different. The 36 different types could take a little time to process or a lot. Some required multiple operations, and these often had to be done in a specific order. All of the account reps had computer terminals at their desks through which they could access USA Services' computer system. Some of the required changes could be made directly online, but others had to wait for the nightly batch run, and, if the changes were complex enough, multiple nightly batch runs had to be made. To manage the pending work, the account reps filed the letters or notes from telephone calls into a series of 12 trays at their cubicles, with each using a different system.

The time it took the account reps to work through the letters given them depended on several factors:

1. the mix of items to process (some changes were more complex and time-consuming to make than others);
2. the volume of work on the account rep's desk; and
3. the telephone traffic from banks or universities.

The controls in place were rudimentary: incoming mail counts and tallies by the account reps themselves on what they did each day. Management did not know precisely how many letters it received of different sorts, nor did it know exactly how many items the account reps completed during any period of time. There was no mechanism to verify that a particular letter had made it to the department and, if the computer system did not show the requested change, there was no mechanism to track its location. The management team wanted more controls in place. In particular, it wanted to know:

- which client letters had not been processed within the standard turnaround times;
- what current turnaround times actually were;
- the current processing capacities so that accurate staffing decisions could be made; and
- how much work individual account reps had done during the year.

Senior management had made it clear to the Loan Disbursement Services department that it could not expect any new investment in technology as the means to solve this dilemma. The company's capital investment was being directed elsewhere and the department was simply going to have to make do with what it had.

A good place to start to analyze a messy situation like this one is to create a process flow chart that captures what's going on. Figure 5.1 is a flow chart for this process.

In Figure 5.1, the rectangles indicate processes that are worked on, the circles are inspection or control steps, the triangles are inventories of mail or phone calls, and the diamond indicates a decision step. A process flow diagram such as this can be tagged with any of several metrics that can help to isolate what is going awry. For example, the steps in the process could be tagged with their capacities, a useful metric to see if a bottleneck is evident. Or, it could be tagged with times, a useful way to spot where waste may be lurking and causing certain activities to take too much time to accomplish. Yields are another useful metric to study how quality could be improved. And, costs can be tagged to the various steps to see where costs accumulate.

What was a real concern for the managers at USA Services was that such a simple process was not producing in a timely fashion. Too many requests were taking much too long to complete.

When people read this case, they often moan about senior management and the dictate that investment in new technology cannot

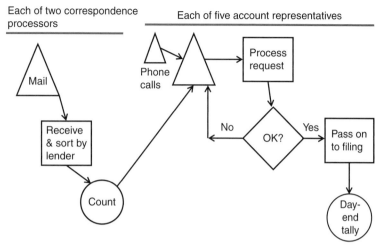

FIGURE 5.1 "As is" process flow diagram for USA Services

be made to save the day. They want to invest in scanning equipment, new systems, and new software. This fond hope presumes that this process has a bottleneck that some investment in capacity can break. Indeed, bottlenecks are the classic reason why throughput times are long and inventory builds up. When they are reminded that senior management is serious about not investing in this particular process, they grumble, but then move on.

Another one of the frequent suggestions offered is to side with management and advocate the institution of some controls, so that management can figure out what is getting done or not getting done. Indeed, at the time this case was written, the manager involved had instituted a new control mechanism that had one of the account reps logging more data about what he did. That, of course, took time, and lowered his capacity, and USA Services didn't learn anything more of interest about the process. The situation remained one of deteriorating results for the company's customers.

What, then, to do to raise the productivity of this process? How should one look at this case? What does swift, even flow say to do? Swift, even flow asks two key questions about any process:

- Where is there variation in the process – variation in quality, quantities, or timing?
- Where does the throughput time lengthen?

By answering these two key questions, an analyst of this process can uncover where productivity is suffering, and the path forward can often be revealed. Let's make a careful investigation of this process.

Variation

There are a number of sources of variation in this process.

1. The account reps could receive any of 36 different types of request.
2. Some of these requests took lots of time to process and some took just a little.
3. There were no common protocols for processing the requests; each account rep used a different system.
4. The phone calls that came in for the account reps interrupted their work.

Throughput time

The throughput time for getting requests processed was obviously very variable, too. If one account rep's banks and universities were busy with requests, that account rep would get a flood of mail and phone calls. That could happen while another account rep's banks and universities were much less busy in generating mail or phone calls. And, it would not be evident, necessarily, what the highest priority request was. The account reps had to read each one to find out.

The correspondence processors did not care how much inventory of mail a certain account rep received. They simply kept filling the account rep's cubicle. The correspondence processors could figuratively bury an account rep with mail.

What swift, even flow suggests

If this process is to become more productive, then the variation has to be reduced and also the throughput time for the average request. How can this be accomplished?

The 36 kinds of request cannot change but the requests could be segregated so that the account rep does not have to go from working on one type of request to working on another, completely different, type of request. Like requests could be grouped together much as family of parts are grouped together for a manufacturing cell. Thus, rather than assign account reps to banks and universities, USA Services could assign them to a type of request. Thirty-six is rather a lot, but one could think of aggregating the 36 into much smaller groups, say three to five, with roughly similar turnaround times. In this way, one could think of easy requests, complicated requests, and medium-time requests.

By reducing the categories of request, one could also begin to think of imposing the same processing protocols on the account reps. Right now, they put whatever they want to put into the 12 trays in their cubicle. With a simpler system, the processing itself might be standardized.

The phone calls could be segregated as well so that that source of interruption is eliminated. This means, of course, that the account reps would no longer be the sole contacts between USA Services and the banks that they currently serve. Some of those studying this case object to that, but most do not. They observe that if the process can work more quickly and satisfy the banks that their requests are being handled expeditiously, the banks will not object to working with a team rather than an individual.

The throughput times for the requests are highly variable because there is no way, currently, to know which ones have the highest priority. And, the current assignment of account reps to banks and universities hinders a balancing of the loads across account reps.

The throughput times for the account reps are also variable because the correspondence processors simply push more and more letters into each cubicle, swelling the account reps' inventories. The account reps do not get a chance to control what comes into their work areas. They risk becoming inundated.

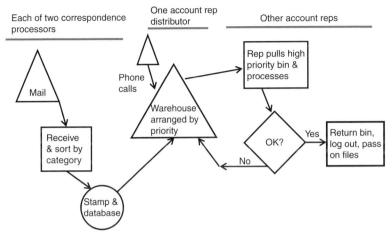

FIGURE 5.2 "Should be" process flow diagram for USA Services

What can be done to counter this "push" of inventory onto the account reps? Like with the Lean Manufacturing Philosophy, one can think of the account reps "pulling" work into their work areas. Where would they pull work from? Instead of thinking of individual inventories of work in the cubicles of the account reps, one can think of one big, centralized inventory of work. And, that inventory of work – a warehouse, if you will – can be arranged so that the highest priority requests, those in danger of being late, get worked on first.

The process can thus change from Figure 5.1 to Figure 5.2.

Here, one of the account reps takes over the "warehouse." He would be charged with arranging the priorities, handling all of the phone calls (many of which inquire after the status of a previously sent in request), and perhaps working on particular jobs himself. The standard containers could be color-coded, and work of a particular priority placed in the same way each day, so that the account reps would immediately know what to select once they entered the warehouse.

The other account reps would then go to the warehouse and "pull" a standard container (a bin) of the highest priority available, filled with a standard quantity of similar time frame requests (e.g., complex, easy, medium). They would work on these requests unimpeded by phone calls and other distractions and then return them to the warehouse when completed. The warehouse could have a board outside of it, listing the account reps and keeping tabs on which containers they have taken and which ones they have completed. Such a board could provide the data by which to evaluate the workload on the account reps and to gauge how productive any one of them is.

By reducing the variation that the account reps were subject to, the throughput time for the average request will be reduced. With fewer interruptions and with grouping similar requests together, the work for the account reps should be easier and their productivity higher.

In fact, the managers in the Loan Disbursements Services department did change their process in much this way. They established a central "warehouse" where standard containers of ten requests each that had been sorted into two-day, three-day, and ten-day "families" were pulled by the account reps. By doing this, they began to attack the aging items that had slipped through their fingers before. Service times improved dramatically, and the volume of telephone calls declined. Banks and universities began to compliment them for their work instead of hounding them with complaints. All of this was done through low-tech means. In fact, the new system performed so well that the company saved money for years by avoiding investment in the department.

By standardizing things, management was able to analyze the work that was being asked of the department. What they found stunned them. They discovered that 30 percent of the work in the department was really duplicate work, sent in by banks and universities when their initial requests took so much time to process. And, 20 percent of the work really didn't belong to this department anyway; it needed to go elsewhere in the company.

Suppose that the company had been willing to invest in technology to solve this problem. What would the solution have looked like? Probably not much different from how the nontech solution turned out. All of the letters would have been imaged and held in a large database, not unlike the warehouse that was created. The imaged documents would have been prioritized by urgency, not unlike what was done. As the account reps finished working on items, the computer would have shunted other, probably similar, items to them. The computer would have kept track of individual productivity, much like the board outside the warehouse did. The logic would have been much the same.

SOME TAKEAWAYS FOR MAKING FLOWS SWIFT AND EVEN

By employing the concept of swift, even flow to this situation, the variation and lagging throughput time of the "as is" process was revealed and addressed. A new process was devised, and productivity soared. Besides the key questions relating to variation in quality, quantity, and timing, and to the bogging down of throughput time, what else can we take away from this case as aids for reducing variation or reducing throughput time?

- Group like things together into families.
- Segregate unlike things into separate categories.
- Avoid "push" and embrace "pull" as the best way to keep local inventories low.
- Standardize procedures and protocols.
- Plan the process so that no one's schedule gets consistently overloaded while others' schedules are under-loaded.

Let's keep these things in mind as we tackle some other situations.

NOT A BOOMING BUSINESS

The drop-off in coal mining in the United Kingdom had a very deleterious effect on explosives manufacturers. Here's an encapsulated version of what happened with ICI-Nobel's Explosives some years back.[2]

ICI-Nobel Explosives

ICI-Nobel Explosives was the division of Imperial Chemicals Industries that derived from Alfred Nobel, the inventor of dynamite, and that served the British market with explosives, chiefly for quarries, especially since coal mining was in decline.

ICI-Nobel's products included detonators (for which it was the only producer and thus it supplied its competitors), ANFO (a mixture of ammonium nitrate with fuel oil) either loose or in "sausages" for use when the drilled blasting holes were dry, and slurries and emulsions, in "sausages," which could be used when the holes were wet. ANFO (the cheapest alternative), slurries, and emulsions could be mixed on-site or mixed off-site and carried to the site. ICI-Nobel had two different stockkeeping units (SKUs) for ANFO, 16 different SKUs for slurry, and nine different SKUs for emulsion. There were strict regulations on how much explosive could be stored at a quarry (typically less than two metric tons) and how much could be trucked in (eight tons mixed and 16 tons unmixed). A typical quarry blast would require over two tons of explosive, so it was generally the case that the quarry called ICI-Nobel a day or so ahead of need for the explosives it required.

A quarry was most productive when the explosions ("shots") used resulted in rock on the ground that was uniform in size (that is, none so big that further processing was made more difficult) and that was not thrown too far from the rock face (and thus was easier to harvest). Productive shots depended on the use of the proper amount and type of explosive, holes drilled in the right places (which in turn depended on the rock face geometry), and an optimal firing sequence for the shots (whose timing between shots in the sequence was measured in milliseconds). Quarries usually fired shots every five days or so. They could employ their own workers to determine the shot geometries and firing sequences and to drill the holes, or they could contract out such services.

Explosives were seen as commodities, and ICI-Nobel (54 percent market share) had competition from two main competitors.

ICI-Nobel's competitors approached the market differently. Exchem, a subsidiary of a French company (36 percent market share), was a longtime competitor with a product line that was almost as broad as ICI-Nobel's (no emulsions). Explosives Development Ltd., on the other hand (10 percent market share), was a more limited supplier of mainly packaged slurries and emulsions, and the company competed largely on price. Neither company had as much experience or knowledge of things such as blast geometries or firing sequences as ICI-Nobel, which had developed a software package to help it understand the optimal shot for a given rock face.

ICI-Nobel served its customers from a manufacturing site in the center of England, a warehousing operation in a different central England city, and a series of five smaller depots scattered about England, Wales, and Scotland. Customers called the depots whenever it suited them to schedule next-day delivery of the type of explosive they needed. There was little customer loyalty.

ICI-Nobel was desperate for ideas/policies that would lessen the commodity nature of its business. Sales and profits had been declining for years.

At first blush, this is a terrible industry to be in. Sales have declined because there is less mining of coal. The resulting over-capacity and the existence of a price competitor assured all in the industry that margins and profits would remain low.

Many who have looked at this case grasp for straws. Some want to charge more for detonators and others want to earn the consulting fees that the company might get by playing up its expertise with blast geometries and firing sequences. Still others look to close down a depot or two, or the warehousing operation. Unfortunately, none of these options offers a lot of "bang for the buck."

Can the productivity of the current process be enhanced somehow? Here is where the concept of swift, even flow enters the scene. We can ask the standard questions: where is there variation in the process, and where does throughput time lengthen?

Variation

There are a number of sources of variation in this process.

- The quarries could call in an order at any time. ICI-Nobel had little idea when the quarries were blasting or even how much explosive they needed.
- The weather was a source of uncertainty. If conditions were dry, the low cost of ANFO would assure its selection by the quarry. Otherwise, more expensive slurries or emulsions had to be used. Which SKUs would be needed was thus difficult to predict much ahead of time.
- The uncertainty of which quarries would call in orders when, combined with the requirements on what could be transported on the truck, meant that ICI-Nobel would often have to run a hub-and-spoke transportation system. The truck would load at the depot, make its run to the quarry that called in an order, and then return to the depot to be loaded again. With an average delivery of just over two metric tons, this meant that the truck's much bigger capacity was being wasted.

Throughput time

The throughput time slowed down because of the many handoffs in the distribution channel: factory to warehouse to depot to quarry. Also, there were varying levels of inventory at each of these stages and that added to throughput time. Even the hub-and-spoke transportation added time to the process.

WHAT SWIFT, EVEN FLOW SUGGESTS

Let's move downstream first, toward the customer quarries. After all, managing the flow of goods and materials in the process depends heavily on managing the backward flow of information from the customer on up the supply chain. The quarry customers in this case are a significant source of the variation that plagues the process. Because of that, any meaningful improvement to this process's productivity will likely have to deal with the quarries.

The variation caused by the fickle and unpredictable quarries forces ICI-Nobel to run a hub-and-spoke transportation system and to carry a great deal of inventory. What would be better? Running a bus route. With a bus route, and a known demand for each quarry, ICI-Nobel could load up the truck fully and deliver its explosives in sequence. If only ICI-Nobel could itself dictate when the quarries would fire their shots and what they would use to do so.

How could ICI-Nobel dictate explosives use to its customers? This is an interesting question. One way to do so would be for ICI-Nobel to take over the design and decision-making about their customers' blasts. ICI-Nobel has the expertise to do so. It does mean morphing itself into a company that provides a service to its quarry customers, but that can be done. It does not have to stay a simple manufacturer.

How then would it get paid? Would services be billed separately from the explosives used? Could some other means be devised? One alternative is to be paid for the result of its service, namely, the rock that lies on the ground after a blast. The quarry weighs its rock anyway, and ICI-Nobel could be paid for the weight and quality of the rock its actions put on the ground. The company would not bill its quarry customers for explosives; those quarries would not care which kind of explosives were used as long as the result was good.

If the customers are not specifying the explosives that are used, ICI-Nobel could benefit by standardizing its operations. It could, for example, reduce the number of SKUs it produces, say, by always using a slurry or emulsion.

Such standardization could also lead to some simplification of the supply chain. Perhaps the warehouse could be eliminated. Or, particularly if the trucks could be filled more completely, they might be able to operate over longer distances, and this could mean eliminating one or more of the depots.

The benefits to all involved are clear, however. For the quarries:

- no shot-firing themselves, which saves on overhead personnel;
- no inventory of explosives;
- less explosive used because of better-designed shots; and
- better-sized rock to harvest, assuming that ICI-Nobel has better expertise than the average quarry.

And for ICI-Nobel:

- better utilization of its assets;
- fewer SKUs to produce and handle;
- possibly fewer or smaller facilities; and
- barrier to entry.

This last benefit for ICI-Nobel may well be the most important. ICI-Nobel can steal a march on its competitors by engaging in this service. The competitors do not have as much expertise in shot-firing as ICI-Nobel does and thus could not readily copy ICI-Nobel. In the meantime, ICI-Nobel can lock up lots of customers in long-term contracts, thus guaranteeing their loyalty.

Much of this discussion actually occurred. ICI-Nobel's Australian operations (now known as Orica Mining Services) pioneered this "rock on ground" concept where a commodity good was replaced by a difficult-to-copy service that was perfectly attuned to the needs of the quarry customers. ICI-Nobel, in Britain, purchased special 16-ton trucks that could mix, on site, a slurry that worked in any weather. The slurry could be poured directly down the drilled holes, and that improved the contact of explosive with the rock, making for better blasts. It also meant that the packaging that existed before was unnecessary, saving cost in the manufacturing process.

ICI-Nobel people could do everything for the quarry, from designing the blast, to drilling the holes and firing the shot. Quarries could buy the service and not worry about blasting again. The result was hugely successful for ICI-Nobel and it did alter the competitive landscape. When ICI was broken up in the 1990s, ICI-Nobel was purchased by the Australians who had concocted this clever solution to what seemed to be an intractable problem.

This morphing of manufacturer into service provider is sometimes called servitization. The popular example for it is the "power by the hour" program of the jet engine manufacturer, Rolls Royce. Rather than purchase jet engines outright, airlines can now rent propulsion from Rolls-Royce, which then assumes all of the maintenance of the engines. To cite another example, IBM, under Lou Gerstner, shifted more to selling "solutions" rather than keeping the focus on computers and other "hardware." Other examples abound.

SOME TAKEAWAYS FOR MAKING FLOWS SWIFT AND EVEN

Here we have an example where the variation caused by the customer is so great that actually taking charge of the customers' demands, and reducing the variation in those demands, makes sense. Doing so saved customers money, and thus a new business model was born.

Yet, this new business model has its inspiration in the analysis of variation and throughput time. An investigation into what would improve productivity directed a light on the alternative that was possible. What can we glean from this investigation?

- Go first to the point in the supply chain closest to the customer – go downstream – and assess the variation caused by the customer that affects operations upstream.
- Do not be bound by thinking that a manufacturer must always stay a pure manufacturer. Service can be a useful part of the product offering. It may even serve to raise barriers to entry.

A change in a business model is a big, strategic change that can stem from examining swift, even flow. Smaller, but still important, changes can also result.

ALL CLOGGED UP

This is a disguised case of a situation that, once analyzed properly, was turned around quickly.

Stewart Instruments, Ltd.

Stewart Instruments was a manufacturer of laboratory equipment in Islington, UK, just outside of London.[3] The company was losing money but not for lack of demand. Business was good, but the factory simply could not ship on time.

The plant produced 550 different pieces of lab equipment from 10,000 separate part numbers, mostly sheet metal, plastic and metal parts, and electrical and electronic components. Purchased parts accounted for 40–50 percent of standard cost. A typical product (e.g., a water bath) was assembled from 60 different parts with a bill of materials (BOM) that stretched to five levels, the top of which (Level 0) was the finished product. The time it took for materials to move through the various departments in the factory, from start to finish, was governed by the levels of the BOM. The time was estimated as the time spent in each department, or two weeks, whichever was greater.

Several of the mid-level managers in the operation were particularly frantic:

- The production planning manager was coping with an increasingly high number of scheduling changes. The scheduling changes – either increases or decreases in the schedule – were made by the company's four product managers in the third week of each month and could affect the following month. They wanted to improve the quality of the forecast.
- There were some other decisions that affected production planning:
  - A goal of zero inventory/zero backlog. Manufacturing was to produce to order only.
  - Finance, worried about the increasing inventory, had dictated that six weeks was the maximum time that should elapse between two successive lots of the same item.
- The manager of the Fabrication Department, the first department to handle any materials for an order, was concerned that the time standards in the system did not correspond with actual times. Work had piled up all around that department even though overtime was a regular occurrence. Some fabrication work had been outsourced to help with this situation, but the drawings used were seldom up to date and the subcontractor was shipping parts that did not meet the current specifications.

- Only 40–50 percent of jobs were picked clean. There were many discrepancies between physical counts of inventory and what the MRP system said was available. The taking of physical inventories generally was required twice a year in order to reconcile the differences.
- The volume of expedited orders was swamping the Purchasing Department.

The untimely death of the former general manager thrust a new guy into the job. What was he to do to get product out the door? The company had shipped more in recent years than it was shipping now. What was clogging up things and what could be done about it?

When people confront this case, the initial thought could be that there is a shortage of capacity. After all, the issue is not getting sufficient output out the door. However, the company has shipped more in the previous years than it has shipped at the present time, and there is no reason to think that it could not do so now. Capacity is not the problem.

Production planning is the problem. People studying this case understand this, at least in a vague way, but then they freeze. There is simply too much to consider and it is difficult to put together the kind of "story" that explains things clearly and leads to the concrete steps that can remedy this situation. When they hear that the actual company, once it got its arms around this problem, went from losses to profit in a matter of months, they suffer even more anxiety.

GETTING ARMS AROUND THIS PROBLEM

Here is where the structure of swift, even flow can provide comfort. The questions to ask are the usual ones: where is there variation of any kind and where does throughput time lengthen?

Variation

- Obviously, the product managers are changing the schedule and that is a major source of variation. And, they are changing the schedule as close as two weeks beforehand.

- It is also clear that inventory is not controlled well at all. The company does not have a firm grip on what it has in inventory. Physical inventory counts have to be scheduled twice a year, when, in many companies, physical inventory counts have not been engaged in for years.
- The labor standards are also suspect. If, indeed, the standards for jobs are low – they are underestimates of the time it actually takes to do the job – then the master production schedule that relies on those standards will shovel more materials to the factory floor each week than that factory floor can handle. The result will be a buildup of inventory. That is what is being observed.
- More difficult to see as sources of variation, but still critical to this case, are the rules that have been set up, presumably to cope with the growing inventory that the company has experienced.
  - One rule is the "zero inventory, zero backlog rule." That rule, meant to keep inventories under control, actually increases variation by removing the buffer of finished goods inventory that could be used to dampen the production schedule.
  - The other rule is finance's six-week rule that limits the production of any product to no larger than the forecast of the next six weeks. That rule could defeat a "level" production strategy that tries to smooth the quantities that the factory makes.

Throughput time

The principal impediment to swift flow is the buffer lead time that is assigned to movements between levels in the bill of materials. That is, as materials move from one department to another, lead time is added to make sure that the production schedule is easily kept. It only serves to slow things down, and all for the sake of the information system.

The buffer lead time is longer, also, because the bill of materials is five levels deep. A more shallow BOM would help. A five-level BOM ensures that the throughput time for something like the water bath is at least eight weeks long (four level changes of two weeks each). Given that the product managers are changing the schedule in as short as two weeks hence, it is no wonder that the Fabrication

Department is going crazy. They simply do not have enough time to react to any of the changes for the next month. Moves to expedite orders through the department will only sap capacity as the change-overs proliferate.

The company sees increasing inventory as the problem, but it has adopted a series of rules and policies that only add to its difficulties. The zero inventory/zero backlog rule eliminates the use of finished goods inventory so that the factory must make to order. Yet, the long throughput times derived from the many levels of the BOM and the two-week buffer lead times for going from one level of the BOM to another ensure that the factory is not very agile. And, it cannot anticipate or react to orders that are longer than six weeks out. Yet, the product planners demand agility by changing the schedule. This dooms the factory to groan under more inventory.

WHAT SWIFT, EVEN FLOW SUGGESTS

The production planning for Stewart Instruments is fraught with variation and impediments to swift flow. If the company is to get out of the bind that it is in, it must reduce that variation and improve its throughput time. In this case, reducing variation will be a quicker fix to the problem, but reducing the throughput time is something to pursue as well.

What can be done to reduce variation and throughput time?

- The zero inventory/zero backlog rule can be abolished and finished goods inventory held. Holding some of the more popular models that are sure to sell would avoid any obsolescence. The amount of finished goods would not have to be all that large. It simply needs to be enough so that expediting is reduced and production plans can become more stable.
- The six-week rule can also be abolished and the production plan can then become more "level" and less "chase" in nature.
- The production schedule can be frozen for a period of time so that the product planners cannot change the schedule on short notice and wreak havoc on departments upstream, such as the Fabrication Department. The frozen period needs to be at least as long as the throughput time of the product.

- Labor standards can be altered in a general, rough way for the major work centers, with the idea of making the production schedule more feasible. Significant study of the work by industrial engineers would take longer, but it, too, is something to consider.
- Avoiding the physical inventories of the past will take more discipline throughout the factory. Cycle counting, where only selected items are reconciled, could be useful.
- Reducing the throughput time will take revisions to the bills of materials and to the use of buffer lead times. Calming the factory's production planning is a step forward but it would be most beneficial if the flow of materials through the factory did not depend on the computer system.

The company did implement these suggestions. A finished goods inventory was held and the production schedule was frozen for a period of 12 weeks. The six-week rule was abolished. Labor standards were improved in a rough-cut way. A cycle counting program was implemented so that those parts expected to be used in the next nine weeks were cycle counted, except for those that had already been cycle counted in the prior four weeks. More than this, the new general manager met with all of the workforce and sought their ideas for improvement. Many improvements streamed out of the workforce and lower levels of management. The percent of jobs picked clean rose from 40–50 percent to 92 percent in a matter of six months. The company became profitable in a quarter's time.

SOME TAKEAWAYS FOR MAKING FLOWS SWIFT AND EVEN

In the previous case, ICI-Nobel Explosives, the customer quarries were the chief source of variation. Here, the company's own production planning, strapped with counterproductive rules and policies, was to blame. Finance and product managers may have had the best of intentions, but their actions added significant variation to the factory and caused inventory to increase steadily. One must be constantly vigilant about the addition of new rules and policies; they can be devilish.

The structure of things such as bills of materials can do much to shoulder the process with unnecessary and long throughput times. Buffers, be they inventory or planning times, should be the objects of continual scrutiny. A little of each is often all that is needed. Here, better process design and controls are needed.

BOTTLES, BOTTLES EVERYWHERE

This is a disguised case, but a true story, and one that has broad implications.[4]

Spirit Bottling

Spirit Bottling Company was a bottler of soft drinks. It bottled and canned nine different flavors in an assortment of sizes. In the past year it sold 22.3 million cases of soft drinks in 20 different packages. It was currently suffering from very high inventories, however. On average, it was holding 7.5 days of sales in finished goods inventory, but those days of sales varied from 1.6 days on the low side to over 100 days on the high side.

The company did not have enough space indoors to hold all of its finished goods inventory. It was forced to hold some of it outside where cold and rain could damage both cartons and bottles. Management was contemplating the construction of more warehouse space.

Exactly how management decided how much to produce of any item at a particular time was not terribly clear. For the most part, management looked to the days of supply for each flavor and package combination, electing to bottle (or can) those combinations whose days of supply were the lowest. However, this rule was not followed all the time. The decision of how much to produce relied on a number of things: raw materials inventory, production times, safety stock levels, warehouse space, sales promotion, inventory costs, and sales forecasts. It was rare to schedule the filling equipment for anything less than three hours, even when the product was a "low-runner" where a three-hour production run could mean months of sales.

> The data for one product was illustrative.
>
> Product: Spirit, in 10 oz. returnable bottles
>
> Cost (per case of 24): bottles ($4.30), cartons ($0.20), syrup for soft drink ($0.72), water ($0.06)
>
> Sales (cases per month): 31,690
>
> Production line: operated for one ten-hour shift a day, four days a week, and an average of 17 days of production per month. (Fridays were used for maintenance.) 1,000 cases per hour. Eight other products, with total monthly sales of 116,800 cases, were also produced on this production line. Changeovers of the production line for different packages and/or products took 30 minutes each. Changeover cost: the labor time for a changeover of the line was valued at $12.
>
> Inventory carrying cost: 15 percent per year.

Here we have a case where management is flying by the seat of its pants, and the result is excess inventory and no clear consensus on what should be done about it.

The notion of using days of supply to schedule production smacks of the reorder point system (sometimes known as the EOQ system) where a particular value for the days of supply (the reorder point) triggers production of a standard quantity (the economic order quantity, or EOQ). Such a system is often embedded in the various lot sizing routines of material requirements planning (MRP) systems, or more generally now in enterprise resource planning (ERP) systems. Thus, its logic can be widespread, especially as it can be readily calculated.

What would such a calculation look like for 10 oz. returnable Spirit? The formula, derived from calculus and minimizing the total cost of carrying inventory and changing over production, is

$$EOQ = \sqrt{2DS / iC}$$

where D is the demand for the product, S is the setup or changeover cost, i is the inventory carrying cost, and C is the variable cost of the product. For 10 oz. returnable Spirit, the calculation, using monthly figures (note: the inventory carrying cost figure is 15% per year, or 15/12 or 1.25% per month), is

$$EOQ = \{(2* \ 31{,}690*12) \ / \ ((0.15/12)*5.28)\}^{1/2} = 3{,}395 \ \text{cases}$$

Is this a big number or a small number? It is really a fairly small number. Monthly demand is 31,690 cases and thus this calculation requires that the production line be changed over almost ten times per month, or pretty much every other day. That's a lot of change-over, especially when we recall that the production line also serves eight other products with small EOQs. That much changeover can rob a production line of considerable capacity, and it may even be true that the production line does not have enough run time left from its 40 hours per week to bottle all that it is required to bottle. Because of this, we can appreciate why the managers at Spirit Bottling are so confused about what they should do. They may be trying to balance capacity against the dictates of an EOQ calculation that calls for lots of short runs.

What is more, the reorder point (EOQ) system is really not meant to plan production. Its assumptions are very suspect if production is the goal. For example, the reorder point system assumes that someone is always looking at whether the reorder points for products have been struck. When they are, replenishment of the EOQ quantity is assumed to progress right away. And, there are no assumed capacity constraints. The replenishment can always progress on schedule. In short, the reorder point system is not a good one to be embedded in MRP and ERP systems. If one is not careful, some very inappropriate lot sizes could be triggered and the operation of the plant compromised as a result.

What is the alternative? What else could Spirit Bottling do? The counter-type system to the reorder system is the periodic reorder system. While the reorder point (EOQ) system calls for constant monitoring and replenishment of a fixed quantity (the EOQ), the periodic reorder system calls for regular (not constant) monitoring and the replenishment of a variable quantity that depends on how much has been used during the preceding period and how much is projected for the current period. The following chart captures some of these distinctions.

	Reorder point system	Periodic reorder system
Quantities	Fixed (EOQ)	Variable
Timing	At any time	On a regular basis, e.g., weekly

With a periodic reorder system, management would choose a set period, say a week. The order of production of products on the production line would stay the same from one week to the next. What would change would be the quantities produced – more if the forecast called for it, more if demand had been stronger than previously forecast, and less if demand had not been strong or if the forecast did not call for as much. One could take a look at the total time involved, run times and changeover times. If the total time was less than the 40 hours of the week, then some items could be changed over more often and inventories reduced as a result. If, on the other hand, the total time were greater than 40 hours per week, then the review period should be lengthened from a week to some longer figure. Getting the total time (run times plus changeover times) to match as precisely as possible the schedule of the production line will assure that the schedule is feasible and that inventories are as low as could be expected.

Figure 5.3 shows how changing the periodic reorder system's timescale can lower the inventory that the company carries. In Figure 5.3A, production occurs just once during the review period. Inventory is depleted in a steady way. In Figure 5.3B, given the same steady depletion of inventory, the review period is half of what it is in Figure 5.3A, and the resulting average inventory is also half of what it is in Figure 5.3A.

In this case, we have roughly 148,000 cases that need to be produced in 17 ten-hour days a month. At 1,000 cases an hour, 148,000

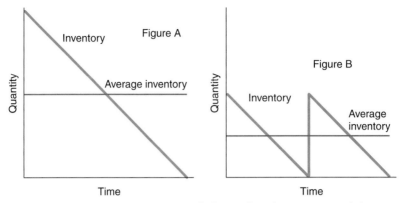

FIGURE 5.3 Average inventory declines when the review period shortens

cases would take 148 hours, leaving 22 hours for changeovers. There are nine different products produced on the line, thus, nine different changeovers were the absolute minimum for a month. That way, each product would be produced only once a month. However, that would leave inventories higher than they should be.

If the periodic review period could be limited to a week, then 36 changeovers would be required, using up 18 hours of time. With 22 hours available for changeover, a review period of a week would be feasible. In fact, it leaves four hours of extra time. With these four hours, some of the higher volume products could be produced even more frequently, and that could reduce inventories even more.

WHAT DOES SWIFT, EVEN FLOW SAY ABOUT THIS? A CRITICAL TAKEAWAY

Where does swift, even flow enter into this conversation? It is easy to see that the increased frequency of production pares down the level of inventories and that reduces throughput time. All to the good. And, swift, even flow likes it when variation is reduced. That variation, as we have seen, can be with quality, quantities, or timing. Here we have a situation where the reorder point system reduces variation in quantities but permits sometimes significant variation in timing.

The periodic reorder system does the mirror image. It reduces variation in timing but permits variation in quantities.

Which is the more important variation to reduce? Timing. Having a set schedule is very much more important than producing set quantities. If a schedule is interrupted at will, so much can be thrown into turmoil. Variation in quantities, on the other hand, is relatively easy to cope with, as it means adjusting run times, often by relatively small amounts.

This is an important and practical insight for many companies. Over time, variation creeps into many operations. It's a natural progression. Product lines expand. Options proliferate. Customers are added and companies want to please them. Special requests are acceded to. The operation, bit by bit, becomes more complex. Just as the laws of thermodynamics teach us, entropy – that measure of disorder – always seems to increase, for the universe as a whole but also, it seems, for companies.

How can one reverse this entropy? The operation needs to become more regular and controlled. And, what is the regularity that should be most prized? Timing. Working with a set schedule is critical. Changing quantities within that schedule is more easily accommodated. Timing is the source of variation that commands the more immediate attention.

SOMETIMES THERE ARE MORE CHOICES THAN YOU THINK

Companies in a host of industries must deal with either regulation or deregulation. When regulation or deregulation comes knocking there is little choice; one must comply. But, the company has a good deal of leeway in how to cope with the change. How should a process be changed when such mandates are thrust upon you? The following case is an old one, dealing with the deregulation of trucking. It is a condensed version of what happened to Yellow Freight back in the latter part of the 1970s.[5] Its lessons, however, are timeless.

Yellow Freight

It was 1976 and the US Congress was once again taking up the passage
of trucking deregulation. A similar measure had been defeated five years
previously, but some legislators were persistently pursuing passage.

Yellow Freight was one of the major national trucking companies,
able to ship full-load (60 percent of sales) or "less-than-truckload"
(LTL) quantities (40 percent of sales) almost anywhere in the United
States (interstate shipping), and it had consistently been the most
profitable. It had done a particularly good job of taking advantage of
the current regulations.

Trucking regulation in the United States dated from 1935 and was
modeled on railroad regulation. Trucking companies were usually
either interstate shippers such as Yellow, or they were same-state
shippers with the right to travel anywhere within the state but not
outside of it. Manufacturing and service companies could own and
operate their own trucks but they could not pick up freight from
anybody other than their own plants or warehouses. In order to serve
a particular pair of cities, trucking companies such as Yellow needed
to acquire the right to offer service and bore the responsibility of
serving anyone who needed shipping done, provided the company
had trucks available. Prices varied by type of cargo and were fixed by
cartels of trucking companies overseen by federal government. The
right to ship also spelled out the specific path the truck had to drive
between the cities. Companies wishing to extend their services had
to purchase existing companies and their regulatory rights to use
set paths for their trucks; they simply could not announce their
intention to serve a new market. Furthermore, new companies could
not enter the business unless they, too, purchased the rights to do so.

Yellow Freight had been successful for several reasons:

1. It had a strong balance sheet, which permitted acquisition of failing companies that had rights to cities Yellow had not previously served.
2. Yellow had an extensive number of terminals (where freight originated or
   was sent) and break-bulks (where shipments were regrouped for continu-
   ation along Yellow's routes), although not as extensive as several other
   firms in the industry.

3. Yellow practiced a relay system for their trucks rather than a roll-and-rest system. That is, trucks drove to preselected spots where relief drivers took the shipment further. Such a system helped to provide information and control of what was happening. Yellow knew exactly where any of its shipments were, something companies that practiced roll-and-rest could not guarantee.

4. To keep track of its trucks and their shipments, Yellow had invested large amounts of money in computers and computer systems.

5. Yellow owned and operated new equipment. It did not want to be in the business of significant truck repair. It sold used trucks usually after three years of use.

6. Yellow identified the most profitable accounts and concentrated on procuring business from them.

Congress was considering the abolition of the shipping rights-of-way, so that any firm, given certain safety requirements, could enter the industry, ship anywhere, and charge whatever price it wanted.

The deregulation of trucking didn't happen in 1976, but it did happen four years later. Some of the major trucking companies were more prepared than others, and some of these other companies left money on the table when deregulation hit. Processes certainly changed as a result.

Let's examine the company's operations under regulation. Yellow Freight had done a brilliant job of mastering the regulatory environment. It specialized in key accounts that it had identified as being major users that shipped a product for which the cartel-agreed tariff was attractively high. It could offer the shipper greater control over its shipments than other companies. And, it offered a country-spanning network so that it could ship nearly anywhere in the United States. The elements of its operations (points 1–6 above) supported this strategy.

What would deregulation do? The most significant aspect of any deregulation is the increased entry permitted to the market. Trucking deregulation would be no different. Capacity would be greatly increased. The value of operating licenses for routes, previously the reason companies were purchased by other companies, would vanish. As long as safety could be maintained, new trucking companies, and, indeed, individual operators could enter the business. Prices would definitely drop.

The issue at the heart of this deregulation is what aspects of the current, regulated business would be attacked and not defended very well, and, what aspects of the current business could be defended well. Here is where students reading this case began to stumble. They often were unclear about which aspects of Yellow's operations were vulnerable. After all, the company had been so successful under the regulatory umbrella.

ATTACKING THE OLD REGIME – WHAT SWIFT, EVEN FLOW HAS TO SAY

Enter swift, even flow. The most productive aspects of the prevailing operation have to be those for which variations in quality, quantity, and timing are low and for which throughput times are short. Any new entrant will want to go after the business that displays those characteristics. Which aspects of the business are they? The truckload business certainly has lower variability than the LTL business, especially if it involves general commodities and not more exotic ones that demand refrigeration or special handling. The LTL business also involves terminals and break-bulks that lengthen the throughput time for the items being shipped. The local area business is also less variable than the long-distance one; a relay system is not needed around a metropolitan area.

Suppose that new entrants choose to deliver truckload quantities point-to-point and that they do not need break-bulks. Where will this leave Yellow Freight? The company will likely be left with the most variable and longest throughput time business, namely the LTL business between cities and states. If it is to succeed, it will have to do better than the other major trucking carriers at improving this LTL portion of its business. This, in turn, will mean devising ways to remove variation and to decrease the throughput time for LTL shipments.

How can this be done? It will mean concocting a hub-and-spoke system that works for the entire country. You do not want shipments broken down and repacked too many times. You want to diminish that double handling. Doing that will mean opening up more terminals and break-bulks. You do not want to build bottlenecks or constraints into the system by forcing shipments through too many of the same break-bulks.

Getting such facilities quickly may mean acquiring some other companies whose own facilities and their locations complement Yellow's own. The operating licenses for such companies used to be the reason for the acquisition. Now, it is their physical assets that are valuable.

The name of the game will be the quickness by which shipments can proceed from origin to destination. This may, in turn, mean that a labor-intensive rather than a capital-intensive operation in the break-bulks might work better. The company will be better served with a reputation for quick, seamless transportation than for a reputation as a low-cost handler, but one that may not get the shipment there quickly.

In fact, Yellow Freight was caught flat-footed by the Motor Carrier Act of 1980. It took the company a number of years to regroup. But, regroup it did. It became the largest LTL carrier in the United States and, in 2003, it acquired Roadway, the second-largest carrier, to become, as Yellow Roadway Corporation, one of the world's largest transportation providers.

TAKEAWAYS

In this case, swift, even flow was used to analyze a policy change and its potential impact on an industry and the leading firms of that industry. Once the federal government let go of its old regulations of the trucking industry, companies had to figure out where the most productive, and thus possibly the most profitable, niches within the industry would be. Swift, even flow helps to do just that.

LESSONS LEARNED: TURNING AROUND POORER-
PERFORMING OPERATIONS

These various case studies bring to the surface some fruitful ways of thinking. First, asking the questions of (1) where there is variation in the process, and (2) where throughput time lengthens, can uncover a raft of problems and show the way to improvement. They are useful ways to begin to diagnose what ails any process. And, from the Yellow Freight case, we see that asking these questions can reveal a company's vulnerabilities to changes in the level of competition, such as where new entrants are likely to focus their attention.

Second, these case studies demonstrate some mechanisms by which one can remedy both variation and lengthy throughput times.

Coping with variation

1. Segregate items into families. Variation within families is, by definition, less than variation across families. This is what cells do for a process.
2. Standardize procedures, if they are not already standardized.
3. Manage customers, as they are a frequent source of variation. If they can be managed by means such as reservation (appointment) systems, then so much the better. Sometimes offering a service with a product embedded in it, rather than selling the product outright (what is sometimes termed servitization), is another way to manage the customer.
4. The production plan can overload any process. Build buffers into a process, all the more so when the process is more job shop or batch in character. Avoid unnecessary rules, or even rules of thumb, that can inadvertently foster deleterious variation in production plans.
5. Time is likely to be a more important source of variation than quantities. Smooth the "drumbeat" of time before you smooth the quantities involved.

Coping with long throughput times

1. Break bottlenecks. It's the time-tested remedy to increase capacity and can sometimes be done simply.
2. Reduce inventories. Inventories are the classic way by which throughput time is lengthened.

3. Adopt pull systems. Pull systems, as opposed to push systems, control inventory levels better and thus act typically to shorten throughput times.

4. Head downstream first. Given the power of pull systems, it is often much more helpful to start downstream and then work back upstream. The sources of variation and of long throughput times (e.g., inventories) are often best dealt with in this way.

5. Remove non-value-added steps.

6   Linking the supply chain

So far, we have discussed swift, even flow from the standpoint of the individual company, but there is nothing that constrains the concept from extending to the entire supply chain. Throughput times and variation are as readily apparent in a supply chain as they are within a service or manufacturing process. What follows are more condensed versions of case situations that a variety of different companies faced as they contemplated issues in their supply chains.

TICK, TOCK

The first case documents what Ernst Zängerle confronted upon taking over manufacturing and logistics at Omega Watch in the late 1980s.[1]

Omega, autumn 1988

In the autumn of 1988, Ernst Zängerle joined Omega Watch as VP for Manufacturing and Logistics. Omega was part of the SMH Group that included a number of other famous Swiss brands such as Longines, Tissot, and importantly, Swatch. The merger that created SMH under its new head, Nicholas Hayek, had resulted in one of SMH's subsidiary companies, ETA, producing the watch movements for all of the brands, and in a clear positioning of the brands, with Omega as the most expensive brand with CHF 250 million in annual sales from the factory (average price at retail of CHF 1,200).

Hayek had not changed any of Omega's manufacturing or distribution, and this prompted the many concerns that Zängerle had. A tour of the supply chain revealed the following:

Suppliers: the 60 suppliers, of which ten were used extensively, took an average of six to eight months to deliver an order.

Manufacturing: it took six to seven minutes of labor to assemble a watch and another two days to test it. There were 500 distinct models produced (down from the number that Hayek inherited) and an estimated 400,000 watches of all types were made during the year. Watches were assembled in batches to minimize changeovers (one to two minutes in going from one style to another) with the batch size being 200. The throughput time for a manufacturing batch was 30 days.

Factory warehouse: the factory warehouse contained an average of four months of inventory. This warehouse filled the orders placed on it (typically monthly) by the 120 country-specific distributor companies. The percentage of orders filled completely and on time (the service level), however, was only 40–50 percent.

Distributor companies: the distributor companies, the major ones of which were owned by Omega, filled the orders of the retailers in each country. The service levels were again only about 40–50 percent. Salesmen for the distributors called on retailers two or three times a year at which time the retailers were encouraged to place their orders for delivery weeks later. Distributors tried to sell what was in their inventory. The distributor companies held between six and 12 months of inventory, on average.

Retailers: retailers were of all types – chains and independents, large and small. On average they held 12 months of inventory in their shops. Few, if any, could carry all 500 models. Most tried to sell customers what they carried in stock.

Omega had no real idea of what was actually selling in the marketplace; it only knew what it was shipping out of the factory warehouse.

After reviewing the situation, Zängerle developed a vision of what Omega needed to do to improve.

The first thing that strikes people when they look at this situation is how much inventory there is floating in the supply chain! Omega does not own all of it, of course. The retailers own their share and the suppliers control the parts they ship but Omega does control the major country distributors and so the company itself has to finance 11–17 months of inventory. With factory sales of CHF 250 million, this implies that the company carries a comparable amount in inventory. The potential for saving on inventory carrying costs is enticing.

People also take note of the fact that Omega really doesn't know what is selling at the retailer level. The company loses control after it ships from its warehouse in Bienne, Switzerland, and the distributors really cannot help much.

After these observations, however, people generally stumble over what to do about it. Many look upstream to see what can be done with the suppliers. Others want to cut down on the 500 models that the company produces, and are disappointed to learn that Hayek has already trimmed the number of models to 500 and will not easily trim those numbers more. The distributors are a likely source of improvement, but exactly what to say about them is not easy. Many then sit back, resigned, more or less, to living with the status quo and thankful that the Omega brand is as well respected as it is.

SWIFT, EVEN FLOW FOR THE SUPPLY CHAIN

From our investigations in the last chapter into improving single processes, we know that two questions are critical to answer: (1) where there is variation, and (2) where throughput time lengthens.

There is clearly a good deal of variation inherent here. The service levels in the supply chain were only 40–50 percent, which naturally implied a good deal of expediting to get watches to the countries that needed them. Manufacturing was driven by forecasts as opposed to orders, as it did not know what was actually selling in the field, and those forecasts likely fluctuated. The wide variety of models had sales that probably followed the standard 80–20 rule, with a low number of models (say 20 percent) accounting for the bulk of sales (say 80 percent). Thus, especially for the low-volume items, sales could be expected to bounce around quite a bit.

More dramatic is the long throughput time for this supply chain. From suppliers to retail sale, the throughput time varies between 29 months on the low side to 37 months on the high side. There are big inventories at each step of the way and they all soak up time. Having lot sizes of 200 contributes to this. If there are roughly 400,000 Omega watches sold (assuming that the retail mark-up on the watches is 100 percent) and 500 different models, then the average model would sell about 800 watches per year, or four lots. For the many models that sell less than 800 watches in a year, the lot size of 200 would be an even larger fraction of total annual sales. This relatively large lot size, then, would, for certain models, extend their throughput times.

If Omega is to become more productive, it will have to reduce both the variation and the throughput time for its watches. But, how can this be accomplished?

The previous chapter suggested that analysis begin as close to the customer as possible and then work back upstream. This same prescription works just as well for a supply chain. Start near the customer and follow the supply chain back upstream to the suppliers. In this case, the closest we can come to the customer is the retail store. Stores were drowning in inventory, a year's worth on average. It is clear that the retailer could make more money if it could cut down on that inventory and the carrying charges associated with it. However, Omega's own operations did not make that easy for them to do.

The stores were supplied in bulk at select times during the year. Omega essentially pushed inventory on to the country distributors and from them to the retail stores. The service levels were low despite the expediting done. Omega could not supply the retailers quickly and reliably. Hence, inventory built up in the supply chain. Importantly, there was no mechanism to prevent the buildup.

How can this phenomenon be countered? Here is where the vision of the Toyota Production System can help. If inventory is to be kept low, then the "push" of the current system has to be changed to the "pull" of a revised system. The high throughput times of the Omega supply chain must be reduced; the inventory has to be pared down. To do that, Omega needs to think of its distribution channel as a series of replenishments, just as Toyota thinks of replenishing its production line. The retailer sells a watch. The country distributor replenishes it rapidly. The Bienne warehouse replenishes the country distributor. The Bienne factory replenishes the Bienne warehouse. And, Omega's suppliers replenish the factory. Furthermore, the information flow needed to trigger these replenishments will provide Omega with the information it craves about what is selling at the retail level. In this instance, an improved operation can lead to better marketing.

One could envision that the retailer holds a carefully considered target inventory of watches of less than a year's worth of sales, a target inventory that Omega helps them devise. The sale of a watch from that target inventory could then trigger, via some quick communication, its replenishment from the country distributor in the next day or two, say, via air freight or courier. The country distributor, in turn, could be replenished on a weekly basis from the Bienne warehouse. What sells out of the Bienne warehouse could then serve as the basis for the scheduling of the factory and the management of the suppliers.

This vision of replenishment completely changes the relationship that the retailers have with the company. The country distributors "hawk their wares" to the retailers in the push system that now prevails. A new, revised pull system would require the country distributor to be more of a partner, counseling the retailer on what to hold, facilitating the communication on replenishment that can now be daily (via computer link, phone, or fax), and troubleshooting any problems. The country distributor would also have to learn how to fill the replenishment orders quickly and accurately. If the retailers are to be happy with less inventory in their stores, they need to trust the distributors to get the replenishments to them quickly.

The same will have to be said of the operations in Bienne, both warehouse and factory. The warehouse will have to fill the, say, weekly orders from the distributors quickly and completely. And, the factory must be able to replenish the warehouse quickly, too, and with any model that may be needed in stock. The more flexible the factory the better off everyone will be, but, in order to be more flexible, the batch sizes of 200 will have to be pared down. They are far too big for most of the models offered.

To reduce the batch size will require more, smaller lot sizes. These smaller lot sizes will, in turn, require more setup or change-over time and a reduced labor efficiency. More changeover time will mean less time for actual assembly and this could cut into capacity. The company might have to hire additional assembly workers. Would such a cost be justified? Would it make sense to reduce lot sizes if the result is added direct labor?

The answer is a relative no-brainer. As noted above, Omega carries an inventory of about CHF 1 million for every business day of the year. Assuming that the carrying cost percentage for that inventory is 10 percent, this means that Omega incurs a carrying cost of CHF 100,000 for every day of inventory held. Reduce inventory by a day and costs decline by CHF 100,000. Cut inventory in half and the company saves CHF 12.5 million a year. A lot of direct labor can be added and the company still saves big money.

ZÄNGERLE'S VISION

Ernst Zängerle had come to Omega from Hilti, a Lichtenstein manufacturer of products for the construction and building maintenance industries, and he was well versed in lean manufacturing principles. He looked at the bloated supply chain at Omega and was determined to reduce it. He realized that Omega needed to abandon its "push" approach in favor of a "pull" approach. His own targets were to reduce the retailer's average inventory to four months or less and that of the country distributors to between two and four weeks.

(This would likely mean more sales from the catalogue, but if replenishment could be done quickly, this option became more attractive.) Zängerle wanted to eliminate the Bienne warehouse completely, but to do so meant being able to produce any of the 500 models of Omega watch in three days. Unfortunately, he could only reduce the manufacturing throughput time to 10–15 days and that wasn't enough to completely eliminate the Bienne warehouse. He was able to reduce its inventories, though, to two weeks, and to have the warehouse add flexibility to the operation by matching watch heads and watch bands, so that the exact combination needed in the market could be "postponed" until the last possible moment. Getting the suppliers to adopt lean manufacturing principles was not easy but Zängerle made advances there, as well.

SOME TAKEAWAYS FOR MAKING SUPPLY CHAIN FLOWS SWIFT AND EVEN

The concept of swift, even flow is as readily applied to a supply chain as it is to an individual operation. A number of lessons can be drawn:

- A long throughput time can reveal a lot of waste in a supply chain, and in the distribution channels especially.
- To investigate a supply chain, it is most useful to start at the customer and work back upstream to the suppliers.
- Pull systems (replenishment systems) can work throughout a supply chain and typically can improve a great deal on a "push" system.
- A potentially useful tactic in ridding a supply chain of waste is to manage the retailer/customer better. Think partnership. Doing so may require establishing a better operation so that the retailer/customer has faith that orders will be fulfilled quickly and accurately.
- Reduction in the throughput time of a supply chain can free tremendous quantities of investment for other purposes. Labor efficiency can pale in comparison to the savings from collapsing the throughput time of the supply chain.

This next case builds nicely on the first.

BRICK BY BRICK

In the late 1990s and early 2000s, LEGO, the iconic producer of toys and known for its interlocking plastic bricks, lost money for the first time since its creation in 1932. Among other things, its supply chain needed attention.[2]

LEGO's supply chain

Since LEGO's creation in 1932 by Ole Kirk Kristiansen in Billund, Denmark, there had been a steady march of increasing sales and profit. From its start with wooden toys, new products had been added at a steady clip, notably the interlocking plastic brick in 1958, the LEGO train in 1966, Duplo in the late 1960s, the LEGO figure in 1974, the Technic series in 1977, the first of a series of story-themed play with the Space series in 1979, the Star Wars license in 1998, and Bionicle in 2001. In 1998, however, the company began to lose money. Losses were registered in 2000 and again in 2003 and 2004. Sales even dropped in 2003 and 2004. Inventories were growing. Something had to be done.

The market for toys was both highly competitive and seasonal. New products accounted for 75 percent of LEGO's sales and 45 percent of its total sales occurred within the three months before Christmas. Sales were also concentrated; 20 customer companies accounted for 70 percent of LEGO's sales. Importantly, although LEGO's customers needed the company to be a flexible supplier to them, they did not require daily or next-day deliveries.

LEGO produced its bricks and other toys in some of the largest plastic injection molding operations in the world. Its main production facility was in Denmark with another production facility for Europe in Switzerland. The American market was sourced from a factory in Monterrey, Mexico. There were packing and other facilities in the Czech Republic, the United States, and Korea, and an assortment pack assembly operation in Denmark. The production facilities were running at 70 percent utilization.

The company's supply chain included over 11,000 suppliers who helped to supply a total of 12,500 stockkeeping units (SKUs) in over 100 different colors. Within Europe, there were three tiers to the distribution network that LEGO oversaw. To begin, there were centralized distribution centers (DCs) in Denmark and Switzerland, paired with the factories there. There was a second-level central warehouse in Germany that housed finished products. There were four third-level distribution centers in Europe: two in France for the UK and southern Europe, one in Germany for the central and eastern European markets, and one in Denmark for Scandinavia and the Benelux countries. Almost 14,000 customers received direct deliveries from the four distribution centers. LEGO used more than 60 logistics/transportation companies within this supply chain. Only 62 percent of orders, however, were delivered on time.

Management viewed this European supply chain as too complex and costly.

LEGO, as this case relates, was the victim of its own success over the years. It designed more and more toys, in different colors and with different story themes. The number of stockkeeping units soared. In an effort to make sure that the fickle market for toys was well served, LEGO set up a number of different distribution centers, in three tiers, that tried to deliver toys quickly to its retailers. The result, unfortunately, was escalating inventories, declining on-time deliveries, and falling profit. The new toys that were being added contributed less and less to the company's success.

What should be done? Here, again, it is useful to ask the questions of where the variation in the process exists and where throughput time starts to balloon.

VARIATION AND THROUGHPUT TIME WITHIN LEGO

This case is replete with increases in variation. Prominently, the number of stockkeeping units is up to 12,500. With so much of the company's sales dependent on new toys (75 percent), it is no wonder that the number of SKUs has mushroomed. What, apparently, has not accompanied this growth is any trimming of the low-volume items that the company still produces and must distribute.

The number of suppliers – now 11,000 – is staggeringly high, as is the number of logistics and transportation companies that LEGO employs – over 60. Both of these numbers are candidates for reduction.

The case notes that inventories have risen with both the increase in sales and the proliferation of SKUs. Moreover, these inventories are strewn around among three levels of a tiered system of distribution centers. These undoubtedly extend the throughput time for the company's bricks, figures, and accessories.

WHAT SWIFT, EVEN FLOW SUGGESTS

The LEGO supply chain has become so complex and clogged that it is easy to see how adhering to the fundamentals of swift, even flow could point to some quick remedies. Does LEGO really need 100 colors and all 12,500 SKUs? Can it not slash the number of suppliers and still be competitive? And, within the EU it is now fairly easy to identify large logistics companies that can provide the service that LEGO needs to all of the countries to which it sells. The 60 companies that it currently deals with can be markedly reduced.

More challenging is what to do with the three-tiered distribution system that LEGO operates and the series of plants that it also runs. An important point to note is that LEGO's customers were not lobbying for next-day delivery. They would have been satisfied with, say, weekly deliveries if LEGO could have consistently delivered what they had ordered. Currently, only 62 percent of orders were filled on time. Having three tiers to the distribution system assured that inventories remained high and, thus, also throughput times. Logistics/transportation costs suffered the same fate.

What can be done to shrink throughput times? Clearly, the three-tier distribution system can be abandoned in favor of a single-tier system. Europe is a small enough continent, and logistics and transportation are now so efficient that one can easily conceive of a single distribution center to deal with LEGO's needs for Europe. Going to a single distribution center should also improve the company's ability to ship all of an order and on time, especially if the shipments are changed to weekly shipments.

In concert with these changes to distribution, it might also make sense to define clearly what the LEGO factories ought to be producing. In particular, segregating high-volume production from lower-volume, more technically demanding production has a lot of appeal.

WHAT LEGO DID

LEGO realized that its supply chain had been bloated and less responsive than it needed to be. In a study of where to put a new, single distribution center, the company alighted upon the Czech Republic. It was close to the center of LEGO's market in Europe and it promised cheaper costs than Denmark or Switzerland. The company collapsed all of its three-tier system in favor of a single, large distribution center in Kladno, Czech Republic. Half of the 100 colors that LEGO produced were dropped and the company's SKUs were reduced almost in half, to 6,500. The roughly 60 transportation companies serving LEGO distribution were trimmed to seven. Logistics costs dropped 9 percent even while sales jumped 35 percent. On-time delivery went from 62 percent to 96 percent and the company's logistics costs slid from 10.8 percent to 7.9 percent of sales, a drop of more than a quarter. Profit returned. For its efforts, LEGO won a 2008 European Supply Chain Excellence Award.

LEGO also changed its manufacturing. It closed its factories in Switzerland and Korea and moved that manufacturing to Hungary and the Czech Republic. It concentrated its standard and high-volume production in Hungary and the Czech Republic, while keeping its more technically demanding production (e.g., Bionicle, Technic) in Billund, Denmark.

Several more lessons relevant to supply chain management can be drawn from this LEGO case:

- Given today's improvements in transportation and logistics, companies have less need for the construction of multitier distribution systems. Being near customers is now less important than it used to be. More centralized distribution can cut costs and still be very effective.
- Slashing the number of SKUs and the number of companies serving the supply chain can yield dramatic cost savings.
- Coordinating manufacturing strategy with distribution strategy can mean even more savings.

The next case looks at how devastating variation in the supply chain can be.

DINNER, ANYONE?

This case is a condensed version of a case that Barilla, the Italian multinational maker of pasta, faced on its home turf in Italy.[3] It illustrates a classic issue with supply chains.

Barilla SpA

The logistics managers at Barilla were deeply concerned about the weekly fluctuations in demand for pasta production for its main factory and the fact that these fluctuations seemed to be increasing. To counter this demand fluctuation, Barilla wanted to introduce a new program that it termed Just-in-Time Distribution (JITD). With JITD, Barilla would take into account information on shipments and stock levels from its distributors and would then determine the best allocation of inventory all along its distribution channels so as to dampen the fluctuations that its factory was experiencing. Trouble was, the distributors for Barilla's pasta were not the least bit interested in providing such data and Barilla's salespeople were even willing to sabotage the proposal. The logistics managers didn't know what to do.

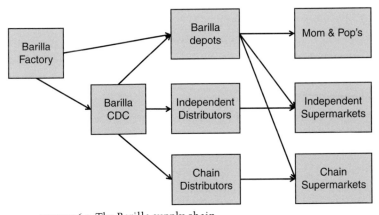

FIGURE 6.1 The Barilla supply chain

The distribution channels for Barilla pasta involved four levels:

1. Barilla factory
2. Barilla CDC (Central Distribution Center)
3. Distributors of various types (independent distributors, chain distributors, and Barilla depots)
4. Retailers of various types (Mom & Pop stores, independent supermarkets, and chain supermarkets).

Figure 6.1 captures how these levels tied together.

It was customary for the retailers to hold two weeks' worth of pasta inventory on their shelves. Similarly, the distributors each held two weeks' worth of inventory in their warehouses, as did the Barilla CDC. Each level of the distribution channel acted independently from the others. The retailers placed orders on the distributors. The distributors, in turn, placed orders on the Barilla CDC. And, the Barilla CDC placed orders on the factory.

Barilla's sales people were paid, in part, based on promotions that the company ran. Distributors could secure discounts for those promotions and for volume purchases and full truckload orders.

The JITD program would change how this system operated, but the independent distributors and the chain distributors would have nothing to do with this innovation. The logistics managers felt stymied.

The variation that is plaguing Barilla, and especially its factory upstream in this supply chain, is of a classic variety. Consider a situation where a Barilla promotion leads to a 10 percent increase in sales, but only for the promotion period, say, a week. Then, demand returns to its standard level and stays there. What would that mean for the orders placed at each level of the supply chain, paying attention to the fact that the orders placed will be those needed to keep two weeks' worth of inventory for each level?

We can capture this situation on a spreadsheet, Table 6.1.

Let's review this spreadsheet. Sales at the Retailers level are 50 each week, except for the 10 percent increase that occurs in Week 2. The Retailers keep two weeks of sales as inventory, so the inventory they need is 100. With sales of 50, the remainder is 50 and the order placed to bring the inventory back up to 100 is 50, as well.

As we work back upstream, a similar situation prevails. Sales at the Distributors level are 50 and their inventories are also two weeks' worth. Thus, they hold 100 in inventory and order 50 to keep up those inventories. Similarly, for the Barilla CDC. The factory, then, has an order placed on it to produce 50. All is well and seemingly tranquil.

Now, consider what happens when sales at the Retailers' level increases to 55 and the same rules for inventory carrying and order placement are followed. You may want to try working through the spreadsheet on your own.

The results of your following the rules with this spreadsheet should result in the following Table 6.2.

As this spreadsheet reveals, the seemingly innocuous increase of sales by 10 percent for a single week results in havoc throughout the supply chain. The orders gyrate wildly from week to week, and, what is worse, the orders become increasingly volatile as you move back upstream. The increase of five units at the Retailers level results in an immediate increase of 45 at the Distributors level (95–50=45) and an increase of 135 at the Barilla CDC and the Barilla Factory levels (185–50=135).

Table 6.1. *A model of the supply chain – starting point*

	Barilla Factory	Barilla CDC	Distributors	Retailers
Week 1				
Existing inventory to start	**100**		**100**	**100**
Sales	50	50	50	50
Inventory needed (two weeks' worth)		**100**	**100**	**100**
Existing inventory after sales		50	50	50
Orders/production	50	50	50	50
Week 2				
Existing inventory to start		**100**	**100**	**100**
Sales				55
Inventory needed (two weeks' worth)				
Existing inventory after sales				
Orders/production				
Week 3				
Existing inventory to start				
Sales				50
Inventory needed (two weeks' worth)				
Existing inventory after sales				
Orders/production				

Table 6.1. (cont.)

	Barilla Factory	Barilla CDC	Distributors	Retailers
Week 4				
Existing inventory to start				
Sales				50
Inventory needed (two weeks' worth)				
Existing inventory after sales				
Orders/production				
Week 5				
Existing inventory to start				
Sales				50
Inventory needed (two weeks' worth)				
Existing inventory after sales				
Orders/production				
Week 6				
Existing inventory to start				
Sales				50
Inventory needed (two weeks' worth)				
Existing inventory after sales				
Orders/production				

Table 6.2. A model of the supply chain – completed

	Barilla Factory	Barilla CDC	Distributors	Retailers
Week 1				
Existing inventory to start	**100**		**100**	**100**
Sales	**50**	**50**	**50**	**50**
Inventory needed (two weeks' worth)		**100**	**100**	**100**
Existing inventory after sales		**50**	**50**	**50**
Orders/production	**50**	**50**	**50**	**50**
Week 2				
Existing inventory to start		**100**	**100**	**100**
Sales	185	95	65	55
Inventory needed (two weeks' worth)		190	130	110
Existing inventory after sales		5	35	45
Orders/production	185	185	95	65
Week 3				
Existing inventory to start		190	130	110
Sales	0	0	40	**50**
Inventory needed (two weeks' worth)		0	80	100
Existing inventory after sales		190	90	60
Orders/production	0	0	0	40

Table 6.2. (cont.)

	Barilla Factory	Barilla CDC	Distributors	Retailers
Week 4				
Existing inventory to start		190	90	100
Sales	0	60	50	**50**
Inventory needed (two weeks' worth)		120	100	100
Existing inventory after sales		130	40	50
Orders/production	0	0	60	50
Week 5				
Existing inventory to start		130	100	100
Sales	20	50	50	**50**
Inventory needed (two weeks' worth)		100	100	100
Existing inventory after sales		80	50	50
Orders/production	20	20	50	50
Week 6				
Existing inventory to start		100	100	100
Sales	50	50	50	**50**
Inventory needed (two weeks' worth)		100	100	100
Existing inventory after sales		50	50	50
Orders/production	50	50	50	50

The next week the bottom falls out of the market when the sales level at the Retailers level returns to the long-run average of 50. Everyone in the supply chain has enough on hand and no orders are placed. The factory goes from feast (185) to famine (0) in the space of a week. And, the famine for the factory lasts a while. Production does not return to the steady state level of 50 until Week 6. And, all of this happens to pasta, whose consumption in Italy, from week to week, is as steady as we could hope for any product.

Why does this happen? The key points are these:

- The levels (or stages) of the supply chain operate independently of one another.
- The dealings among the levels are "myopic"; they operate level to level and do not extend across levels.
- The lot size ordered is greater than one period's (week's) usage.

The upshot of all of this is a great deal of waste. The distributors and the Barilla CDC have to carry more inventory than they need to and they probably have to hire more labor than necessary to handle that inventory. The warehouses may even have to be bigger than they would ordinarily be. The same thing is true for the factory. It, too, will suffer from excess inventories and capacity. And, it will suffer inefficiencies.

This phenomenon is known as the "bullwhip" effect. It's well named because, with a bullwhip, a simple flick of the wrist leads to a loud crack that is really the tip of the whip breaking the sound barrier. In this case, while the manufacturing and logistics managers are not seeing so violent a feast and famine situation at Barilla – presumably because there are some buffers along the way – they are troubled enough to press for a different way of managing this supply chain. Their solution is to have Barilla control the ordering throughout, so that the supply chain is managed as a whole, with complete transparency at every level. They are lobbying to abandon the independence of each level of the supply chain and to operate across levels. In the actual case, the Barilla managers could not get the independent distributors to embrace their JITD solution until those managers showed them, with the Barilla-owned depots, that the new system worked wonderfully well to both reduce costs and increase service.

WHERE DOES SWIFT, EVEN FLOW ENTER THE SCENE?

The bullwhip effect goes against everything that swift, even flow stands for. Swift, even flow argues for as little variation in quantities and timing as possible, and as compressed a throughput time as possible. The bullwhip lengthens the throughput time by injecting lots of inventory into the supply chain, and it induces tremendous variation in quantities and timing. Thus, advocates of swift, even flow would be advocates for all that the logistics managers at Barilla are calling for.

Indeed, not only would swift, even flow want (1) to banish the independence of the levels of the supply chain and tie them together, and (2) to manage the ordering across levels, but it would want (3) to reduce the orders themselves. The lot-for-lot replenishment philosophy that is part of the Toyota Production System is another way to calm the volatility of the bullwhip. The goal is to "use one" and then to "make one" to replace it.

The earliest evidence for the bullwhip effect that I have been able to identify is again from the renowned business historian, Alfred Chandler. In his book *Scale and Scope* he tells the following tale:

> Firms that had relied on wholesalers until World War I began after the war to replace these intermediaries with expanded organizations of their own. Not only had their output reached a scale that permitted them to distribute as cheaply as the intermediaries, but direct sales to retailers had also assured them a far better control over inventory and, therefore, of factory throughput. In 1919 Richard Deupree, the general sales manager of Procter & Gamble (later its chief executive officer), advocated direct selling to retailers. He emphasized that although consumer demand for soap and cooking oil remained steady, the orders of individual wholesalers fluctuated widely.

"If we supplied the retailer with what he needs on a week-to-week basis, the outflow from our plants would likewise be a steady week-to-week flow. If we are to avoid periodic layoffs, the solution seems to be to sell so that we will be filling retail shelves as they are empty. In that way, our outflow will be as steady as the retailer's. And we can stabilize our employment year-round to match the retailer's year-round sales ... The only way we can control our own production schedule is to produce to the consumption line."

His associates agreed, even though the cost was high. Overnight the sales force had to be expanded from 150 to 600; 125 more warehouses had to be acquired; 2,000 contracts had to be written for deliveries by trucks; and the accounting department had to be reorganized to handle 450,000 accounts. The investment paid off. Other soapmakers followed Procter & Gamble's example. By 1939 only 8.8% of the soap produced in the United States was distributed through independent wholesalers.[4]

Deupree recognized the effects of the bullwhip and he convinced his company to invest heavily to thwart it. How did they do it? They eliminated the independence of the wholesalers by making a complete end run around them. It was costly to put in an entire distribution channel that they controlled, but it was worth it. They saw that the entire supply chain had to be controlled so that the orders on the factory matched what was truly occurring at the retail level.

TAKEAWAYS

This leads to some useful takeaways:

- Supply chains can be subject to the bullwhip effect, which can be vicious.
- Eliminating the bullwhip effect means managing the supply chain as a single unit with visibility across its levels.
- Production that matches sales at the customer level is the goal; "sell one, make one."

SOME SUPPLY CHAIN HISTORY

Procter & Gamble's experience is emblematic of a lot of change to supply chains that occurred in the latter half of the nineteenth century and the first part of the twentieth. Importantly, the concepts of swift, even flow that were applied to those supply chains helped to fashion some major company competitors despite their not having great manufacturing practice. That is to say, the power of swift, even flow could apply to a company's supply chain separately from its manufacturing facilities.

Up until the late 1800s, the distinctions between manufacturing and service firms were clear-cut. There were clean handoffs in the supply chain between manufacturers and those firms that took manufactured products to market or that supplied manufacturers with their raw materials. In the late 1800s, however, the development of high-volume production (often continuous flow processing) and the development of products that could be sold widely (i.e., nationally and internationally) but with specialized marketing needs, caused many brand-name producers to augment their manufactured goods with selected services, often by integrating forward into distribution and sometimes, too, backward into purchasing and supply. Thus, supply chain steps that had previously been independent services and left to market forces were subsequently assimilated into the management of an integrated manufacturing company. Some examples are illuminating.

THE HIGH-VOLUME PRODUCERS

Consider first some high-volume, continuous flow process manufacturers. In 1884 James Buchanan (Buck) Duke purchased two then-new Bonsack cigarette-making machines. These two machines' production was sufficient to flood the nascent American market for cigarettes. Selling cigarettes then became Duke's chief concern. In response, Duke created an extensive international sales organization. These offices were responsible for marketing and distribution to the wholesalers and jobbers who kept cigarettes in stores. At the other end of the pipeline, Duke began buying tobacco directly from farmers at auctions and storing and curing tobacco for himself, something hitherto not done. By integrating his manufacturing operation with previously independent services, Duke was able to assure a steady, high volume of tobacco for his factories and a steady, high volume of cigarettes for the trade. Still, while Duke developed mechanisms to manage his distribution and supply networks, he did not own those networks, and the integration of service with manufacturing was designed simply to increase the sale of a new product.[5]

As mentioned in Chapter 3, the milling of grain was one of the first continuous flow processes to be developed. Two products were critical to the industry: flour and oatmeal. Flour, for baking, was, of course, a high-volume commodity product with a well-established supply chain. Oatmeal, on the other hand, was not a high-volume product, although oats were particularly amenable to continuous flow processing. Producers such as Washburn-Crosby (forerunners of General Mills) and the Pillsbury brothers were leaders in the production of flour. But, it was Quaker Oats that led these processors into the integration of manufacturing and service by creating the breakfast cereal market where none had existed before. Quaker Oats used extensive advertising and promotions for its product, much as American Tobacco did. Sales offices were opened to manage jobbers and to help schedule factory runs. Quaker Oats also bought directly from farmers, as Duke did. It was only later, when the price of flour dropped and the market stalled, that Washburn-Crosby and Pillsbury began integrating sales offices into their operations. They were not nearly as proactive as Quaker Oats had been. All of these companies eventually developed integrated operations that placed previously independent supply and distribution steps under the control of a central administration.

High-speed canning was another newly developed continuous-flow technology. H. J. Heinz; Campbell Soup; Borden Milk; Libby, McNeil and Libby; and Wilson & Company were the initial industry leaders. Food in cans was new, and it quickly became important for the canners to establish networks of sales offices and to advertise widely. Heinz pioneered a large purchasing and storage organization as well, so as to be able to can year round.[6]

The wholesalers and retailers in these food supply chains did, however, stay independent, but the manufacturers still had some control over them.[7] To wit:

> The manufacturing companies, however, continued to use wholesalers for the physical distribution of the goods (on a fixed markup or commission basis), because mass sales of these branded and packaged products demanded little in the way of specialized facilities or services. In the words of one economist, existing wholesalers became "essentially shipping agents for the manufacturers."[8]

THE MEATPACKERS

The producers of perishable products, notably the new product of refrigerated, dressed meat, were different. Their bundling of new services with established goods (i.e., meat) provided significant benefits to retailers and their customers. These producers required not only reliable supply and distribution, but also speedy distribution. The integration that these producers – Swift, Armour, and some smaller companies – pioneered was established to do both.[9] The refrigerated railroad car was, in this instance, a key technology, and one owned by the meatpackers and not by the railroads, but it was not the full story.[10] The meatpackers invested dramatically in their distribution systems, including refrigerated warehouses (branch houses) close to retail butchers:

> The refrigerator car was not the reason that Swift became the innovator in high-volume year-round production of perishable products. He became the first modern meatpacker because he was the first to appreciate the need for a distribution network to store meat and deliver it to the retailer. He was the first to

build an integrated enterprise to coordinate high-volume flow of meat from the purchasing of cattle through the slaughtering or disassembling process and through distribution to the retailer and ultimate consumer.

When Gustavus Swift, a New England butcher, moved to Chicago in 1875, nearly all meat went east "on the hoof." Western cattle were shipped alive by rail in cattle cars to local wholesalers who butchered and delivered to retailers. The economies of slaughtering in the west and shipping the dressed meat east were obvious. Sixty percent of an animal was inedible and cattle lost weight and often died on the trip east. Moreover, the concentration of butchering in Chicago and other western cities permitted a high-volume continuous operation which not only lowered unit cost, but also made possible fuller use of by-products.

... Though Swift did rely on advertising to counter prejudice against his product, it was clearly the prices and quality made possible by high-volume operations and the speed and careful scheduling of product flow that won the market. Once the market was assured, Swift had to expand his production facilities to keep up with demand. He increased his speed of throughput by subdividing the processes of butchering and by using moving "disassemblying" lines.[11]

Butchers and wholesalers not associated with the major meatpackers were irrepressibly pushed out of business.[12]

McCORMICK AND SINGER

Even greater integration of manufacturing and service occurred with the producers of more specialized, high-tech products that were not produced by continuous flow processes and, indeed, whose manufacturing processes were not considered state-of-the-art: McCormick and Singer.[13] Consider first Cyrus McCormick and the reaper, the most complex piece of farm equipment of the era. McCormick's business strength lay in bundling manufacturing and service, and not in manufacturing itself. In the 1850s, with the expansion of the railroad and the telegraph, a company such as McCormick could begin to think about a national market for its products. Initially, McCormick used the prevailing distribution model, which relied on territorial agents to distribute product. These agents received small salaries plus commissions. They built their own organizations to reach the farmer for sales, service and repair, credit, and collection. In the late 1870s, McCormick took a big step toward taking over this entire distribution channel. The independent agents became salaried managers within the McCormick Harvesting Machine Company and the lower-level sales organization became franchised dealers. Service and repair people also became salaried workers of the corporation. McCormick integrated backward as well, even to the point of buying timberlands and sawmills.[14] McCormick's adoption of precise machining and interchangeable parts came only after 1880, however, with Cyrus McCormick's firing of his brother, Leander, as factory superintendent, and the hiring of Lewis Wilkinson from the Colt armory. "The arrival of Wilkinson and his tutelage of Princeton-educated Cyrus McCormick, Jr., played a major role in bringing about radical change in McCormick's production methods."[15]

Even earlier, the Singer Sewing Company had gone even farther toward the customer. Singer owned and operated its own retail stores where sales and repairs were made, where inventories were kept, and where a cadre of women demonstrated the sewing machine for customers. And, it started doing this in the 1850s, as soon as the patent confusion for the sewing machine was resolved.[16] Singer also eliminated all of its independent sales agents and replaced them with salaried executives.[17] Singer also instituted a "hire-purchase system" whereby customers could buy in installments.[18] Significantly, Singer's position in the market was not, at least initially, due to its manufacturing expertise, as David Hounshell states bluntly:

> Although the Singer sewing machine was the product of the
> colorfully scandalous Isaac Singer, the successful enterprise

known as I.M. Singer & Co. (incorporated in 1863 as Singer
Manufacturing Company) was primarily the handiwork of
lawyer Edward Clark. Clark's success rested on marketing, not
on production techniques. The Singer company initially held no
technical advantages and no decisive patent monopoly over major
competitors because in order to construct a workable sewing
machine, four organizations (including Singer) had been forced to
pool their patents.[19]

The moves made toward the customer and the bundling of service
with its products distinguished both Singer and McCormick from
their competitors.

> At both Singer and McCormick the branch offices assured a
> steadier flow of machines from the factory to the customer –
> and of payments from the retailer to the central office – than
> had independent distributors. In both companies the internal
> organization also provided customers with more reliable service
> and more uniform credit for the expensive products whose
> operation had to be demonstrated and whose maintenance and
> repair required trained mechanics.
>
> The reliability of service and the availability of credit were
> particularly important in the sale of agricultural machinery. A
> reaper was a large capital investment for a farmer, but he only
> needed it during the two or three weeks of harvesttime. If it
> broke down, the result could be disaster. McCormick's company,
> therefore, reduced production at the Chicago factory during
> harvesttime in order to send workers into the field to help the
> regular mechanics at the branch offices assume immediate
> maintenance and repair of the machines. Existing intermediaries
> were rarely able to recruit experienced personnel for this
> seasonal work, nor did they have the experience or financial
> resources to provide the essential consumer credit. McCormick's
> leadership, based on product reliability and credit, prevailed even
> though its prices were higher than those of most competitors.[20]

McCormick's was not the first reaper; Obed Hussey held the first patent.[21] However, McCormick and Deering were the only companies to make investments in franchised dealers and branch office networks that reached out to the customer, and, in 1902, it was McCormick and Deering that merged to form International Harvester.[22]

Singer's competitors, such as Wheeler & Wilson, and Willcox & Gibbs, were much stronger in manufacturing. They employed the best techniques of the "armory system" (aka "the American system of manufactures") with its commitment to interchangeable parts and the models, gauges, jigs, fixtures, and technology change that went with it. These manufacturers, however, did not direct their efforts downstream and they were left in the dust by Singer, especially as Singer adopted better manufacturing practice.[23]

George Eastman was another who invented a new product – camera film – that required an extensive marketing network, salaried salesmen and demonstrators, and, within several years, its own retail stores.[24] And, there were many other examples of new, technologically based products whose pioneering managers sought control over manufacturing, sales/service, and purchasing, among them typewriters (Remington) and cash registers (National Cash Register).[25]

SWIFT, EVEN FLOW FOR THE SUPPLY CHAIN

In all these cases, the bundling of goods with services and the integration forward and backward along the supply chain were done to assure reliable, steady deliveries of raw materials and reliable, steady distribution to customers. They bundled their goods with services that were valued by customers (e.g., product demonstrations, product repair, product financing). And, even with manufacturing prowess that lagged competitors, it was these companies that flourished.

It is important to recognize as well that none of these moves of integration would have been possible without the dramatic improvements in transportation and communication that came in the mid-to-late 1800s. The completion of a national railroad network permitted shipments anywhere, and much more quickly than ever before. And, the completion of telegraph links permitted near instant communication. The coordination and management of geographically dispersed offices and plants without these technological advances simply would not have been possible.

The history of supply chains shows clearly that swift, even flow is at the heart of their success. The companies that exploited transportation and communication improvements and that developed their own channels of distribution downstream of their factories and their own sources of supply upstream of them did better than the others that remained strictly manufacturers, however proficient they were at that.

LESSONS LEARNED: MANAGING THE SUPPLY CHAIN

Much as factories and service operations have matured over time, so have supply chains. What was once disjointed and subject to the vicious consequences of the bullwhip effect is now much better understood and coordinated. Today, as it was in history, companies compete as much through their supply chains as they do with their own operations.

As we have seen, the concept of swift, even flow can be applied to the supply chain.

- Throughput times can reveal waste in a supply chain.
- When examining a supply chain, start at the customer and work back upstream to the suppliers.
- Pull systems are typically an improvement over push systems.
- Reduction in the throughput time of a supply chain can free tremendous quantities of investment for other purposes.
- Companies do not need multitier distribution systems as much anymore. More centralized distribution can be much lower cost and still very effective in reaching customers.
- Slashing the number of SKUs in the supply chain can yield dramatic cost savings.

- Supply chains can be subject to the vicious bullwhip effect if they are not managed as a single unit with visibility across its levels.
- A useful goal for many supply chains is make and deliver today the product that was sold yesterday.
- Supply chain strategy involves coordinating manufacturing with distribution strategy.

7   Amid uncertainty

The previous chapters have examined production processes from both service and manufacturing settings that were floundering and screaming for improvement, and whole supply chains of linked processes that were suffering in one way or another. Yet, there are other kinds of processes that are fair game for swift, even flow. What is more, they can be critical to the profitability of a company and thus getting them "right" is a worthy goal. These are processes where uncertainty flourishes. Chief among these is the product development process, where the success of the outcome is seldom known in advance. This chapter also investigates outsourcing, where the make vs. buy decision is often fraught with risk.

The following is a summary of a case on Eli Lilly's development of Evista, currently a billion-dollar drug for the company that treats osteoporosis and reduces the risk of breast cancer in postmenopausal women. It describes a product development project and poses some choices about what can be done in similar situations.[1]

Eli Lilly: the Evista project

Pharmaceuticals are tremendously expensive to research and develop. It could take years for a drug to progress through the succession of:

- Discovery (2–10 years).
- Preclinical testing (laboratory and animal testing).
- Phase I (20–80 healthy volunteers used to determine safety and dosage).

- Phase II (100–300 patient volunteers used to look for efficacy and side effects).
- Phase III (1,000–3,000 patient volunteers used to monitor adverse reactions to long-term use).
- US Food and Drug Administration (FDA) review/approval (deciding what the "indication" would be on the label and thus what it would be approved to treat). Approvals for Europe and elsewhere also required.
- Commercialization (how the "indication" would best be exploited).

The major research-based pharmaceutical companies, such as Eli Lilly, were ever vigilant for the new blockbuster drug that could sell $1 billion a year or more. Naturally, the best of all possible worlds was enjoying such revenues for a long time. Thus, getting a blockbuster drug to market quickly was important. This meant successfully moving through the different phases of discovery and development in preparation for FDA approval and subsequent product launch.

With Evista and to a lesser extent with Zyprexa, before it, Lilly had adopted a new mechanism for ushering drugs through the final Phase III trials more quickly. What remained was for Lilly to decide whether this same mechanism ought to be continued through the commercialization phase.

What Lilly executives had done with Evista was to create a special, full-time, colocated team to do the work of Phase III. (Zyprexa was already in Phase III when its special team was assigned.) The team was led by a Ph.D. with deep research experience on bones. Reporting to him were people from marketing, medical research (e.g., clinical trials, biostatistics, physicians) and program administration (including manufacturing and project management). The champions for the team were the president of the women's health business for Lilly and a vice president for research.

It was estimated that the team saved 18 months from a typical Phase III process. How had the team done this?

Item	Traditional way	New way
Project management	Four or five projects at a time	One project only
Team members	On four or five projects at a time	Dedicated, co-located, cross-functional
Meetings	Monthly	At any time
Project plans	No detailed plans	Project book, with deliverables and timetables
Geographic scope	US focus	Global focus, including both Europe and Japan
Data entry on patients from around the world	Done centrally	Done remotely on patients
Locking the database (clean data ready for analysis)	Lots of work between last patient visits and having clean data on those patients, typically six months	Cleaned data all along the way, so that database was ready for analysis after one month
Regulatory reports	Worked on once data and analysis had been done	Agreed with FDA beforehand on format for report and how analysis would be presented
Scientific publications	Scientific papers, key for marketing launch, done after regulatory reports	Scientific papers were worked on in parallel with regulatory reports

This new team approach did have its detractors. Noting that the team received almost everything that it requested, people had nicknamed the team the "Big Pigs." (The Zyprexa team had been known by the less pejorative nickname of the "Big Dogs.") Some wondered whether the success of the team was really due to the resources lavished on it rather than anything that the team had done itself.

The question remained as to what to do about commercialization. Should the team be continued or should commercialization be handled in the traditional way, by the functions themselves?

People generally perceive that it takes a long time for research-based pharmaceutical companies to develop new drugs. When they examine this case and see the success of a dedicated team with Evista, they embrace the approach. There is good reason to do so. When months that could be saved in the Phase III stage can mean months of high revenues in the latter stages of the drug's patent protection, there is much to recommend this dedicated team approach.

Yet, designating a team for such a task is expensive. Moreover, the expenses are known with certainty while the benefits are only known with uncertainty. Drugs fail at the Phase III stage and not all drugs that look promising at this stage end up as blockbuster drugs for the company. This helps to explain why some who analyze this case balk at adopting such teams.

There is also concern for the dispersal of talent to teams and away from functional groups. It is thought by many that expertise is more likely to be developed within a functional group and that the expertise may atrophy if it is dedicated to a team for too long a time.

Discussion of this case then often hinges on the weighing of these trade-offs. Frequently, the majority opinion is that the team should be broken up at the commercialization stage, with, perhaps, only a few key members continuing to help the functional groups that should be charged with commercialization.

THE ROLE OF SWIFT, EVEN FLOW

What can swift, even flow have to say about this situation? Before we tackle this question, however, we need to understand that productivity and profitability, although linked, are not the same thing. This is especially true when thinking about product development. Product development is an inherently variable and risky endeavor. One only undertakes it in the hope of finding a new product with an attractive revenue stream stretching out into the future that could be worth the risk of developing it. Decisions about product development always need to keep the product's economics in mind. Thus, seeking always to decrease variation in the development process may not always be the best option, if, in fact, a burst of creativity – which can be disruptive and highly variable – can lead to significant new sources of revenue.

That said, attention to swift, even flow can be useful in assessing the product development process and its productivity. For example, if a dedicated team approach is to be more productive than the traditional approach to product development, what must be true? The concept says that it must reduce variation and/or throughput time. That is the only way to guarantee that productivity advances, although, I hasten to add, it may not be the way to advance profit.

Clearly, in this instance, throughput time has been reduced significantly, but the thought lingers that such a reduction may be solely because resources were lavished on the team and not because the team was doing anything differently. For dedicated teams to do an effective job, they need to do things differently so that waste is eliminated and variation reduced.

For Evista, many things were done differently. The international clinical trials captured the data remotely. A team "cleaned" the data, making sure that it was all correct, even while other data were being collected. Such cleaning "all along the way" – a task done in parallel with the data acquisition itself – meant that the database could be "locked" and thus readied for analysis in a month's time versus the more typical time of six months. Not to have a cleaned and locked database would mean increased variability to the analysis and likely much rework before the FDA could approve the drug.

Other activities were done in parallel as well. The format for the regulatory report was agreed upon with the FDA while the analysis was proceeding. The relevant data and its analysis could then be "dropped" into the report quickly. Scientific papers were also worked on in parallel with the regulatory reports and not as an afterthought. Such papers are critical to the marketing of a drug with doctors.

As it turned out, Eli Lilly did not continue with the dedicated team in the commercialization stage of the product's development. The functional groups took charge, as they had done with the company's other products. In fact, Lilly no longer uses a dedicated team approach to its new drug development. The dedicated, colocated teams were seen as requiring too much time from the various functional groups, creating an imbalance that needed to be rectified. Indeed, dedicated, colocated teams are a rarity within the pharmaceutical industry. They are much more prevalent in other industries, however, and they merit more discussion.

THE PARALLELS IN THINKING

Many companies have changed how they engage in product development. They have adopted many new traits. The distinctions are reminiscent of the changes that have been made in manufacturing itself. Table 7.1 captures this.

What happened with manufacturing when the lean philosophy was introduced is mirrored with what has happened with product development. Many companies have adopted a much more collaborative approach that overlaps tasks and emphasizes communication. The tasks that make up the product development process are done differently in these companies. The result has been fewer surprises (i.e., less variation) and a much quicker development timetable (i.e., reduced throughput time).

Table 7.1. *Comparing product development to manufacturing thinking*

Item	Manufacturing	Product development
Panel A. The conventional way: batch thinking		
Batch size	Large	Information in large batches, sent sporadically
Layouts	Job shop	Functional, departmental
Process flow	Sequential	Sequential engineering
Scheduling	Centralized	Centralized
Suppliers	Little coordination	Little involvement
Quality	High rework	Engineering change orders numerous
Automation	Islands	Isolated systems
Lead times	Long	Long
Panel B. The new way: the lean philosophy		
Batch size	Small	Information in small batches, sent routinely
Layouts	Product-specific	By project team
Process flow	Coordinated	Concurrent engineering, parallel work
Scheduling	Local	Local
Suppliers	Close coordination	High involvement
Quality	Low defects	Engineering change orders reduced
Automation	After simplification	Simple but integrated
Lead times	Short	Short

With less time spent on product development, some wonder what happened to the time that had been spent before. Is the product development process truly as effective even when the time taken for it is less? Where did the time go, anyway? These are important questions to understand.[2] Typically, here is where the time vanishes as the new model of product development takes over:

- fewer designs means fewer engineering hours spent on those designs;
- fewer levels of approvals required;
- fewer engineering changes and other false starts;

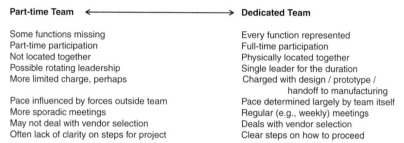

FIGURE 7.1 A spectrum of product development organization

- less waiting on tooling and fixtures; and
- less time spent in prototype production.

The engineering hours spent before were not all spent on value added. There was considerable waste in the typical process. The new way of handling product development carves some of that waste out.

Another way to understand these distinctions is to contrast the nature of the teams devoted to the development process. At one end of the spectrum is the traditional, part-time product development process and at the other end, the dedicated team. Figure 7.1 illustrates the distinctions between the two.

DOING THINGS DIFFERENTLY

What are some of the things that companies are now doing differently for their product developments? Here are some things that research has revealed.[3]

1. *Concurrent engineering.* Concurrent engineering, where tasks are taken on in parallel fashion rather than in serial fashion, works. It takes teamwork – designs can no longer be "thrown over the wall" – but it can dramatically reduce the time taken for product development. It can also improve the quality of the product itself by getting operations involved in the early stages of product design.

2. *Full-time participation.* Full-time rather than part-time team participation appears to facilitate speedier product development. Specialized

skills required in different phases of the project may make full-time participation difficult to implement.

3. *Coordinator.* Projects benefit from having a dedicated coordinator for the team, preferably one that works full time on the project.

4. *Meetings.* Regular formal meetings (say, weekly) are good, but the content of the meetings should strike a balance between the very general and the too specific.

5. *Colocation.* Locating close to one another is extremely beneficial to the speed of the project. A "war room" that is used for meetings and that houses documents, messages, and "bulletin board stuff" also is useful to team members.

6. *Team membership.* Teams will typically be rich with engineering and design personnel, and they will involve operations. Marketing should be involved early and fully because marketing volume and price numbers are important to certain design and operational trade-offs. If they are not forthcoming, speed and team morale suffer. It is very useful to have costing on the team, especially as it can feed data to marketing.

7. *Control documents.* Having a control document of some kind speeds up the project. Critical path charts are good, but other network charts, Gantt charts, etc. also can be employed.

8. *Oversight.* The team is generally best left alone with few formal reviews but with the knowledge that top management is interested in them. Top management send a useful signal to the team when it shows speed and decisiveness in its own spending and choice decisions related to the new product.

9. *Vendors.* Using single sources from the start, and having the important vendors of the group sitting in with the team on its meeting can quicken the project's pace and effectiveness.

10. *Prototyping.* It is attractive to have physical prototype models developed in continual, incremental fashion to keep interest up in the project, the design and technical skills of the staff honed, and to keep the project moving ahead. Having the model shop under the team's control can also help.

This list of things that high-performing product development teams do smacks of swift, even flow. Much of it is dedicated to reducing variation of one sort or another, and its avowed goal is reducing the throughput time of product development. What is striking is how focus on the swift flow of decisions in the product development process can actually lead to improved products, right out of the blocks. When the process is scrutinized for what truly adds value and what does not add much value, the result is an improvement for all concerned. And, with a shorter product development process, the company can iterate the design quickly and benefit from market feedback in ways that it could not when product development cycles were longer.

A CHAMPION FOR FLOW

Although I am far from being an expert on product development, I find the views of one such expert, Donald Reinertsen, particularly compelling.[4] Reinertsen has been an advocate for some new ways of thinking about product development, ways that emphasize the often asymmetric economics of that process – where the return from a blockbuster product can be huge and the cost of delay in getting products to market great. Reinertsen borrows from how the Internet is managed (e.g., breaking tasks into smaller bits) and from the military's approach to dealing with uncertainty (e.g., balance of centralized and decentralized control) and from the revolution in thinking about manufacturing that the Japanese launched (e.g., putting constraints on queue size). He grounds his thinking in economics and in insights from the queuing phenomenon.

For Reinertsen, the traditional stage-gate way of controlling product development projects – where a project is periodically reviewed and nothing is to proceed until the review is complete – is fraught with difficulty. In fact, in his experience, companies never manage that way. There is always an underground system that starts tasks early and does not wait for the large batch transfer of information that is the traditional stage-gate process.

Reinertsen is all for swift flow of product development projects. For him, the cost of delay can be huge and thus managers need to know how much a delay costs them and then pay attention to the ways by which that delay can be reduced. In the same vein, managers also need to know that they amass inventory every bit as costly as the inventory that a factory amasses. Most product development managers, according to Reinertsen, have no clue that their projects and the component pieces of those projects build up into queues of value-added work that can, and should, be managed. Keeping control of the queues of design-in-process inventory can work wonders in reducing delay and its cost.

Importantly, he also recognizes that while reducing variability is often important (e.g., steady, frequently timed reviews), the economics of new products often requires that variability (think creativity) be prized and managed, and not always curtailed. After all, new products are all about change. The upside potential for the unexpected opportunity can be tremendous, and quick feedback and action can make all the difference.

Thus, Reinertsen could be said to support swift, even flow, but only when the productivity of the product development process does not interfere with the creative potential needed to develop the new product. The economics of the situation will determine this. In this light, it makes more sense for the lessons of swift, even flow to apply to the more minor updates and extensions of existing products than to the major, more revolutionary and radical product innovations that can create entire new product categories.

LOSING IT IN THE LAB

It is one thing to improve a product development process. It is quite another to be surrounded by new products and the chaos that they can inflict on a company. This next case takes us to a young company that will live or die with its new product offerings.[5]

Instrumentation Laboratory, Inc.

Instrumentation Laboratory, Inc. (ILI) was a young, privately held company making medical instruments. Sales had been growing at a fast pace as a succession of new products and models had been introduced. The founder/president held 85 percent of the stock and was responsible for providing the company's financing. The backlog of orders had tripled in the past year, but output had only grown by 35 percent. In fact, for the company's two key products, output had actually fallen in the past two months, while sales had continued healthy growth. The lack of production was threatening the future of the company.

The problems with a flame photometer were illustrative. Here is a list of them:

- Severe parts shortage for a particular material used for the base.
- Shortage of skilled machinists for ILI's own shop and a shortage of test technicians, too.
- Failure of a motor likely caused by a vendor applying too much pressure to fit a part on it, but the motor itself was sourced as the lowest cost one and was being run at higher speeds than had been specified.
- New circuit board design that cut test time but that made the board more temperature sensitive.
- An opening used to draw air into the instrument kept clogging up with specks of dirt and no one knew precisely where the specks of dirt came from. A copper tube with cadmium plating was the latest suspect.

These problems had surfaced after over 1,000 units had been successfully produced. What had changed? Five things were mentioned: (1) older parts were now being used sometimes; (2) the location of the assembly had changed, although the same people were involved; (3) a cleaning operation had been inadvertently eliminated; (4) cadmium plating had been introduced; and (5) the material for the base had changed, although this did not seem to be part of the problem.

It seemed that as one problem was solved, another surfaced. The analysis of these problems often required experimentation. The remedy often meant an engineering change and it sometimes involved recalls of product from the field so that corrections could be made. These remedies sapped capacity from the factory floor.

The founder/president was considering a reassignment of responsibilities. He was thinking of assigning one of the problem products to the vice president of engineering, a part-owner of the company, and away from the vice president of operations. The VP of engineering's approach to the issue was likely to be considerably different from the approach that operations had been following.

The conventional analysis of this case is often sympathetic to the operations people in the company. This analysis notes that ILI had done well in its early years and needed desperately to get over this present situation. The proposed solution is often to freeze product designs and to limit the number of engineering changes. The operations function needs to be given some breathing room, in this view of things, so that it can wrap its arms around the problems that have been encountered.

Engineering, for its part, needs to improve its documentation and controls, even though that may mean a decline in the number of new products that the company introduces to the market. The VP of operations may be weak but the VP of engineering is frequently seen as the villain of this piece, angling to seize the troubled products from operations.

We can see in this analysis of the case real appreciation for the woes that bedevil operations that suffer from a lot of variation. This is a company for whom variation is a constant theme. So, it is understandable why a number of the people examining this case would turn to freezing designs and to lessening the number of engineering changes as remedies for the current situation. If factory floor productivity were the sole goal, then, this is the way to go.

A BROADER ROLE FOR SWIFT, EVEN FLOW

The important qualifier in the previous sentence is "if factory floor productivity were the sole goal." From the standpoint of the business itself, is factory floor productivity the single goal of the company, or, even, the most important goal of the company? Here, I think, a lot of people would say no. ILI has grown as it has by producing an array of technologically advanced products that the market values. It has not grown because it is the low-cost producer.

One has to put away factory floor productivity as the chief goal of the company and, instead, embrace the fact that ILI is a company that lives and dies with its new products and new models of existing products. The goal has to be the productivity of both the product development process and the factory operation that actually produces those products. It is to reduce the throughput time of the new product's development, but also to reduce the throughput time for its production.

But, how do you improve the productivity of these joint processes? The remedy must span both product development and the factory floor. The throughput time for the product handoff from engineering to operations counts here. And, the throughput time for the solving of production problems with the design counts here, as well.

Much as product development benefits from overlapping tasks so that they can be done in parallel and not in series, this joint process of product development and production needs to manage the overlap between them. This is the variation that has to be endured and coped with. But, is there other variation that can be diminished, in compensation? Yes, by narrowing the focus of the product development–production interface to a single family of products, you can help to rid the joint process of the extra "noise" that could make it much less productive. Rather than distinct heads for engineering and the factory floor that are charged with all of the company's products, you could assign distinct heads for the various product groups of the company. These product group managers would oversee the engineering and production functions for their own product groups and only these product groups. Such a reorganization could then work on the coordination needed to reduce the joint time of product development and initial production.

The productivity on the factory floor cannot be expected, under this new form of organization, to match what it would be if designs were frozen and engineering changes reduced to a trickle. However, with this organization, the company can keep up the flow of new products and manage resources so that the operation produces the quantities that the market requires, and the company can thrive as a result.

LESSONS AMID UNCERTAINTY

From these last two cases we can see that the concept of swift, even flow can apply to processes quite apart from those related to the supply chain and its component parts. There are easy parallels between swift, even flow in, say, the factory, and in the development process that creates new products for that factory. These changes may not make sense for all companies, but for many the move to dedicated teams, parallel and not serial processing of tasks, greater degrees of collaboration, a focus on nailing down data and specifications early and completely, and the other facets of the lean philosophy as applied to product development has been a rewarding one.

The concentration on a goal that is characteristic of the product development process also helps when the issue is coping with the uncertainty of a company that lives or dies with its new product offerings. Much as a product development team rallies around the product itself and can cut development times significantly, so a product-specific team that combines engineering and operations can slash the time it takes both to develop the product and to introduce it successfully into the operation.

OUTSOURCING

Another company process that introduces more uncertainty into the picture is outsourcing. It is often a highly charged decision for the company, too. It can be an emotional decision as years of tradition can be overturned. And, it carries with it the political consequences of jobs moving elsewhere. It is not an easy management decision, either. There are a host of decisions that even the contemplation of outsourcing forces on a company:

- Should the outsourcing involve parts or entire products?
- Which parts or products?
- Where should any outsourcing be done?
- How should the company decide which companies ought to be used for the outsourcing?

- How do you know that you are getting a good deal with the outsourcing? Does it beat establishing your own operations in a different country?

To put these issues into perspective, here is a summary of a case on Mattel and its outsourcing in Asia.[6]

Mattel, Inc.: vendor operations in Asia

Mattel, Inc., the premier toy company in the United States, had long had operations in Asia, both plants that it owned and vendors that it used to produce some of its products. The issue now was the company's own Hot Wheels toy cars and the Matchbox toy cars that the company had recently acquired from its merger with Tyco. Sales were expected to grow and new capacity was needed. Mattel's management faced the choice of developing new, company-owned operations or outsourcing the needed production to other firms in Asia.

Mattel currently made its Hot Wheels cars in a company-owned factory in Penang, Malaysia. The merger with Tyco introduced two other company-owned operations, in Bangkok and Shanghai, where Matchbox cars were made. Relatively smaller quantities of the cars were outsourced to vendors in the area. That outsourcing had not been widespread was due primarily to the fact that Hot Wheels and Matchbox toy cars were seen as "core products" of the company, much as Barbie was, Mattel's signature product. (Noncore products were more promotional in character or had life cycles that were expected to be short.) In addition, the technologies involved with producing the cars were not readily mastered by the suppliers that did other products for the company.

Figure 7.2 depicts the major steps of the process flow for producing either Hot Wheels or Matchbox.

Die-casting was regarded as the toughest technology to outsource. There were few suppliers that did it, it needed more capital than many operations, its margins were thin, and quality could vary quite a lot. Vacuum metalizing was also regarded as more difficult and more expensive to do. The barbell assembly, where wheels and axles were placed on the car, had been developed by Mattel and was seen as a comparative advantage. The assortment process required

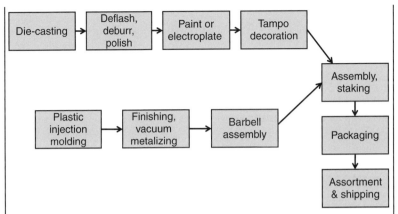

FIGURE 7.2 The process flow for Hot Wheels and Matchbox cars

some skills and favored centralization, particularly for the rolling mix strategy where Mattel rotated the multitude of models that it produced so that, at any time, only selected models were in the retail store. The other processes were fairly standard, even the staking operation that brought together the body and the chassis of the car.

Mattel's long-standing Hot Wheels factory at Penang was well regarded but it could not be expanded. Some productivity advances could increase its production (+20 percent), but major boosts in capacity would require physical expansion, which could no longer be done on site. The former Tyco facilities in Bangkok and Shanghai had experience but were not as highly regarded. The equipment was older and quality was suffering. The Hot Wheels car was deemed to be more difficult to manufacture than the Matchbox car.

The match of forecasted demand and existing capacity could be summarized as follows:

Expected demand (in millions of units)					
	Now	+1 year	+2 years	+3 years	+4 years
Hot Wheels	155	169	184	200	218
Matchbox	64	68	72	76	81
Existing capacity (in millions of units)					
	Penang	Bangkok	Shanghai	Outsource	
Hot Wheels	120 (to 144?)			35	
Matchbox		21 (to 50?)	33	10	

> The company could locate a new plant in the area. A location in southern China had been selected preliminarily, but currencies were sliding elsewhere in Asia and locations in Indonesia (where Barbie was produced) or in Malaysia were also possibilities.
>
> Should the company go with a new plant, and, if so, where, and how big should it be?

Mattel faces a host of decisions in this case:

- Should it outsource more Hot Wheels and Matchbox cars or should it outsource some aspects of their production, say, painting or assembly or packaging?
- Should it outsource Matchbox, leaving the somewhat more difficult Hot Wheels in-house?
- Where should any new plant be located? What should that plant do? How much capacity should be added?
- What should be done with the Bangkok and Shanghai facilities that Tyco previously controlled?

Let us pursue the outsourcing issues first, before we tackle the nature of Mattel's plants in Asia.

Mattel has labeled Hot Wheels and Matchbox as "core products" and such products are produced in Mattel-owned facilities. Noncore – promotional and short life-cycle – products are the ones that are outsourced. Does that make sense?

CORE PRODUCTS AND CORE COMPETENCE

Certainly, Mattel's core products are high-volume products that can be produced fairly steadily. They do not go in and out of fashion abruptly. These facts, in and of themselves, however, do not say much about whether outsourcing makes sense or not. What swings the argument, for me, is what swift, even flow can bring to the discussion. With steady and high-volume demand, a production process that focuses on the productivity that swift, even flow can promise becomes attractive. Such a facility can become very productive and low cost.

Swift, even flow also argues for keeping the full process together and not trying to break it up into pieces that are accomplished by a series of suppliers. This is particularly true in light of the difficulty Mattel has incurred in locating vendors that can do die-casting.

The debate that one can have on "core products" is reminiscent of the debate on "core competence," sparked by the work of C. K. Prahalad and Gary Hamel.[7] (Prahalad and Hamel define a core product differently from Mattel, but both point to particular competencies within the company.) Prahalad and Hamel provide three tests for identifying core competencies. A core competence:

1. provides potential access to a wide variety of markets;
2. makes a significant contribution to the perceived customer benefits of the end product; and
3. should be difficult for competitors to imitate.

For them, core competencies develop and evolve through continuous improvement, and they require the company to harmonize and coordinate technologies and skills. They are more fundamental than strategic business units and their portfolios of products. An argument for outsourcing is precisely to keep attention on the company's core competencies. The company may risk losing focus on its core competencies if it tries to do too much by itself.

This notion of core competence has had a broad impact. Yet, how does a company know when it has a core competence, especially one that relates to the productivity of its operations? Or, how does a company know that it is indeed evolving a core competence in its operations? Couldn't a company fool itself easily that it has a certain competence when, in fact, it is far off what world-class is? If we are to believe in swift, even flow, the answer, and the test for it, are straightforward. A core competence exists in operations if both throughput times and variation are low. Indeed, the metrics to use to know when a company has succeeded in developing a core competence in operations are the ones that measure throughput time and variation (quality, in particular). And, if the trends in those metrics look attractive, then a core competence is evolving. These are metrics that can be benchmarked.

A core product, in the sense of Prahalad and Hamel, is not an end product (such as Hot Wheels or Matchbox) but an intermediate product that can quickly be adapted to help produce end products of different types. The core product itself does not suffer from lots of variation, although it can lead to diverse end products. Thus, core products, as well as core competencies, exhibit the character of swift, even flow.

BACK TO MATTEL

Mattel's policy of designating both Matchbox and Hot Wheels as core products makes sense from the perspective of swift, even flow. They are high-volume products where speed to market means a good deal. And, keeping the processes that make them together also makes sense. Throughput time is lowered by doing so. But, what should be done about the facilities and the capacity that the company needs?

The big growth is expected to be with Hot Wheels. The Penang plant, though a good one, cannot keep pace with the demand and cannot be expanded. At issue, then, is whether Mattel should build a new plant for Hot Wheels, or do something else. The appeal of low cost can be a siren call for many companies, and the prospect of low exchange rates can turn heads within a company. But, operations decisions of this type are long lasting, and the long view is what is needed.

What's intriguing in this case is that the old Matchbox facilities in Bangkok and Shanghai have some capabilities that could be exploited. These facilities have not been invested in and they need an upgrade, but the personnel have experience with a car that is similar to Hot Wheels, although a little less complex to make. One could invest in both Bangkok and Shanghai and switch them to Hot Wheels. The new plant could thus be devoted to Matchbox. And, this is what happened. Bangkok and Shanghai were converted to Hot Wheels, and a new plant in southern China was built for Matchbox, of 65 million units of annual capacity initially, but capable of being expanded easily.

This line of reasoning sees the plant as an entity that evolves over time. It masters a succession of capabilities and can become increasingly valuable to the company. Much as products are thought to follow life cycles, one can think of life cycles for plants.

THE PLANT LIFE CYCLE

The common view is that the factories that close are ancient rattle-traps, victimized by uncompromising labor unions. Some of that has happened, no doubt, but the statistics point to other causes, many of which relate to production technology and the management practices surrounding the plant.[8] It is more likely that that plant closing was due to:

- gagging on product variations;
- expanding repeatedly to the point where materials handling, production and inventory control, and personnel management becomes oppressive;
- adding too many people and thus spawning more bureaucracy;
- souring labor relations;
- ignoring modifications in technology.

Many of these points highlight what variation and added complexity can do to a facility that in its early, highly productive years was probably characterized by swift, even flow. If the factory is to have a useful life, it needs to battle against what creeping variation and complexity can do to it. Understanding that factories go through life cycles – birth, adolescence, maturity, and decline – can prepare the company to cope much better. The company can appreciate what makes the plant uncompetitive and take action to limit it. Often this means resisting product and technology proliferation, and working to take advantage of the added skills of the workforce. Having a formal document that sets out a plan for the plant and its life cycle is often a good way to resist the persistent changes, however small, that can sap a plant of its productivity. Swift, even flow works at all stages of a production process's useful life, but it can erode as well. Keeping that always in mind is important.

This next case summary goes directly to this point. It chronicles the life of Hewlett-Packard's Singapore operation.

Hewlett-Packard: Singapore

HP's Singapore plant was established in 1970 to produce computer memories when doing so meant stringing together small ferrite "cores." Technological advance brought obsolescence to that product. However, in subsequent years, HP Singapore took on a succession of ever-more complex and sophisticated products and challenges:

- 1973 calculator assembly;
- 1977 keyboards, displays, application-specific integrated circuits (ASICs) design;
- 1981 sophisticated calculators and a cost engineering program to reduce expenses;
- 1983 keyboard engineering, assembly of the ThinkJet printer;
- 1984 a second-generation keyboard;
- 1986 a third-generation keyboard, mouse, data tablet;
- 1988 the Alex project;
- 1990 a split of the operations in Singapore into an Asia Personal Computer Division and an Asia Peripherals Division.

These responsibilities meant increasingly complex products, multiple manufacturing technologies, investment in training and the selection of talent, heavy emphasis on testing, development of design skills, and development of vendor relationships and networks. HP managed these escalating capabilities by sending mentors to Singapore and by bringing Singapore workers and managers to the United States to see how HP operated on its home turf.

The Alex project was HP's attempt to create a low-cost inkjet printer to challenge the even lower cost dot matrix printers that populated the lower end of the printer market. Responsibility for the engineering of the product was centered in HP's Vancouver operation, while the cost reduction and manufacturing were centered in Singapore. The project quickly fell behind schedule and stayed that way. Performance and cost reduction targets were missed as well. The project was finally canceled after more than two years of effort. It was the first failure associated with the Singapore operation.

In late 1990, the Singapore operation was split into two divisions, including the Asia Peripherals Division. With this division, Singapore's managers wanted to design and sell a printer in Japan, where HP was not then selling. The ThinkJet printer was to be the vehicle for this initial foray into Japan, with software developed to print Japanese characters. Nevertheless, the ThinkJet was bigger than the existing inkjet printers on the Japanese market and it would not have the capability of printing addresses on postcards, a feature that its competitors offered. Still, the people at HP-Singapore wanted to try their hand with the Japanese consumer.

Just months after the failure of the Alex project, should HP-Singapore have been permitted to develop this product for Japan?

The story of HP-Singapore dovetails nicely with the notion of a plant life cycle, as discussed above. The plant began as a way for HP to save costs in the very labor-intensive process of stringing cores, but, bit by bit, the plant added capabilities so that it could assemble complex products such as calculators and printers, design things such as keyboards and ASICs, and engage in substantial cost reductions, in part because of its abilities to manage vendor relationships in Asia. For its part, HP did a fine job of bringing the plant along, with mentoring and education.

Yet, the plant did fail with the Alex project, although, to be fair, the failure was shared by HP's operations in Vancouver. Several things can be listed for the causes of this failure:

- The project was too ambitious to begin with. The targets for performance, cost, and timetable could be argued to be simply too difficult to meet, even for the best engineering and manufacturing.
- The project was hampered by the need to coordinate with Vancouver, across the Pacific and many time zones apart.

- There were cultural differences between Vancouver and Singapore that hindered the progress of the project and the decisions that needed to be taken.

A useful debate for those studying this case has been on the point of whether the Alex project was a step forward or a step backward for Singapore. They did learn from it, but, for many, the assignment of the Alex project was a step backward. Those who argue that the Alex project was a step backward note that HP-Singapore was ready for a project all its own. It had successfully designed components of computers, such as keyboards, had assembled complex products, and had engineered cost savings well. The next logical step was a complete product that it could call its own.

There is considerable merit in this position. It certainly captures the spirit of the plant life cycle. Furthermore, what we know of product development argues for a colocated team, which is something that the distance between Vancouver and Singapore rendered impossible. The Alex project started as a compromise, in this view, and it ended badly as a result.

Those who favor this point of view tend to be more sympathetic to Singapore's ambitions in Japan. Everyone recognizes that the initial product that they have for the market there is not a great one. Many counsel to wait and work on a smaller version that can do postcards. They worry that HP's reputation will be sullied for the long term if a better product is not offered to the Japanese. For those pushing to enter the Japanese market, the contention is that the Singapore plant is ready for this step and that any step is a step forward. With time, these people feel confident that Singapore will figure things out and will create and make products that will sell well in Japan. For them, the life cycle of the plant is as important as the life cycle of the product.

HP-Singapore was given the green light to enter Japan. The initial product was not a big success, but it did sell. The next product offered was a color printer and that did very well. With time, Singapore engineered a much smaller printer that was a huge success.

Singapore then became the global center for HP's portable printers. Its journey to full capability was thus complete.

This is a case that combines the uncertainty of product development with the uncertainties inherent in the growth and development of the plant itself and its capabilities. As we found, swift, even flow and the guidance it provides for debates on core competencies, core products, and plant life cycles can help the company to cope with these uncertainties.

LESSONS LEARNED: SWIFT, EVEN FLOW AMONG UNCERTAINTY

This chapter has delved into topics where uncertainty lurks – new product development and outsourcing. Even here, the insights of swift, even flow can be helpful.

- Product development, like any other process, can be analyzed and improved. It can be measured for throughput time and variation, just as any process can, and it can be looked at through the lens of the lean philosophy.
- Product development, however, requires a balance between expected profit and the cost of development. Encouraging variation can be rewarding.
- Ideas such as the parallel processing of tasks and the removal of the more obvious roadblocks to swift decision-making have been exceedingly useful in reducing the time it takes to develop new products.
- Product development generates inventory, albeit an inventory of plans and specifications, and that inventory can be substantial, causing delay that can be very costly given the potential for new products to generate sizable revenues.
- The cost of delay needs to be traded off against the cost of speeding up the process.
- The handoff of product development to the operations function can be fraught with variation. Managing them jointly, say by grouping product development and production together, can be useful.
- Outsourcing brings up issues of what is "core" to the company. Swift, even flow is one way to define what is core. Core competencies and

core products can both be measured by throughput times and variation; where both are relatively low, there lies what is "core."

- Factories have life cycles, just as products do. Youthful factories with swift throughput times and little variation can give way to older factories where variation and complexity creep in. Understanding this can be helpful.

8   Strategy

Although I have devoted a chapter to "vision," most of the cases we have discussed to date involve improvements that are typically labeled "tactics." They have not involved spending huge amounts of money nor have they taken a significant amount of time to implement. In this chapter, we dismiss any such constraints and address the more strategic decisions that face companies. Again, we will see that when productivity issues surface, the concept of swift, even flow can point to the way forward.

CAMERAS, COUNTERS, AND CHAOS

The first case, although dating from the mid-1970s, is a classic that remains as applicable today as when it was first written.[1]

Searle Medical Instruments Group

The Searle Medical Instruments Group was a pioneer in nuclear medicine. Its "counters," made by its Analytic division, could analyze samples that had been tagged with radioactive isotopes and its "cameras," made by its Radiographics division, could picture where radioactive isotopes clustered in the body. The market for counters included not only hospitals but clinics and laboratories in both the public and private sectors. The market was growing at 5–10 percent per year and was crowded with 17 competitors, some of whom competed on price. No patents protected anyone, but Analytic engineers were committed to providing the best-performing instruments on the market. To do so, they were continually engineering new models.

The market for cameras, although smaller, was very successful, growing at 15–20 percent per year, and it was essentially recession-proof as the cameras, unlike the counters, were always associated with insurance-covered patients. Searle held a patent on the camera that was good for another three years, and its engineers had made several technological advances to the camera that made it more useful to doctors. These were well received. Radiographics could also customize its cameras for the doctors who purchased them. The company held a 60 percent share of its market and had licensed production of the camera to four other producers, and earned royalties from their sales. Profits for Radiographics were good, but they were slipping for Analytic.

The two product families, although distinct, used some common components. The fabrication areas of the plant produced a wide variety of parts and subassemblies for both product families, including the minicomputers that the instruments needed to process the data they generated. Once assembly began, the product families were differentiated into separate lines, with "counters" more labor-intensive than "cameras." Parts for a counter or a camera were picked from inventory and then "kitted" together and taken to the factory floor. The production plan called for one month each for (1) the picking of parts, (2) the building of subassemblies, and (3) the final assembly and test of the product. Typically, however, these phases of production took far longer than three months to produce a counter or camera. Production would begin on the kitted parts, but completion of the product depended upon the receipt of an order. The company did not want to accumulate finished goods inventory, especially since the product families had 950 product options available between them.

It did not help that there were significant parts shortages and other difficulties in sourcing. The company wanted to have three vendors for each part but, for 45 percent of its parts, there was only one vendor. Lead times from those vendors were often longer than desired, and for some parts, such as housings and ball bearings, the lead time could be a year or more. Sometimes, products would be started into production without all of the parts in stock. As parts came in, they would be completed.

The Searle plant in suburban Chicago had been repeatedly enlarged to accommodate the company's steady growth. However, the plant could not be expanded any more. In fact, the engineering, marketing, and administration for the Radiographics product line had been relocated to other quarters nearby.

On the face of it, this is a case about the growing pains of a successful business. The company had been a technological pioneer and its newest product line, with its patent protection, was selling well. The need for new space was apparent. However, there were storm clouds on the horizon. Profits for the Analytic division were dropping. Parts shortages and other supply problems were plaguing the factory. And, the patent for the Radiographics camera was expiring in three years.

What should be done about this? Here, readers of the case typically engage in some hemming and hawing. The company should manage its vendors better. Expansion is needed. Better controls should be put in place. Specifics, however, tend to be lacking.

The analysis improves when it is pointed out that the two divisions, Analytic and Radiographics, are really fairly distinct from one another. Analytic, although selling to a larger market than Radiographics, had no patent protection and suffered from considerable competition, some of which was on price. That could well explain the decline in profits. Radiographics was patent-protected and operated in a much livelier market that was growing quickly. Its market valued technological advance as well as customization of the product. Thus, the markets were asking for different things of the two product lines, at least until such time as the patent ran out.

WHAT SWIFT, EVEN FLOW CAN CONTRIBUTE

Productivity is clearly an issue here. Analytic, especially, is having difficulty meeting the prices of the competition. There is variation galore – models have proliferated, customization can occur for cameras, production can begin without all of the parts in stock. And, the throughput time is long, at least three months.

Not only is there variation within each of the divisions, but there is significant variation between Analytic and Radiographics. The market demands on the two product lines are distinctly different with one calling for low price (Analytic) and the other calling for innovation and customization (Radiographics). If we harken back to the discussion about different processes (Figure 2.5), it is reasonable to expect that Analytic needs to have a process that is farther down the diagonal than the process that serves Radiographics. Analytic needs to reduce costs. That aim is more consistent with an assembly line that offers a swifter flow of materials and can thus be a more productive means to put together its counters. The less labor-intensive Radiographics, on the other hand, requires more of a batch process that can customize output and be flexible enough to implement lots of engineering changes, reflecting the innovation that Radiographics thrives on.

As another way to reduce costs, Analytic should take a close look at its wide array of product models and drastically reduce their numbers (a fundamental source of its variation). The costs to the company of keeping up such a broad range of product models undoubtedly overshadow any real benefits such a range provides the company's sales. Analytic should zero in on the most popular and useful features of its product line and make those standard. This mandate might be a tough one for Analytic's engineers to swallow, but it is absolutely necessary. Indeed, the parts shortages that are plaguing the operation could well be the result of engineers who are so in love with the performance of their instruments that they have neglected to think of what it takes to make them low cost. They have thrown out standardization in favor of engineering elegance, and that mentality has had dramatic consequences for its purchasing and supplier base. Housings and ball bearings that take a year to acquire cannot be standard, high-volume parts that are in steady supply. (Aside: too often we hear that companies want their suppliers to be "world-class" without those same companies thinking about what it takes for them to be "world-class customers.")

Standardization will be required if the advantages of an assembly line are to be enjoyed. The drumbeat of the assembly line needs to be steady, and this underscores the desirability of building up a finished goods inventory of the best-selling models. Assembly line production for Analytic also implies abandoning the picking and kitting of parts and instead adopting the classic system for assembly lines where parts are delivered to the part of the line that will use them. The workforce, too, will need to change. The job content for the line's workers will be lower than one would expect for workers doing custom work. Job skills may not need to be so high, as well.

Searle's current manufacturing choices are more compatible with the demands on the Radiographics product line. A batch operation, with kitting, limited finished goods inventory, and high-skilled workers, is more suited to a product line that is undergoing continual tweaks to its technology and whose customers are willing to pay for custom versions.

The distinctiveness of the processes that make sense for Analytic and Radiographics call into question their sharing of the factory. Much of the operation is designed to accommodate both divisions, and neither one is particularly well served as a result. This especially compromises what could be done to lower the costs of Analytic's products. These observations argue for a separation of the two product lines into distinct entities whose engineering and manufacturing are distinct.

THE FOCUSED FACTORY

These insights are behind the important and very useful notion of a focused factory. This is a concept that was put forward in a famous *Harvard Business Review* article in 1974 by Professor Wickham Skinner. In that article, Skinner advocates that factories "focus" on a limited range of products or processes, understanding that a factory cannot do well by every measure. This requires examining the demands of the marketplace and what those demands imply for the manufacturing function (e.g., low cost, quick delivery). The choices then made for manufacturing should be consistent with those "manufacturing tasks." Most frequently, a focused factory is a factory devoted to a single product line, such as, in our case, Analytic or Radiographics.

Focused factories have a number of things going for them.

1 Factory focus reduces the impact of variation

Factory focus is a strategic way to reduce the impact of variation. Focused factories, for their part, resemble manufacturing cells, only writ large. They typically incorporate a broad cross section of operations and support functions (e.g., engineering, quality, production planning and control, accounting); all that are required for the production of the product line that the factory is "focused" on. Direct costs of all kinds can be assigned to focused factories. With this matching of resources to responsibilities, focused factories frequently both perform better and make a managerial situation more manageable. They reduce the impact that variation can have on all of a company's manufacturing.

What is more, the limited strategic needs of a focused factory ease the implementation of advanced manufacturing hardware and software and new ways of thinking about manufacturing management (e.g., lean thinking). Because focused factories typically concentrate on a single product line or a particular technology, they seldom require the expensive, supermachine that can do a wide variety of things or its software equivalent. With the more limited and less complex requirements that are typical of a focused factory, technology and new ideas can work more quickly, and often more effectively.

This reduction in variation's impact, and this often more effective exploitation of new technology and/or thinking, liberates capacity that might otherwise be directed elsewhere. This can lower costs. And, a portfolio of focused factories can deal with significant variety in a company's product line. This is what helps to keep the breadth of process and product variety wide for the firm (typically wider than can occur with advanced technology alone) and costs lower at the same time.

2 Factory focus allows flows to surface to be studied and improved

As this entire book has argued, swift, even flows of materials and information are essential to productivity gain. Factory focus, by segregating products (or processes), isolates flows effectively and this can accelerate the rethinking and redefinition of those flows. When the complications of other products (or processes) are removed, often those close to the process can see the next logical steps much more clearly. Bottlenecks can be determined and broken. Waste can be more easily identified and removed. Quality-related feedback loops are shorter and less convoluted and this, too, can help.

3 Firms learn more quickly in focused factories

Learning can be quicker in a focused factory, not only because the flows of materials and information are readily identified and clear to all, but also because of two other factors:

1. Focused factories tend to have fewer layers of overhead personnel, largely because there is less need for coordination; the flow of the product is more visible and comprehensible. More people are thus directly placed into situations where they can learn and experiment, and this helps the learning process. Middle managers, famed for derailing so many initiatives, are less of a concern in focused factories because there are so few of them there.

2. Because most sources of cost are directly attached to the focused factory (and thus to the product line it produces) rather than allocated to it, product costs are better known. Accounting and performance measurement is simpler, less arbitrary, and thus typically more effective in a focused factory. (The greater labor-intensity of the Analytic product

line, and the fact that Searle allocated its overhead based on direct labor, meant that Analytic carried a greater overhead cost than it arguably should have. After all, with all of the engineering required for the Radiographics product line, Radiographics, and not Analytic, should have been saddled with the larger overheads.)

Indeed, Wick Skinner, in his classic article, argued that: "Focused manufacturing is based on the concept that simplicity, repetition, experience, and homogeneity of tasks breed competence" (p. 115). For me, learning is breeding competence.

4 Factory focus is a key means by which "rigid flexibility" can be enjoyed

Elsewhere,[2] Bob Collins and I have argued that flexibility in manufacturing is best accomplished by concentrating on simplicity and discipline. Table 8.1 reproduces some of the examples of this "rigid flexibility." We continued by arguing that simplicity and discipline are easier to achieve when manufacturing is organized into focused factories. (The quotation from Skinner, above, points to the same insight.) Naturally, in focused factories, the organization of activities is simpler, primarily because there are fewer products and/or processes to master. In addition, discipline is easier to enforce, indeed, easier to envision. Ideas such as lean manufacturing principles or Six Sigma or engineering–manufacturing integration or throughput time reduction are more clearly conceived and implemented in focused factories.

BACK TO SEARLE

This discussion about factory focus naturally leads to the conclusion that Analytic and Radiographics should split, with a separate factory devoted to each product line. That "factory" could be physically separated into two brick-and-mortar structures, but it could also be a "plant-within-the-plant." The important distinction is that the two divisions should be separate for their key functions such as engineering, manufacturing, and cost accounting.

Table 8.1. *How simplicity and discipline support different needs for responsiveness*

Need for responsiveness	Simplicity	Discipline
Customization of products	Standard footprints, modular designs, automated assembly	Design for manufacturability, design for assembly
Supplier responsiveness: frequent deliveries of small quantities	Fewer suppliers, lower number of purchasing transactions, less materials handling	Suppliers on design teams, sharing of forecast and order data with suppliers, continuous improvement feedback loops
Cellular manufacturing and flexible manufacturing systems (FMSs)	Product or part families	Preventive maintenance, operator checking of quality, cross-training, even-paced production planning
Just-in-time manufacturing	Clear pull system signals, great visibility on the factory floor and less need for traditional controls, lower levels of inventory	Setup reduction, problem solving and continuous improvement, more level production plans, good housekeeping, experimentation
Setup reduction	Less wasted motion and effort, re-layout of work area, reengineered fixtures	Practice, following prescribed methods exactly
MRP systems	Easy access to and visibility of stocks and flows of material in the supply chain	Great data integrity, rigorous updates of bills of material, part numbers, engineering changes, inventory counts, etc.
Worker empowerment	Clear task definitions	Training and follow-up with personnel affected

With plant space squeezed as it is, and with the prospect of growth, especially for Radiographics, it may make more sense to create two distinct structures. Given that Analytic needs more of a makeover than Radiographics, extracting Analytic from the existing factory is my preference, leaving Radiographics in the current space and giving Analytic a fresh start. This could be an expensive alternative, but it is the cleanest alternative. And, as the adage goes, if the business is worth keeping, it is worth investing in.

One could try to keep both "plants" within the current plant, arguing that a redesigned Analytic would not take up as much room as an assembly line as it now takes up. But, managing the space needs of the current operation and the transition to a new layout would be difficult to do at the same time. One way to save space would be to outsource more of what is now fabricated in-house. Surely, Searle does not need to make its own minicomputers. It may mean designing its instruments to fit existing minicomputers from the major manufacturers of the day (e.g., Digital Equipment), rather than the other way around. That this is an issue at all is another reason to be suspicious of the attitude of the engineers in the company. Getting them to focus on cost reduction may be a high hurdle to clear.

What happened in this case? Unfortunately, nothing. No consensus was reached on what to do and no significant changes were made. A year after the case, with Analytic losing money, some key manufacturing executives were terminated. Two years after the case, the Searle Medical Instruments Group chairman resigned. Three years after the case, with nothing much altered, the Analytic division was sold. Five years after the case and after the patent had expired, GE jumped into the market with both feet and the Searle Radiographics business was sold to Siemens. For lack of attention to the implications of swift, even flow for manufacturing strategy, what had been a pioneering business was lost.

SOME TAKEAWAYS

The big takeaway with this case is the power of factory focus. It is the highest level mechanism for reducing variation and throughput time. It can mean the segregation of an entire product line and of the business functions that support it. It can train management attention on the process flow and so uncover what it takes to keep that flow of materials highly visible and its throughput time low. It can even mean the development of parallel, focused supply chains. Dell, for example, distinguishes the supply chain that it now uses for retail sales from the supply chain that it has traditionally used for online sales.[3]

Moreover, factory focus can, paradoxically, mean greater flexibility for the entire operation. The focused factory is where simplicity and discipline, the keys to flexibility, can meet to great effect.

BOOM GO THE PROFITS

This concept of the focused factory has wide application. It is not simply for manufacturing. It can apply to services as well, as this next case attests.[4]

Hartford Steam Boiler

It was 1974 and the Hartford Steam Boiler Inspection and Insurance Company (HSB) was losing money on its insurance underwriting for the first six months of the year, especially on larger, more complex objects. The top officers were also concerned about the length of time it took for completed policies to be delivered. Hartford Steam Boiler was the leader in the insurance niche market for insuring boilers and other machinery. The company insured a range of equipment, from simple air tanks to complex boilers, printing presses, and huge compressors.

Hartford Steam Boiler differed from most equipment insurers in that it inspected all of the items it insured. Other companies often did not inspect and instead used an actuarial approach to the smaller, standard items they insured. They might pass on insuring more complex equipment. About 90 percent of the items HSB insured were smaller, more standard equipment, but 10 percent were more complex items where an inspection could lead to one of five results:

1. the company could take the risk;
2. the company could reject the risk;
3. the company could adjust the premium and/or the deductible to compensate for the risk;
4. the company could adjust the coverages for the object; or
5. the company could have the object physically modified to reduce the risk.

HSB did more of the latter than any other firm, largely because it had the largest staff of inspectors. Inspectors could inspect between five and 20 standard objects in a day, but they could only inspect between one and 20 complex objects during a week.

Inspectors did a range of tasks. Their first priority was responding to accidents. The second priority was completing first inspection orders, so that new policies could be issued. The next priority was doing inspections required by law, and the last priority was doing routine inspections for the company's loss prevention service. Inspectors in each branch reported to a chief inspector who operated independently of the branch manager. Inspectors rarely came into the branch office. Instead, they covered a territory that was a portion of the geography served by the branch office. About 15–30 percent of an inspector's time was spent traveling, 15 percent was spent writing reports, and the rest was spent doing inspections. Each inspector had considerable leeway in planning what he did on any day.

A typical policy was initiated by a request from the customer to an independent agent who represented HSB. An HSB special agent was then called in and he performed a cursory inspection. The customer filled out an application, and then HSB issued a binder that covered the customer's object until a more detailed, completed policy could be issued. The inspector was then called upon to do the first inspection order and write it up for review by the supervising inspector at the branch. Only when the object was cleared by the chief inspector at the branch could the completed policy be written and the customer's premium payment received. The home office goal for issuing policies was 21 days, but that goal was only being met for the simplest policies. For others it would take much longer. For example, a typical first inspection order might take 29 days itself with 11 more days of review by the supervising inspector. It would be another ten days to underwrite the risk and ten days more for filing and recording the policy. Some objects, of course, took much longer.

Why was Hartford Steam Boiler losing money on its underwriting operation? The long time that the company was taking to get inspections done was imposing extra costs:

- losses during the binder period that could have been avoided with modifications to the equipment or repricing of the policies; and
- opportunity costs incurred by not receiving premium income as early as it could have been received.

What then to do about the situation?

This case becomes a lot easier to digest and to see through to a recommendation when you take into account swift, even flow and the focused factory concept. Where is there variation in this operation and where does the throughput time lag? It is clear that both variation and throughput time are greater for the more complex objects that HSB insures. The smaller, standard items can be inspected quickly and their policies are the ones that are completed closer to the target of 21 days. Indeed, some insurance companies do not even inspect these smaller, standard items in favor of getting policies written quickly and premiums paid quickly.

Hartford Steam Boiler has a competitive advantage in dealing with the more complex objects that customers need to insure, yet, the company is squandering that advantage by taking too long to inspect the objects and to write policies to cover them. This tardiness incurs more opportunity cost with premium income and subjects the company to greater losses than need be the case.

The inspectors are asked to do everything from accident investigation to loss prevention. And, they are charged with both small, standard items and the more complex items. There is great variation in the times that they can take in making such divergent inspections, from minutes to weeks.

This case screams for some segregation of the risks being handled. At least two "focused factories" could be established to remedy the situation. One focused factory could handle the smaller, standard items. HSB could still inspect these items, but they could be dealt with routinely and without the disruption that occurs when a complex item comes up for inspection.

The other focused factory could cover the major risks. One could expand the geography for these risks and have them covered by inspectors who are less "local" in character and who could be based in more regional centers rather than the typical branches. The inspectors would have to travel farther but they would be staying on site longer. Accident investigation could still be the province of the local branches. The same could be said of the loss prevention service that the inspectors provided. What is critical is isolating the major risks from the minor ones. And, this is what Hartford Steam Boiler did. They established a special accounts division to handle the major risks and left the standard risks to the branches.

Note that this recommendation is exactly analogous to the recommendation made for the USA Services case, the first one examined in Chapter 5. There we argued to group the complex requests together and the simpler requests together for the account representatives to work on. Similarly, the telephone calls were segregated to the "warehouse" that was established. Here we are doing the same thing, only on a much grander scale. Swift, even flow can apply in both situations, great and small.

THE BATTLE FOR EUROPE

Arguably the most important stimulus for manufacturing strategy change in the past 20 years has been the creation of the Single Market in Europe. The following is a case involving a consumer products company and the pressures it was under in the mid-1990s.[5]

Prentiss Products Europe

Prentiss Products was a privately held US-headquartered producer of consumer products. Its array of products included aerosol products (laundry aids, air fresheners, furniture polish, insecticides, and carpet care), liquid products (cleaning and care products for floors, furniture, automobiles, laundry, air freshening, and toilets), personal care products (liquid soap, bath foam, shower foam, shaving gel), solid and powder air care products, and steel wool soap pads.

In 1995, its European operations were housed in five facilities with their sizes and product capabilities indicated:

Plant	Country	Employment	Liquids	Aerosols	Personal care	Air care	Soap pads
Modplant	Nether-lands	292	X	X	X		
Barstow	UK	230	X	X		X	X
Madrid	Spain	80	X	X	X	X	
Portugal	Portugal	24	X				
Lyon	France	?? – newly purchased	X	X		X	
Contractors	159 of them		X	X	X	X	

Significant changes were taking place in the industry. Retailers, particularly hypermarkets, were in the ascendant. They were consolidating, offering more of their own brands, and using point-of-sale information successfully. Manufacturers were having to ship more directly to their distribution centers, often with smaller, more frequent deliveries. Thus, while volumes were increasing, inventory levels were declining.

Many of the major manufacturers in the industry (e.g., Procter & Gamble, Unilever, Henkel, Gillette, Colgate-Palmolive) were creating and marketing pan-European brands. Many had closed plants and consolidated their operations. The pressures on profits were severe.

Prentiss had reacted to this pressure with a number of changes that had altered its manufacturing. Product lines had been trimmed, resulting in better schedules and less downtime. Packaging had been redesigned (bottle heights, sizes, necks, caps, film labels) so that volumes could be higher and changeover times reduced. The company's stable of contractors was producing the lower volume products and the company's newest products.

Modplant, in the Netherlands, had been reorganized into product teams (focused factories that joined manufacturing personnel with support personnel in purchasing, scheduling, engineering, inventory control, and logistics) that improved productivity (up 65 percent) and quality (rejects down 74 percent) and shrank the bureaucracy (five levels to three). Employment had been reduced from 475 to 292 and product codes slashed from 540 to 190. Barstow, too, had seen dramatic change.

Yet, profits were still being squeezed and capacity utilization stood at 59 percent. Something more needed to be done.

One cannot help but feel some sympathy for Prentiss Products and its European operations. It has made some classic moves to improve its productivity – and straight out of the swift, even flow playbook. It has reduced variation by decreasing the number of product codes it made and marketed, and it simplified a number of the design elements for its products' containers. It outsourced the lower-volume products so that its own factories could concentrate on the higher-volume ones. It established some focused factories. Its throughput times have been reduced as well. Yet, more needs to be done.

What is left to try? The low capacity utilization for Prentiss' European factories suggests that a redefinition of the "charters" for those factories is in order. Before, in a Europe prior to the Single Market, many companies produced the same products in multiple factories, so that only one or, at most, a few countries were served out of those factories. With the Single Market, and the changes that make transportation (e.g., backhauls) easier and less costly, it makes

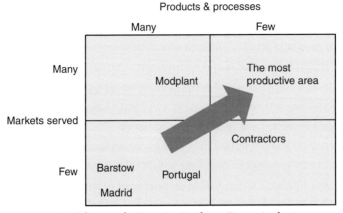

FIGURE 8.1 Charters for Prentiss Products Europe's plants

sense to produce products in product-specific plants whose reach is now the whole of Europe. This is especially important if the products themselves are pan-European ones.

Consider Figure 8.1, which captures the situation for Prentiss Products Europe.

The figure places each of the company's plants within a matrix that arrays products and processes against the markets served. Only the Modplant in the Netherlands was serving a significant number of country markets; the other plants concentrated their efforts on their home countries. As the figure indicates, the most productive area is where a plant focuses on fewer products and processes and serves many country markets. That is the area of the matrix where variation is reduced the most and where the opportunity for swift flow is greatest.

What does it take to move Prentiss into that northeast quadrant of the matrix? The plant charters will have to be redefined, and, given the lower utilization rates, closing the smaller plants may make sense. The Spanish and Portuguese plants, and the newly acquired French plant, are the logical candidates for closing. They are smaller and perhaps less capable than either Modplant or Barstow. Reducing the number of contractors and the volumes that they produce may be another option.

What should occur with Modplant and Barstow? Here is where one can think of product swaps that would leave one plant in control of certain products and technologies and the other plant in control of the complementary products and technologies. Barstow is already the only plant producing steel wool soap pads. It could cede some of its other products – say, aerosols and liquids – to Modplant, and Modplant could cede its personal care products to Barstow. The closing of the other plants would leave Barstow producing soap pads, air care products, and personal care products. Modplant would take the higher volume liquid and aerosol products that had been produced in multiple plants.

This was in fact what the company did. In addition, the company reduced the number of contractors significantly.

As you can imagine, making such decisions can be momentous for a company. Closing plants is always difficult to do and can be tougher to accomplish in Europe than in North America, for example. Moreover, deciding which plant gets the high-volume products, or the high-prestige products, and which plants do not can be fraught with company – and country – politics. Employment levels will certainly fluctuate. Managers who had been managing directors for the operations in their countries may have to give up their titles and become "mere plant managers." The pressures on senior managers can be – and have been – great. However, to shy away from such decisions risks carrying too much needless capacity and dooming a company's efforts to improve productivity. One can see why the Single Market has been the most important trigger for manufacturing strategy change within the past 20 years.

MORE TAKEAWAYS

These last two cases, Hartford Steam Boiler and Prentiss Products Europe, underscore what swift, even flow can mean for any company's strategy development.

- Factory focus works as well for services as for manufacturing. Hartford Steam Boiler provides the example.

- Swift, even flow has to be pursued relentlessly. One cannot think that you can "set it and then forget it." Prentiss Products had made wonderful progress in reducing costs, but it was not enough. They had done lots of the little things, but at least one big thing, the rationalization of production in fewer plants, had yet to be done. Full realization of swift, even flow awaited that strategic move.

UP IN SMOKE

If a company is to be true to the concept of swift, even flow, sometimes it must abandon a lot of old thinking and adopt a strategy that may seem to be counterintuitive. Here is a case that is a bit like an onion.[6] Once the layers are peeled back, the clarity of swift, even flow thinking shines through. It concerns a nasty product, but a wonderful process to see in action. And, this case has quite a bit to teach us.

Alpine Tobacco

The Alpine Tobacco factory in Innsbruck was charged with the task of producing cigarettes for the EFTA (European Free Trade Association) countries. In the late 1980s, volume dropped from 19.5 billion cigarettes a year to 12.5 billion cigarettes because Spain and Portugal were admitted into the European Economic Community (EEC). Thus, the factory was stuck producing a wide variety of brands and packages for the smaller countries of Europe and for the Middle East and Africa.

The factory was proud of its quality, but, compared to the American parent company's other plants, it was not cost competitive, based on the standard measure of cost per thousand cigarettes, and furthermore, the American parent was pressing the factory to reduce its inventory levels from an average of two months' production to one month. (In Austria, placing a pack of cigarettes into inventory meant not only inventorying the value of the pack itself, but also the tax of 8 ÖS [Austrian schillings] per pack that

---

is paid on manufacture and only rebated on export.) Georg Bader, Alpine's managing director, however, had hopes that this adverse assessment of the factory could be reversed with two new initiatives:

1. *Linking.* Already approved by the parent company was the continued linking of the equipment used to make and package cigarettes so that the cigarettes would not have to be handled manually at all anymore and could thus pass through the entire making and packaging operation automatically. Currently, only the factory's fastest making machines were linked with packaging equipment. Consider the following list of equipment:

Making machine	Number	Linked?	Utilization
8,000 per minute	1	Yes	100%
4,000–5,000 per minute	15	10	100%
	5	Unlinked	25–80%
1,500–3,000 per minute	20	No	< 25%

2. *New shop floor monitoring system.* For an expenditure of 37.8 million ÖS, Bader thought he could develop a monitoring system for the shop floor that could instantly determine which machine, making or packaging, was malfunctioning and thus eliminate perhaps 1 percentage point of the 5 percent of the cigarettes created each day that were scrapped. Some tobacco from scrapped cigarettes could generally be recovered but it still cost the factory about 100 ÖS for every 1,000 cigarettes that had to be scrapped. (The standard cost for 1,000 cigarettes was 150 ÖS.)

Bader was eager to know how he should try to sell this idea to top management.

We should be clear at the outset that the Alpine Tobacco factory serves a market that is distinct from the other major factories of Alpine's parent. The major factories serve large markets; Alpine is charged with serving small markets with lots of different cigarette options (e.g., tobacco blends, filters, flavorings, packaging). What is important to such markets is less the cost of the cigarettes and more their availability and quality. That's what Alpine has to get right.

Georg Bader has a bee in his bonnet. He wants headquarters to spend 37.8 million ÖS for a real-time monitoring system that he thinks might save some scrap. What are the economics of such a proposal? Bader hopes to save 100 ÖS for every 1,000 cigarettes, and he produces 12.5 billion of them in a year. Thus,

12.5B cigarettes * 1% of scrap saved * 100 ÖS/1,000 cigarettes = 12.5M ÖS per year

The payback on this investment is thus about three years (37.8 M/12.5M). Not many companies would greenlight such a proposal, especially when the expected savings have not been proved. And, Alpine's parent is no exception. Bader's plan is really a "no go" no matter how fervently he may try to pitch it.

If the money does not lie with the shop floor monitoring system, where does it lie? Alpine's parent has it right; it lies with inventory reduction. What does Alpine inventory when it produces its cigarettes and places them in the warehouse? Ironically, it is not the tobacco itself. Tobacco is purchased at the harvest and it needs several years to age properly before it is ready to be a cigarette. Thus, the decision to purchase a quantity of tobacco is divorced from the decision of how much tobacco to use to produce a run of cigarettes that will be placed in finished goods inventory. The money for the tobacco itself has been shelled out long before this decision of how much of that already-purchased tobacco to use for a run of cigarettes. It is a sunk cost.

Rather, the largest component of cost incurred when cigarettes are produced and sent to the warehouse is the tax that has to be paid. It is as if Alpine pastes 8 ÖS to each pack of cigarettes it produces and sends to finished goods inventory. (There are some other costs that could also be included here, such as the paper for the cigarette and the packaging itself, but those costs are much lower than the tax,

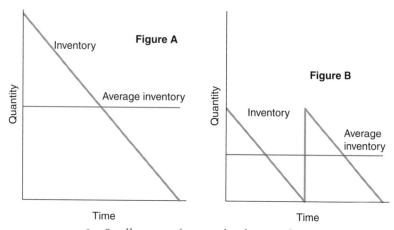

FIGURE 8.2 Smaller, more frequent batches cut the average inventory carried

and I am taking the liberty of excluding them from this illustrative calculation.) When Alpine produces 12.5 billion cigarettes in a year, it is producing 625 million packs per year (12.5 billion cigarettes/20 cigarettes per pack). Two months' worth of these packs is just over 104 million packs. And, at 8 ÖS per pack in tax, that is roughly an investment of 833 million ÖS. For simplicity, let's assume an inventory carrying cost percentage of 10 percent. Thus, an investment of 833 million ÖS yields an inventory carrying cost per year of 83.3 million ÖS. If Alpine can reduce its finished goods inventory from two months to one month, it stands to gain about 42 million ÖS per year. This saving is over three times what Bader hoped for with his shop floor monitoring investment.

What does Alpine need to do to cut its finished goods inventory in half? As Figure 8.2 shows, what is needed is smaller, more frequent runs. With batch sizes that are half as large but run twice as often, the average inventory that is carried is halved.

What will it take to run smaller, more frequent batches? You have to abandon trying to put so much production on the faster machines. Small country markets can be served just fine with slow machines. And, it probably doesn't cost much money, if anything, to make it happen.

HOW SWIFT, EVEN FLOW HELPS

Here is where the concept of swift, even flow comes into play. What is critical to productivity is the throughput time of the cigarettes and not the utilization of the faster machines. Small, frequent runs mean lower throughput times for cigarettes, from their initial making through to their stay in the warehouse before being released to the market. This is where productivity is enhanced. Usually, of course, the cost of residing in inventory is not so great as it is with a tax applied to each unit of production, as in this case, but there is a cost, and avoiding such a cost is often the best way forward.

Thus, what Georg Bader ought to do is assign some of his low-volume products to the slow machines he has and run those machines when he needs the production. Some of those machines can probably stay set up, ready to go when needed. The higher-volume products can be assigned to the fastest machines, but, overall, the utilization of the fastest machines will fall, assuming that the overall production stays at 12.5 billion cigarettes a year.

Now, Georg Bader is a smart man. Why hasn't he thought of this way of dealing with his situation? Why does it seem that he has blinders on? The answer rests, as it too often does, with performance measures. Bader is measured on cost per thousand cigarettes. When are his costs the lowest? When he uses the fastest machines. When does his shop floor monitoring system promise the most return? With fast machines.

To my mind, the easiest way to ruin an otherwise good operations strategy is to use the wrong measures on it. Managers respond to incentives and those incentives should be carefully considered. They need to match the strategy that is in place. Bader and his parent's headquarters operation played the game as if high capacity utilization of the latest and fastest equipment was the best way to lower cost and improve productivity. It's clear in this case that such thinking was not the way to go.

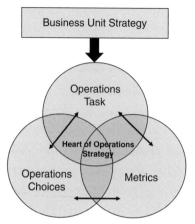

FIGURE 8.3 The heart of operations strategy

THE NATURE OF OPERATIONS STRATEGY

Operations should be about serving the interests of the business unit strategy. For that to happen, operations strategy has to be derived from the company's strategy. (Figure 8.3 shows this relationship.) There may need to be a "translation" of the business unit strategy into what it means for the operation. That is what the "operations task" is designed to do. It is designed to interpret the needs of the company and to specify for the operations function what it is that operations must do well in order for the company to succeed.

Both the metrics created for the operation and the host of choices that can and should be made for that operation need to be consistent with the operations task and, by association, with the business unit strategy. Consistency is the hallmark of good operations strategy.

We saw the need for this consistency in the Searle Medical Instruments Group case. The operations task for the Analytic division was dramatically different from the operations task for the Radiographics division. One highlighted the need for low cost and the other the need for technological advance and customization. The different operations tasks required markedly different operations choices, including a move to an assembly line for Analytic.

The focused factory concept provided a mechanism to resolve this inconsistency. The same was true for the Hartford Steam Boiler case. Different products had different needs, and thus the operations for them had to be separated in order for consistency to reign. Even in the Prentiss Products Europe case, consistency was achieved more readily with pan-European plant charters as opposed to the country-specific operations that prevailed traditionally.

With the Alpine Tobacco case, the inconsistency was with metrics. The operations task and the operations choices were aligned, but the metrics were at odds with them. What should Bader's company have done? The Alpine Tobacco factory served small country markets with customized products – the cigarette blends and packaging that marketing considered most appropriate for those markets. Low price was not the driving force. For this reason, creating a metric such as "cost per 1,000 cigarettes" and applying it to the Alpine Tobacco operation could well be argued to be not the best way to proceed. Much more appropriate would be metrics on quality, on the availability of all of the varieties of cigarettes in those various country markets, and on the total cost of the cigarettes, including the cost of carrying them in inventory. What should have been avoided was providing Bader with the incentive to schedule as many cigarettes as he could on the fastest machines. High capacity utilization of the fastest machines was simply not needed.

And, this leads us full circle back to Chapter 1 and the "usual suspects." It is easy to have the conventional wisdom rule the day. But, it is dangerous. The true path lies with swift, even flow, and that concept needs to guide all of the thinking related to productivity, even to the performance measures used.

A POSTSCRIPT

There is a postscript. Everything has changed now from the time of the case. Today, Alpine (a disguise, of course) is its company's most flexible plant, producing any of 270 blend–filter–packaging combinations. Sales run about 20 billion cigarettes per year, with a capacity of about 25 billion cigarettes per year. The plant sells to the Middle East and somewhat into Eastern Europe now, as well as the small countries mentioned in the case.

When I last visited the plant, I had the pleasure of meeting again the operations manager who had been a participant in a manufacturing management seminar at IMD in which I had taught ten years prior. He thanked me for preaching throughput time reduction at that seminar and how it can aid flexibility. Shortly after that seminar, with the factory in need of a new primary unit, he had directed a big project there that rethought the way they made cigarettes for their fragmented, low-volume market. Throughput time reduction helped to guide his thinking. The new primary can now feed any of the making machines of different speeds, all fully linked to packers, cartoners, and boxers. The fastest machine in production that I saw was 14,000 cigarettes a minute and the slowest was at 4,000–5,000 cigarettes a minute. They have rearranged the secondary unit into cells so that a few workers in each cell can monitor all of those machines. No other company plant is as flexible as they are.

Unfortunately, they are still measured on variable cost per 1,000 cigarettes and the plant doesn't compare with big plants in the system by that measure, but they are not the worst, and everyone now knows that their manufacturing task is different. Their 270 different varieties are an order of magnitude more than the next most flexible factory in the company.

THE ILLUSION OF SCALE

One of the "usual suspects" from the first chapter of this book was "economies of scale." I argued there that true economies of scale, where the production technology differs substantially from small to large scale, are rare and that the constant technological progress that we enjoy keeps shrinking the relevant scale anyway. The initial advantages of innovators such as Richard Arkwright, John

D. Rockefeller, Andrew Carnegie, and Henry Ford, not to mention Michael Dell or easyJet or any of the other contemporary companies we have noted, did not come from scale. They came from speed.

A move to focus factories is typically a move away from scale, as both the Searle and Hartford Steam Boiler cases demonstrate. In Alpine Tobacco's case, costs were reduced by taking volume away from the large, fast making machines, and moving that volume to the smaller, slower making machines.

We have seen how specialized equipment concentrated in cells can provide the flexibility that the market prizes and still keep costs low and productivity high. The same can be said of focused factories. A portfolio of focused factories can be very flexible and yet still very productive.

The implication of swift, even flow for process design is clear. Large-scale equipment should be approached warily. The advantage is in speed of the entire process and not in scale for any single piece of that process, especially for any piece of equipment that could become a bottleneck. Even in industries such as chemicals and pharmaceuticals, going for "big rigs" may not be the most productive choice because they encourage big batches and large inventories. The choice more consistent with swift, even flow is the choice of smaller-scale equipment that produces all the time, at a rate consistent with marketplace demand. If more capacity is needed, another grouping of small-scale equipment can be installed. With advances in lot traceability, this kind of process design becomes more and more attractive. The steel mini-mills have shown us just how powerful a concentration on speed of production rather than scale of production can be.

This discussion suggests that scale should lose out to swift, even flow in capital appropriations requests. As noted earlier, so many capital appropriations requests depend on the direct labor savings or the machine utilization that the investment will bring. That is how the new equipment is often justified. Scale can easily be invoked in such a calculation. A more important question for management is whether the investment will lead to shorter through-put times and/or reduced variation. A capital appropriations request where the economics look compelling but where one cannot be convinced that the new investment will lead to quicker through-put times or reduced variation is a capital appropriations request to scrutinize very carefully.

LESSONS LEARNED

In this chapter, I have advanced the notion that swift, even flow can provide a strategic path for companies.

- Factory focus is a splendid way to reduce variation explicitly, but its simplicity and clarity also promote a visibility that encourages a reduction in throughput time as well. And, although it carries the moniker of "factory focus," we have seen how it applies to any operation, service or manufacturing, with equal force.
- Good operations strategy requires consistency among the operations task, the metrics, and the operations choices. Focused factories have an edge when it comes to this consistency.
- The same kind of thinking, writ even larger, controls the plant charters for entire companies. We see this with the rechartering of plants in Europe as a result of the Single Market. Companies have simplified the charters for their plants so that they produce fewer products and have to master fewer technologies, but they serve a wide geography. This, historically, has been more true of plants serving the American market, but it is now true of plants serving Europe.
- Incentives are intimately tied to strategy. They are often at the heart of strategy's implementation. Here, with the Alpine case, we learn that even incentives have to be true to swift, even flow if they are to be effective.

In all of this, swift, even flow lies at the center of the thinking. Taking the point of view of the materials/information moving through the process is precisely what you want to do, be it for a medical instrument, an insurance policy, a household cleaner, or a cigarette.

9   Resolving the paradox

Why have we not done a better job of managing productivity? What should we do to create a meaningful breakthrough?

THE PRODUCTIVITY PARADOX

In an influential article in the *Harvard Business Review*, Professor Wickham Skinner, generally recognized as the father of manufacturing strategy, reacted to what he was seeing as American companies were trying to beat back the Japanese industrial onslaught that started in the late 1970s and gathered speed through the 1980s. He titled the article, "The Productivity Paradox."[1] In the article, Skinner berated companies for pursuing a narrow policy toward productivity. He claimed that the pursuit of lower costs was leaving companies further and further behind competitively. He chided the managers of these companies for concentrating on direct labor, on efficiency measures of factory workers, and for thinking that conventional cost cutting was the thing that they should be doing. Witness the following paragraph:

> The emphasis on direct costs, which attends the productivity focus, leads a company to use management controls that focus on the wrong targets. Inevitably, these controls key on direct labor: overhead is allocated by direct labor; variances from standards are calculated from direct labor. Performance in customer service, delivery, lead times, quality, and asset turns are secondary. The reward system based on such controls drives behavior toward simplistic goals that represent only a small fraction of total costs while the real costs lie in overhead and purchased materials.[2]

That mode of thinking, for Skinner, ignores the other ways to compete "that use manufacturing as a strategic resource. Quality, reliable delivery, short lead times, customer service, rapid product introduction, flexible capacity, and efficient capital deployment – these, not cost reduction, are the primary operational sources of advantage in today's competitive environment."[3] Skinner ends his article with the following:

> As we have seen, our pursuit of productivity is paradoxical: the more we pursue it, the more elusive it becomes. An obsession with cost reduction produces a narrowness of vision and an organizational backlash that work against its underlying purpose. To boost productivity in its fullest sense – that is to unleash a powerful team of people supported by the right technology – we must first let go of old-fashioned productivity as a primary goal. In its place we must set a new, simple but powerful objective for manufacturing: to be competitive.[4]

Skinner saw clearly that the old focus on inputs such as direct labor and its efficient use was not the best way forward to make operations more productive. The objective needs to be competitiveness. But, how can managers make that particular objective more practical? It is the thesis of this book that competitiveness is best earned by concentrating on the materials and information that flow up and down the supply chain. What is needed is a swift, even flow for them. Everything else of worth tumbles out when swift, even flow is pursued.

To reinforce this view of what should be done, let's examine Skinner's list (above) of the ways to compete that use manufacturing as a "strategic resource." It is my contention that keeping swift, even flow in mind, and working toward that end, will automatically put operations in the role of "strategic resource" for competitiveness. It is the way to resolve Skinner's productivity paradox. Here is Skinner's list:

- *Quality*: this is an explicit goal of swift, even flow. The "even" portion of the moniker is devoted to reducing variation and quality was cited as the number one source of variation in processes of all kinds. To pursue swift, even flow is to pursue quality improvement relentlessly.

- *Reliable delivery*: the other elements of variation reduction (being "even") refer to variation in quantities and in timing, and it is these elements that stand behind delivering things reliably. The operation that is "steady as she goes" is the operation that can deliver what it promises, on time, every time.
- *Short lead times*: here, of course, is where "swift flow" enters the picture. When throughput times are consistently reduced, lead times are short.

These "ways to compete" are embedded in the definition of swift, even flow. Skinner's other ways are not as obviously tied to swift, even flow, but, they are amply demonstrated with the cases we have discussed.

- *Customer service*: good customer service assumes quality, reliable delivery, and short lead times. However, it means more. It means meeting the true needs of the customer. That requires focus on the customer and making sure that the supply chain is governed by the information that the customer can give, the information that emanates from "downstream." Think back on the following cases:
  - USA Services;
  - ICI-Nobel Explosives;
  - Stewart Instruments;
  - Omega;
  - LEGO;
  - Barilla.

In each of these cases, customers were not being well served by either the process or the entire supply chain leading to the customer. And, in each case, swift, even flow led to improvements that cemented those customers to the company, perhaps by providing the product or service in timely fashion (USA Services, Stewart Instruments, LEGO), perhaps by reducing the customer's own costs (ICI-Nobel Explosives, Omega, Barilla), or perhaps by improving the quality of the customer's operation (ICI-Nobel Explosives). Swift, even flow calls first for a look downstream, toward the customer.

That is where the information for the supply chain and the management of its materials is generated. So often, a company's first reaction is to look to its suppliers as the key to improvement. In reality, the suppliers should be later in the process, once the customer and his true needs are understood.

- *Rapid product introduction*: product introduction is as much a process as any other, and can benefit from swift, even flow as the Eli Lilly and Instrumentation Laboratory cases showed. The need to do things quickly yet innovatively, coupled with the desire to reduce waste, hover over the production introduction process. The practices that companies can engage in to improve product introductions are of precisely the same character as the practices that improve manufacturing or service operations.
- *Flexible capacity*: it seems that customers are demanding variety more than ever. To provide a broad mix of products at reasonable cost, companies need to manage their capacity for flexibility. A number of the cases that have been discussed address this issue:
  - USA Services;
  - Stewart Instruments;
  - Spirit Bottling;
  - Omega;
  - Searle Medical Instruments Group;
  - Alpine Tobacco.

Some of the flexibility on display in these cases derives from classic examples of lean operations thinking. A series of smaller-scale, quick-reacting lean processes, for example, can be more flexible in producing an array of products than can a larger, slower general purpose piece of equipment. In the USA Services case, we advocated the grouping of work into families (much as cells work), and in the Searle Medical Instruments Group case, we adopted the macro version of that, the focused factory, as the key insight for unlocking the company's competitiveness. Other cases simply called for running jobs more frequently, so that average inventories could be slashed (e.g., Spirit Bottling, Stewart Instruments, Alpine Tobacco). Doing so meant ignoring old rules and abandoning the old metrics. The Omega case required both new metrics and lean principles.

- *Efficient capital deployment*: in a host of the cases we have discussed, the solution involved redeploying capital to a better use. Consider the following cases:
  - ICI-Nobel Explosives;
  - LEGO;
  - Yellow Freight;
  - Mattel;
  - Hewlett-Packard Singapore;
  - Searle Medical Instruments Group;
  - Hartford Steam Boiler;
  - Prentiss Products Europe.

In several of these cases, an appeal to the focused factory concept was at the heart of the redeployment of capital. The Searle Medical Instruments Group needed to split up Analytic from Radiographics and assign personnel and capital separately to each. Hartford Steam Boiler needed to manage its big-ticket, high-risk items separately from its routine, lower-cost and lower risk items. Doing so led to a complete reorganization of its branch operations. Prentiss Products Europe needed to realign its factories by swapping products and their concomitant technology and capital, so as better to concentrate attention on them. Even Mattel ended up separating Hot Wheels from Matchbox and making them in distinct factories. By so doing, all of these companies could (1) reduce the variation that was clogging up their operations and (2) isolate the flows within those operations and work to reduce throughput time.

Other of these cases involved sweeping redefinitions of the business strategy, with tremendous consequences for operations. ICI-Nobel Explosives was a commodity manufacturer of a wide product range that transformed itself into a service provider that produced its own narrower line of explosives and directed a revised network of depots and a new set of specially designed trucks. LEGO revamped its entire supply chain for Europe. Yellow Freight was caught unawares by trucking deregulation and had to reconfigure its network of depots and break-bulks and, with them, how it managed its fleet of tractors and trailers.

HP did not really redefine its business strategy. Rather, it recognized the advantages of the plant life cycle to specify a new "charter" for its Singapore facility, which had grown in capabilities over the years.

These examples all highlight how comprehensive and flexible the concept of swift, even flow can be. Skinner's call for a "new, simple but powerful objective for manufacturing" is for me a call for swift, even flow to marshal the competitiveness of operations of all kinds.

A CHECKLIST

Faced with a situation begging for improved productivity, what should the manager do? The 16 case summaries and the other examples from the preceding pages can provide us with some guidance. At the risk of sounding formulaic – and formulaic is not something that you want to be because it is the concept of swift, even flow that must remain at the center of any manager's thinking – here is a checklist:

ASSESSING THE SITUATION

1. Is the issue an issue that touches on productivity? If productivity were increased, would it help to remedy the concerns of management? If so, swift, even flow can help. If not, then some other tools or thinking are likely to be better. This concern, as we noted in the chapter on uncertainty, is of special significance to product development, where profitability and not productivity is the goal.
2. Examine the process or processes at the center of the issue. The process can be manufacturing or service. Create a process flow diagram that shows the process from start to finish. The number of symbols on it should typically be between 20 and 50. Less than 20 symbols and the flow chart may be too high level to reveal the aspects of the process whose change could be a significant improvement. More than 50 symbols and the flow chart may be too busy to be of much use.
3. Tag the process flow diagram with metrics that can uncover problems: capacities, times, yields, and costs, among other things. With such

metrics, the process flow chart can reveal potential bottlenecks, waste (where there are lags in time), and quality problems.

4. Once the process is captured well, ask the critical questions:
   - Where is there variation in the process – in quality, quantities, or timing?
   - What is the throughput time and where may it be bogging down?

The answers to these questions will lead to opportunities for improvement.

5. Pay particular attention downstream, toward the customer. Managing well the flow of goods and materials from upstream to downstream frequently requires that the flow of information from the customer upstream toward the suppliers be understood well and appropriately managed.

MANAGING THE SITUATION: VARIATION

1. If there are quality problems, make them a top priority. The tools for diagnosing quality problems and remedying them are well documented. Nevertheless, recognizing quality problems for what they are is a critical task. Dealing with quality variation is often the most effective first step in coping with variation.

2. Segregate items into families. Variation within families is, by definition, less than variation across families. Such segregation can be small scale – creating cells of one sort or another. Or, the segregation can be large scale – dividing operations into focused factories. In either case, variation is reduced (including variation in quality) and productivity is enhanced.

3. Go first to the point in the supply chain closest to the customer – go downstream. If the customer is a substantial source of variation, try to manage him. That could mean creating a reservation system or it could mean offering inducements (price, service) that shift demand off of the peak and into some more manageable time frame.

4. Don't be bound by thinking that a manufacturing situation needs to stay a pure manufacturing situation. Providing a service in which manufacturing is embedded can be the most appropriate way that the customer's true need is met and his variation dealt with.

5. Look carefully at your own process. Is it creating its own variation, say, because of the complexity of its production planning or the structure

of its bills of materials or how it relates to the information system in place? Does one day look pretty much like any other, or are there big swings in what is demanded of the process? Can such swings be eliminated? There often need to be inventory buffers built into a process, even if only small ones, all the more so when the process is more job shop or batch in character. Avoiding unnecessary rules, or even rules of thumb, and trying to simplify the process and make it transparent to all who deal with it can be very helpful.

6. Time is likely to be a more important source of variation than quantities. This means that you want to smooth the "drumbeat" of time before you smooth the quantities involved.

7. Standardize procedures, if they are not already standardized.

8. Trim stock-keeping units if you can.

9. Supply chains can be subject to the bullwhip effect, which can be vicious. Eliminating the bullwhip effect means managing the supply chain as a single unit with visibility across its levels. Production that matches sales at the customer level is the goal: "sell one, make one."

10. Finance and product managers may have the best of intentions, but their actions can add significant variation to an operation. One must be constantly vigilant about new rules and policies; they can be counterproductive.

11. It is useful to understand what may cause an operation so much trouble that it has to be shuttered. As listed earlier, these are some common reasons for that drastic action: too many product variations asked of the process, repeated expansion, more people and bureaucracy. These particular points underscore what variation and the added complexity that surrounds it can do to a facility. Understanding that operations go through life cycles – birth, adolescence, maturity, and decline – can prepare the company to cope better. The company can appreciate what makes the operation uncompetitive and take action to limit it. Often this means resisting product and technology proliferation, and working to take advantage of the added skills of the workforce.

12. Good operations strategy, for both manufacturing and service sectors, is consistent manufacturing strategy. Identify the operations task – what the operation needs to do well for the business unit to do well – and then pursue relentlessly the metrics and operations choices that can be consistent with that operations task. Often operations tasks are different for different products. Here is where the focused factory

concept can be especially helpful so that consistency is more readily achieved. With that consistency, too, swift, even flow will be easier to envision and to make a reality.

MANAGING THE SITUATION: THROUGHPUT TIME

1. The classic reason that throughput time bogs down is capacity related, namely a bottleneck. Typically, with a bottleneck, inventory will build up ahead of it. Stationary bottlenecks are easier to deal with. They can be broken with additional investment in capacity. Sometimes, of course, such investment cannot be made, or made quickly enough. At that point, the bottleneck has to be managed appropriately in order for its consequences to be as benign as possible. Everything needs to be subordinated to the bottleneck. Inventory needs to be aligned in front of it so that it is never down for lack of materials. And, maintenance of the bottleneck, particularly preventive maintenance, needs to be pursued diligently so that the bottleneck operation can be run effectively for as long as possible.

2. Movable bottlenecks may be more problematic because they depend, in part, on the mix of product being scheduled through the process. Investment may need to be made to break movable bottlenecks, but their management, especially for the short run, may depend more on effective production planning.

3. In many situations, inventory can build up because orders (the work to be done) are "pushed" out into the process without much consideration for the capacity of that process. Such an inventory buildup can be very disruptive. Here is where a change of philosophy can be useful. Here is where a pull system may be appropriate, especially if variations in quality, quantities, and timing have themselves been reduced. Pull systems, as opposed to push systems, control inventory levels better and thus act typically to shorten throughput times.

4. Given the power of pull systems, it is often much more helpful to start downstream first and then work back upstream. The sources of both variation and of long throughput times (e.g., inventories) are often best dealt with in this way.

5. Streamline the supply chain. Ask whether it needs the layers and the complexity that may have seeped into it. Remove non-value-added.

6. Reduction in the throughput time of a supply chain can free tremendous quantities of investment for other purposes. Labor efficiency can pale in comparison to the savings from collapsing the throughput time of the supply chain.
7. If product line needs are divergent and the demands on the company supply chain are distinct, consider developing different supply chains for the different needs. Supply chains can be focused as readily as factories can be focused.
8. Speed trumps scale. Beware thinking that big is beautiful.

BACKSLIDING

The emphasis of this book has been how to become productive. As important, however, is staying productive. And, that means avoiding backsliding. It's all too easy to do. US Steel, for lack of attention to swift, even flow, lost their commanding market share in the space of the decade from 1901 to 1911. Even modern-day examples of highly productive companies (e.g., easyJet, Dell) have lost a bit of the vision and commitment to swift, even flow that was so evident in their early years.

Bob Collins, of IMD in Lausanne, Switzerland, and I looked at why some plants stay high-performing and others, within the same division of the company, remain low-performing, even over the course of a decade or more. That is, plants that have the same access to technology, capital, and expertise can have vastly different levels of performance that persist over years. We found that 22 percent of company plants stayed low-performing during the previous ten years and that 13.5 percent of the plants had declined in performance over the same time span, as claimed by the VPs for operations at the surveyed companies.[5] (This research targeted manufacturing plants, but it could just as easily have targeted service operations and, I think, with much the same result.)

What's going on? In short, the answer appears to be "mentality." The plants that do consistently well, those that do not backslide, exhibit a mentality that is distinctly different from their poorer-performing brethren. That is, the management and workforce of these plants think differently about the factory and its operations. Interviews with VPs for operations led us to classify this mentality into five categories: (1) the plant manager and his style, (2) the prevailing philosophy about profit and performance, (3) the attitude toward the plant and its invested capital, (4) the attitude to the environment outside the plant, and (5) how the plant is measured. This way to organize the results of our open-ended interviews may not be the only way, but these five themes became increasingly clear as we studied the records of the interviews. Data analysis of surveys sent to a wider range of operations VPs confirmed these views.

1   The plant manager and his style

Plant managers are important people. Without their leadership, plants can wallow. Effective plant managers can improve poorly performing plants, and sometimes quickly, and bad ones can send formerly well-run plants to the bottom of their divisions. Plants often reflect the attitude and style of their plant managers.

Here are some significant dimensions of the plant manager and his influence:

- Effective plant managers hunger for improvement. They search it out relentlessly. They exhibit a distinct passion for the customer, the product, the process, the plant's people, and its profitability.
- Effective plant managers also do a fine job of communicating a vision, or master plan, for the factory: what it should look like in the future and how it should run. Moreover, they are relentless in the pursuit of that vision.
- Effective plant managers see themselves stimulating people, building on their strengths and helping them to develop expertise in areas where they are weak.
- Effective plant managers get along with people and respect them. Rigid class systems within a factory do not work. The effective plant manager is a good listener and demonstrates a willingness to walk around the plant and to engage the workforce directly. This said, "father figures" can be as effective as more inclusive, supportive managers.

- Effective plant managers need not be engineers. It is frequently better if the plant manager is more "people person" than technocrat. Knowing all the technical aspects of the plant's operation is not what is required of the job.

2   The prevailing philosophy about profit and performance

There is a prevailing philosophy in the best-performing plants about profitability. Our interviews identified four themes:

- Profits come by growing the business and by delivering superb value to the customer. They do not come from slashing costs. As one person put it, "one doesn't save one's way to outstanding plant profitability."
- Rather, performance improvement is rooted in the processes found throughout the factory (both factory floor and support processes) and the conformance quality, throughput time, and flexibility of those processes. This finding, in particular, underscores the importance of swift, even flow.
- The more that the factory's culture is one of curiosity and experimentation, the better. The better-performing factories are the ones more willing to change, especially those that constantly seek incremental, bottleneck-breaking increases in capacity. Such changes are more likely to be changes with a management character to them (e.g., standardization, quicker or fewer changeovers, inventory reduction) than changes that have an engineering character to them (e.g., significant new equipment), although both occur. The poorer-rated plants do not do as well with change.
- Simplicity beats sophistication. ERP systems and supply chain management, while important, are not viewed to be as important as "getting it right" within the factory. Smaller factories are preferred, those of less than 400 people. Big plants often have to be subdivided to be managed well. Simple plant charters (especially now in Europe) are valued, as are focused factories.

3   Attitude toward the plant and its invested capital

The best plants think about their operations and the capital that is invested in them in different ways from the poorer-performing plants. This thinking may strike some as unconventional, but it is very effective.

- Often the best factories exhibit an attitude of making do with the current resources – "squeezing the capital dry" – before advocating for any additional major investments. These factories often evidence a "show me" attitude toward new technology. They do not like new equipment just because it is the latest thing. They are often more willing to "sweat" an existing asset (although never "running it into the ground") rather than to invest significant money in order to achieve only a minor gain. Overengineering is consciously avoided but there is no hesitation about investing for the future once it is clear that current resources are insufficient for meeting the needed capacity, quality, or product performance requirements. The best-performing plants are continually de-bottle-necking themselves. In some of the poorer-performing plants, there is too much equipment and too much of the very latest. Too much of the equipment is dedicated; not enough can be put to multiple uses. In the poorer-performing plant the goal is often to eliminate direct labor. That is not the mentality in the best plants; that is not what swift, even flow would say, either.
- Good housekeeping and good maintenance are necessary conditions and outgrowths of this point of view.
- Workers feel like they own the factory. They trust management and its openness. They are willing to take responsibility themselves. They share across worker teams. They may relish gain-sharing plans.

4   Attitude to the environment outside the plant

The outstanding plants exhibit an attitude that is quite open to the outside. They do not turn in on themselves.

- Plant management is eager to feel the pulse of the marketplace and to spend time understanding customer needs. It seeks close collaboration with marketing and sales. The plant is not fixated on the production schedule. It is willing to do other things that can aid the customer.
- Collaboration extends internally to engineering, R&D, and new product development. Manufacturing is a willing and early participant in product development and change initiatives. In the best plants, managers do not allow design issues to compromise the equipment and the process.

- The factory embraces benchmarking. Nevertheless, the benchmarking that has been done across plants, even within a company, has tended to be informal and of recent origin. It has been observed, as well, that benchmarking works best with the better plants; they use benchmarking effectively to improve. Weaker plants do not use benchmarking effectively and do not improve much, if at all. They do not act on the insights gleaned from benchmarking.

5 How the plant is measured

There is no "silver bullet" for measuring a plant and its performance.

- Our interviews revealed that it does not matter how the factory is measured. All kinds of measures are used and many appear to be valid and useful. No one measure points incontrovertibly to improved performance. A portfolio of measures of different types makes the most sense.
- But not a big portfolio. As one manager put it, "The dashboard of measures can get so big that you can't see out the windshield."
- Sometimes the accounting system inadvertently flags and punishes proper behavior. For example, in reporting performance, many accounting systems place undue emphasis on displacing direct labor rather than on "squeezing capital dry."

Distinguishing high-performing from lagging plants

These observations, drawn from our interviews of senior managers, are broad-ranging. Yet, they are quite consistent with the concept of swift, even flow. Furthermore, in subsequent survey work involving companies from many different industries, the theme of "mentality" distinctions between the best plants and the run-of-the-mill was reinforced. The plants that were seen as lagging had a different character from the plants that were seen as high performers. The high performers had high scores for:

> *Product and process characteristics*: quality management, breaking of bottlenecks.

Managerial characteristics: leadership within the plant, leadership style, culture within the plant.

Style of the plant manager: follow-up and implementation, people skills, decisiveness, communication skills, technical expertise, vision.

Culture at the plant: labor relations.

These results suggest that sustained high performance requires a mix of things. The critical tools and techniques identified are not fancy; they are the tried and true ones of quality management and bottleneck breaking. However, "soft" management skills predominate in this list. Constructive labor relations, strong people and communication skills, decisiveness, and good follow-up and implementation all fall into that category.

The laggard plants, on the other hand, were distinctly low on the following characteristics:

Product and process characteristics: lean manufacturing principles, breaking of bottlenecks, reengineering of plant processes, production planning and control, investment in new equipment.

Managerial characteristics: way plant has been measured, benchmarking.

Style of the plant manager: seeks out input, vision, follow-up and implementation, decisiveness.

Culture at the plant: experimentation and change.

Lagging performance seems to be associated with a mentality in which there is little emphasis on experimentation and change, and where both "tools and techniques" and "soft skills" are lacking.

THE ADVANTAGES OF SWIFT, EVEN FLOW METRICS

Commitment to high performance is a way of thinking ... about the plant and its capital, about its people, about how profits are made, about the outside world. Swift, even flow can play a significant role in this commitment to high performance and in this way of thinking.

Moreover, appeal to swift, even flow is a very practical way to proceed. Consider the following:

- *Reductions in time and in variation are well understood by everyone in a company, and they mean something important at all levels.* Everyone can "own" their slice of swift, even flow. You don't need experts or black belts to think about reducing throughput time or variation. It can be everyone's mantra. What it means at the level of a machine operator is different from what it may mean for the plant manager or the VP of operations overseeing an entire supply chain, but at whatever level, the concept is meaningful. And, importantly, if everyone follows swift, even flow, and if everyone makes suggestions for improving it, then all benefit.
- *The measures are absolute. They can be compared across time.* They are not like cost savings that are toted up, only to evaporate later. Throughput times can be documented and used for comparison. Measures of quality can be, also, as well as measures of the variability in demand.
- *Measures of throughput time and of variation, such as quality, are everyday measures, and they can be analyzed by cause and effect.* These metrics are compatible with *kaizen* initiatives. They are measures that can be taken at any time and they can be correlated with the other forces acting on the operation. Thus, they can be a forensic tool for diagnosing what may be occurring with the operation.

I am convinced that those operations that keep swift, even flow front and center in their operations, by making it a part of their operations' routine metrics, will risk less backsliding than others. Moreover, they can face the future with more confidence. With the lens of swift, even flow, managers can tackle change more effectively; they can filter ideas to see which ones adhere to the principles of swift, even flow and which do not.

THE TEST OF PRACTICALITY

The test of any concept or theory such as swift, even flow lies in its practicality. Is it easy to understand? Can it be applied effectively to lots of different management situations? Are the solutions that tumble out from its use ones that are reasonable and worthwhile? I'm convinced that the answer to all three of these questions is "yes."

Swift, even flow can help to make existing processes more productive. In case after case, the concept has revealed its worth. It works in both manufacturing and service environments. It can be targeted to the entire supply chain as easily as to one portion of it. It can be used, albeit judiciously, to improve new product introduction and outsourcing. It can be applied strategically and employed to provide expansive visions for new processes and new ways of doing business.

It is a concept that undergirds, and unifies, some of the major, proven tools of business improvement – lean manufacturing, the tools for quality improvement, cellular manufacturing and process reengineering, the handling of bottlenecks – and calls into question others – mass customization. Yet, it is broader in its scope than any of these. Its explanatory power can be seen in the grand expanse of business history and economic development, from the creation of the factory onwards. It can provide the vision required to conceive and design a new process or a new supply chain and to rally people to that cause. Its application can bring forth the strategic solutions of factory focus and servitization (i.e., charging for the flow of services from a manufactured product and not for the product itself), ideas that predate the lean movement. These more sweeping issues of history, vision, and strategy are ones on which lean principles and Six Sigma are essentially mute.

Moreover, swift, even flow can mean something useful to everyone connected with a process, be they on the factory floor or in the corner office. It applies to business today and it can help to explain business in the past. It is my fond hope that it will be an important part of your business future.

Notes

I   THE USUAL SUSPECTS

1 P. Krugman, *The Age of Diminished Expectations: US Economic Policy in the 1980s* (Cambridge, MA: MIT Press, 1992), p. 9.

2 For an interesting exposition of this truism, see the column by Jeff Jacoby in the February 6, 2011 *Boston Globe*, entitled "Made in the USA."

3 See R. W. Schmenner, "Service Businesses and Productivity," *Decision Sciences*, 35 (3) (Summer 2004), pp. 333–347.

4 R. Solow, "Technical Change and the Aggregate Production Function," *Review of Economics and Statistics*, 39 (August 1957), pp. 312–320. There have been many commentaries on this article since. For example, see R. E. Hall, "Invariance Properties of Solow's Productivity Residual," NBER Working Paper No. 3034 (also Reprint No. r1625), October 1991.

5 R. W. Schmenner and C. Lackey, "'Slash and Burn' Doesn't Kill Weeds: Other Ways to Downsize the Manufacturing Operation," *Business Horizons*, 37 (July–August 1994), pp. 80–87.

6 Dartmouth Tuck case study: "GM and the Great Automation Solution," authored by Professor Syd Finkelstein, and available on the Tuck School of Business website: http://mba.tuck.dartmouth.edu/pages/faculty/syd.finkelstein/case_studies/01.html.

7 R. W. Schmenner, "International Factory Productivity Gains," *Journal of Operations Management*, 10 (2) (April 1991), pp. 229–254.

8 See F. W. Taylor, *Principles of Scientific Management* (New York and London: Harper & Brothers, 1911) and F. B. Gilbreth, *Motion Study: A Method for Increasing the Efficiency of the Workman* (New York: D. Van Nostrand, 1910).

9 R. Solow, "We'd Better Watch Out," *New York Times Book Review*, July 12, 1987, p. 36.

10 R. J. Gordon, "Does the 'New Economy' Measure up to the Great Inventions of the Past?" *Journal of Economic Perspectives*, 14 (4) (2000), pp. 49–74.

2   SWIFT, EVEN FLOW

1 Swift, even flow was first coined in an article of mine with Morgan Swink entitled "On Theory in Operations Management," *Journal of Operations Management*, 17 (1) (December 1998), pp. 97–113.

2 The books by and about these famed gurus of quality are readily available, especially those of W. Edwards Deming, Joseph Juran, Armand Feigenbaum, and Phillip Crosby. *Juran's Quality Handbook* is particularly comprehensive.

3 This is one representation of Kingman's formula, due to John Kingman, a British mathematician, who published it in 1966. It is an approximation for the mean waiting time, W_q, which is measured on the y-axis.

$$E\left(W_q\right) \approx \left(\frac{\rho}{1-\rho}\right)\left(\frac{c_a^2 + c_s^2}{2}\right)\tau$$

In this formula, ρ is the capacity utilization (the x-axis), τ is the mean service time, λ is the mean arrival rate, c_a is the coefficient of variation for arrivals (the standard deviation of arrival times divided by the mean arrival time, λ) and c_s is the coefficient of variation for service times (standard deviation of service time divided by mean service time, τ). Thus, the wait time depends on the product of capacity utilization, the variation affecting the process (demand and production itself), and the natural speed of the process or rate of production.

4 As will be described later, sometimes families of parts or products can be identified and exist in enough volume to justify the creation of a manufacturing cell (sometimes called "group technology") within the job shop. Such a manufacturing cell gathers various, different pieces of equipment together in a product family-specific configuration.

5 Here, again, the innovation of the manufacturing cell is applicable. Defining manufacturing cells for the batch flow process rather than the job shop is likely to be much easier to do because the identification of a family of parts is likely to be easier.

6 This fact is captured by Kingman's formula, mentioned above, which is applicable to queuing situations and gives a very good approximation of the wait time as a function of three factors: (a) the production rate, (b) the variability of the demand and of the process itself, and (c) the capacity utilization of the process. Thus, the slower the process, the

266 NOTES TO PAGES 24–57

greater the variability of either the demand striking the process or of the process itself, and the greater the capacity utilization, the longer is the throughput time.

7 A story is told of the Boeing Company in the early 1990s, when the delivery times for the C-17 Globemaster transport plane for the US Air Force started to balloon. Simply by withdrawing some of the planes from the production line for a time, and reinserting them later, the situation was remedied and the delivery of all of the planes improved.

8 Frances Frei has done a good job of thinking about such issues. See, for example, "Breaking the Trade-off Between Efficiency and Service," *Harvard Business Review*, 84 (11) (November 2006), pp. 92–101.

9 In this book, variation can typically be expressed with a distribution. That distribution may have a greater or lesser standard deviation, but it can be estimated. Uncertainty occurs when we do not know what the underlying distribution is and we cannot estimate it.

10 As reported in Robert W. Hall, *Attaining Manufacturing Excellence* (New York: McGraw-Hill, 1987).

11 This example is drawn from my own experience and discussion with Dr. Jeffery Pierson, a surgeon in Indianapolis. Also, a paper entitled "Developing Efficiency in a Total Joint Replacement Practice," authored by Jeffery L. Pierson, Lisa M. Brandt, and Mary Ziemba-Davis (2008), personal communication, provided useful detail.

12 My own knee replacement was performed in 39 minutes.

13 See the work of Clayton M. Christensen, *The Innovator's Dilemma: When New Technologies Cause Great Firms to Fail* (Boston: Harvard Business School Press, 1997).

14 R. H. Hayes and S. C. Wheelwright, "Link Manufacturing Process and Product Life Cycles," *Harvard Business Review*, 57 (1) (1979), pp. 133–140; R. H. Hayes and S. C. Wheelwright, "The Dynamics of Process–Product Life Cycles," *Harvard Business Review*, 57 (2) (1979), pp. 127–136.

15 T. Ohno, *Toyota Production System: Beyond Large-Scale Production* (New York: Productivity Press, 1988), p. ix.

16 This quotation is attributed to German social psychologist Kurt Lewin, on p. 169 of K. Lewin, *Field Theory in Social Science; Selected Theoretical Papers*, edited by D. Cartwright (New York: Harper & Row, 1951).

3   THE OLD-FASHIONED WAY TO MAKE MONEY

1 The following are articles of mine that report on this research on productivity: "Explaining Productivity Differences in North Carolina Factories," with Randall Cook, *Journal of Operations Management*, 5 (3) (May 1985), pp. 273–289; "The Merit of Making Things Fast," *Sloan Management Review* (MIT), 30 (1) (Fall 1988), pp. 11–17; "An International Comparison of Factory Productivity," with Boo Ho Rho, *International Journal of Operations and Production Management* (MCB University Press), 10 (4) (1990), pp. 16–31; "International Factory Productivity Gains," *Journal of Operations Management*, 10 (2) (April 1991), pp. 229–254; "Looking Ahead by Looking Back: Swift, Even Flow in the History of Manufacturing," *Production and Operations Management*, 10 (1) (Spring 2001), pp. 87–96.

2 F. C. Lane, *Venetian Ships and Shipbuilders of the Renaissance* (Baltimore: Johns Hopkins University Press, 1934), pp. 129–175; F. C. Lane, *Venice, A Maritime Republic* (Baltimore: Johns Hopkins University Press, 1973), pp. 361–364.

3 A. D. Chandler, Jr., *The Visible Hand* (Cambridge, MA: Belknap Press, 1977).

4 Chandler, *The Visible Hand*, pp. 254f.

5 H. Ford, *Today And Tomorrow* (New York: Doubleday, Page and Company, 1926). Productivity Press reprint in 1988. For the throughput time, see pp. 118f.

6 For an outstanding description of what occurred at Ford, see D. A. Hounshell, *From the American System to Mass Production, 1800–1932* (Baltimore: Johns Hopkins University Press, 1984).

7 From Hounshell, *From the American System to Mass Production*, p. 228.

8 A. D. Chandler, Jr., *Scale and Scope: The Dynamics of Industrial Capitalism* (Boston: Belknap Press, 1990), pp. 205f.

9 Chandler, *Scale and Scope*, p. 128.

10 Chandler, *The Visible Hand*, p. 262.

11 Chandler, *Scale and Scope*, p. 129.

12 Chandler, *Scale and Scope*, pp. 134f.

13 See David S. Landes, *The Wealth and Poverty of Nations: Why Are Some So Rich and Others So Poor?* (New York: W. W. Norton, 1998); Robert C. Allen, *The British Industrial Revolution in Global Perspective* (Cambridge University Press, 2009); Joel Mokyr, *The Enlightened*

Economy, An Economic History of Britain 1700–1850 (New Haven: Yale University Press, 2010).

14 Landes, *The Wealth and Poverty of Nations*, pp. 186–187.

15 Landes, *The Wealth and Poverty of Nations*, p. 256.

16 Indeed, it is at this time when children began to be employed in factories. While one can decry this occurrence, that children could successfully oversee machines of this type is testament to the degree to which skills passed from people to machines.

17 Landes, *The Wealth and Poverty of Nations*, p. 156.

18 Landes, *The Wealth and Poverty of Nations*, p. 219.

19 Landes, *The Wealth and Poverty of Nations*, p. 222.

20 Landes, *The Wealth and Poverty of Nations*, p. 227.

21 Landes, *The Wealth and Poverty of Nations*, pp. 48f.

22 Landes, *The Wealth and Poverty of Nations*, p. 224. See also David S. Landes, *Revolution in Time* (Boston: Belknap Press, 1983).

23 Landes, *The Wealth and Poverty of Nations*, pp. 174f.

24 Landes, *The Wealth and Poverty of Nations*, p. 178.

25 Landes, *The Wealth and Poverty of Nations*, p. 363.

26 Allen, *The British Industrial Revolution in Global Perspective*, p. 202.

27 Allen, *The British Industrial Revolution in Global Perspective*, p. 205.

28 D. J. Boorstin, *The Discoverers* (New York: Vintage Books [Random House], 1985).

29 Boorstin, *The Discoverers*, p. 64.

30 S. N. Broadberry, "Comparative Productivity in British and American Manufacturing During the Nineteenth Century," *Explorations in Economic History*, 31 (3) (1994), pp. 521–548.

31 Broadberry, "Comparative Productivity in British and American Manufacturing During the Nineteenth Century," p. 522.

32 W. J. Abernathy and J. E. Corcoran, "Relearning from the Old Masters: Lessons of the American System of Manufacturing," *Journal of Operations Management*, 3 (4) (August 1983), pp. 155–167.

33 Alexander Rose, *The American Rifle* (New York: Rosewriter, Inc., 2008), pp. 69ff.

34 Hounshell, *From the American System to Mass Production*, Chapter 1.

35 Hounshell, *From the American System to Mass Production*, pp. 179f.

36 Hounshell, *From the American System to Mass Production*, p. 241.

37 See the fascinating description of Fred Harvey in K. A. Brown and N. L. Hyer, "Archeological Benchmarking: Fred Harvey and the Service Profit

Chain, circa 1876," *Journal of Operations Management*, 25 (2) (March 2007), pp. 284–299.

38 S. N. Broadberry and D. A. Irwin, "Labor Productivity in the United States and the United Kingdom During the Nineteenth Century," *Explorations in Economics History*, 43 (2) (April 2006), pp. 257–279. P. Andras and H. J. Voth, "Factor Prices and Productivity Growth During the British Industrial Revolution," *Explorations in Economic History*, 40 (1) (January 2003), pp. 52–77.

39 Chandler, *The Visible Hand*, pp. 58f.

40 Landes, *Revolution in Time*, pp. 308ff.

41 The seminal book on the topic is *Mass Customization: The New Frontier in Business Competition* by B. Joseph Pine and Stan Davis (Boston: Harvard Business School Press, 1993).

42 This is the Wikipedia definition. Others are similar.

43 From Wikipedia's entry on mass customization as of October 10, 2010.

44 Hounshell, *From the American System to Mass Production*, pp. 249ff.

45 Landes, *The Wealth and Poverty of Nations*, p. 215.

4 VISION

1 Most of the information for this example comes from the Harvard Business School case, *Shouldice Hospital Limited*, 9–683–068 (1983), written by Professor James L. Heskett.

2 This section draws on a wonderful article by Vince Mabert and Mike Showalter, entitled "Logistics of the American Circus: The Golden Age," published in the *Production and Inventory Management Journal*, 46 (1) (2010), pp. 74–90. Mabert and Showalter make reference to swift, even flow in the article (p. 81) and I am indebted to them.

3 Mabert and Showalter, "Logistics of the American Circus: The Golden Age," p. 74.

4 Mabert and Showalter, "Logistics of the American Circus: The Golden Age," p. 81.

5 Mabert and Showalter, "Logistics of the American Circus: The Golden Age," p. 81.

6 My colleague of many years, Bob Hall, still provides in his books the best explanation of the Toyota Production System. I commend to you the chapter on Toyota (Chapter 2) in his latest book, *Compression* (New York: CRC Press, 2010).

7 J. G. Miller and T. E. Vollmann, "The Hidden Factory," *Harvard Business Review*, 63 (5) (September–October 1985), pp. 142–150.

8 The following draws from my article entitled "Escaping the Black Holes of Cost Accounting," *Business Horizons*, 31 (1) (January–February 1988), pp. 66–72.

9 Variations on this approach to cost accounting have been adopted by some companies or company divisions, although not widely. For example, as far back as 20 years ago, a division of Motorola put a "velocity" calculation within its cost allocation. Other companies have tried to alter their cost accounting to make it more compatible with just-in-time/lean principles.

5 MAKING A BAD PROCESS BETTER

1 This is adapted from a case that I was invited to write by USA Services.

2 This case is a summary of a case of the same name written by Professor Robert S. Collins of IMD and Michael Gibbs, *ICI – Nobel's Explosives Company (Abridged)*, POM 241, dated February 1, 2002.

3 This case is adapted from an IMD case of the same name originally authored by Owen Dempsey, under the supervision of Prof. Robert S. Collins, *Stewart Instruments Ltd.*, POM 112, 1985. The 2002 revision, *Stewart Instruments, Ltd. (Revised)*, IMD-6–0242, was done by me.

4 This case is a summary of a case that was written by some former students of mine about a family-owned company.

5 This is a condensed version of an old Harvard Business School case, long out of print, written by the late Professor Daryl Wyckoff, *Yellow Freight System, Inc.*, 9–677–046.

6 LINKING THE SUPPLY CHAIN

1 This is a condensed version of a case I wrote while at IMD in Lausanne, Switzerland, *Omega, Autumn 1988*, POM 155, dated October 22, 1992. This case uses information from another IMD case, *Omega S.A., Restructuring the Value Chain: The Convergence of Marketing and Manufacturing*, POM 150, dated March 2, 1992.

2 This short case summarizes Lego's situation as depicted in the IMD case, *Lego: Consolidating Distribution (A)*, IMD-6–0315, (2008) written by Edwin Wellian under the supervision of Professors Carlos Cordon and Ralf W. Seifert, of IMD.

3 This is a condensed version of *Barilla SpA (A)*, Harvard Business School, 9–694–046, written by Professor Janice H. Hammond.

4 A. D. Chandler, Jr., *Scale and Scope: The Dynamics of Industrial Capitalism* (Boston: Belknap Press, 1990), pp. 155f.

5 A. D. Chandler, Jr., *The Visible Hand* (Cambridge, MA: Belknap Press, 1977), pp. 290–292.

6 Chandler, *The Visible Hand*, pp. 295–296.

7 Chandler, *The Visible Hand*, pp. 293–299.

8 Chandler, *Scale and Scope*, p. 65.

9 Chandler, *The Visible Hand*, pp. 299–302 and pp. 391–402, and C. R. Morris, *The Tycoons* (New York: Henry Holt and Company, 2005), pp. 114–117.

10 Chandler, *Scale and Scope*, p. 55.

11 Chandler, *The Visible Hand*, pp. 299–300.

12 Morris, *The Tycoons*, p. 117.

13 D. A. Hounshell, *From the American System to Mass Production, 1800–1932* (Baltimore: Johns Hopkins University Press, 1984), pp. 5–7.

14 Chandler, *The Visible Hand*, pp. 305–307.

15 Hounshell, *From the American System to Mass Production*, p. 7.

16 Chandler, *The Visible Hand*, pp. 302–305.

17 Chandler, *Scale and Scope*, p. 66.

18 Hounshell, *From the American System to Mass Production*, p. 89.

19 Hounshell, *From the American System to Mass Production*, p. 5.

20 Chandler, *Scale and Scope*, pp. 66–67.

21 Hounshell, *From the American System to Mass Production*, p. 54.

22 Chandler, *Scale and Scope*, p. 197.

23 Hounshell, *From the American System to Mass Production*, Ch. 2.

24 Chandler, *The Visible Hand*, pp. 296–298.

25 Chandler, *Scale and Scope*, p. 67.

7 AMID UNCERTAINTY

1 This is a summary of the Harvard Business School case, *Eli Lilly: The Evista Project*, 9–699–016, authored by Matthew C. Verlinden under the supervision of Prof. Steven C. Wheelwright. It has been augmented with some additional information on the project.

2 A splendid book on new product development that addresses these points is *Product Development Performance: Strategy, Organization, and Management in the World Auto Industry* by K. B. Clark and T. Fujimoto (Boston, MA: Harvard Business School Press, 1991).

3 These findings are from V. A. Mabert, J. F. Muth, and R. W. Schmenner, "Collapsing New Product Development Times: Six Case Studies," *Journal of Product Innovation Management*, 9 (3) (September 1992), pp. 200–212.

4 Donald G. Reinertsen, *The Principles of Product Development Flow* (Redondo Beach: Celeritas Publishing, 2009).

5 This is a summary of an old Harvard Business School case, long since out of print, *Instrumentation Laboratory, Inc.*, 6–667–008. It has been the subject of analysis by the eminent Prof. Wickham Skinner, Professor Emeritus at Harvard Business School. The application of swift, even flow to this case is very consistent with Skinner's own view of what management ought to have done in this situation.

6 This is a summary of a 2002 case from the Tuck School of Business at Dartmouth, written by Eric Johnson and Tom Clock, entititled *Mattel, Inc: Vendor Operations in Asia.*

7 C. K. Prahalad and G. Hamel, "The Core Competence of the Corporation," *Harvard Business Review*, 68 (3) (May–June 1990), pp. 79–91.

8 See my book, *Making Business Location Decisions* (Englewood Cliffs: Prentice Hall, 1982). Also, see my article entitled "Every Factory Has a Life Cycle," *Harvard Business Review*, 61 (2) (March–April 1983), pp. 121–129.

8   STRATEGY

1 This is a summary of the second case I ever wrote, *Searle Medical Instruments Group (A)*, Harvard Business School Publishing, 9–675–199. I am happy to report that it was a best seller for years.

2 R. S. Collins and R. W. Schmenner, "Achieving Rigid Flexibility: Factory Focus for the 1990s," *European Management Journal*, 11 (4) (1993), pp. 443–447.

3 See this entry from the Supply Chain Digest: http://www.scdigest.com/assets/FirstThoughts/11-03-18.php?cid=4330. Also, Marshall Fisher, in his article, "What is the Right Supply Chain for Your Product?" *Harvard Business Review*, 75 (2) (March–April 1997), pp. 105–116, argues for different kinds of supply chains (i.e., efficient supply chains for functional products and responsive supply chains for innovative products) for different kinds of tasks.

4 This is a summary of a case entitled *Hartford Steam Boiler Inspection and Insurance Company*, Harvard Business Publishing, 9–675–088.
5 This is a summary of the case entitled *Prentiss Products Europe: From a National to Pan-Regional Orientation*. This is an IMD case, POM 215, written by Kimberly Bechler under the supervision of Professor Robert S. Collins.
6 This is a case summary from an IMD case entitled *Alpine Tobacco*, IMD POM 121.

9 RESOLVING THE PARADOX

1 W. Skinner, "The Productivity Paradox," *Harvard Business Review*, 64 (4) (July–August 1986), pp. 55–59.
2 Skinner, "The Productivity Paradox," p. 57.
3 Skinner, "The Productivity Paradox," p. 56.
4 Skinner, "The Productivity Paradox," p. 59.
5 R. S. Collins and R. W. Schmenner, "Understanding Persistently Variable Performance in Plants," *International Journal of Operations and Production Management*, 27 (3) (2007), pp. 254–281.

Bibliography

Abernathy, W. J., and J. E. Corcoran, "Relearning from the Old Masters: Lessons of the American System of Manufacturing," *Journal of Operations Management*, 3 (4) (August 1983), pp. 155–167.

Allen, R. C., *The British Industrial Revolution in Global Perspective* (Cambridge University Press, 2009).

Andras, P., and H. J. Voth, "Factor Prices and Productivity Growth During the British Industrial Revolution," *Explorations in Economic History*, 40 (1) (January 2003), pp. 52–77.

Banks, R. L., under the direction of Associate Professor W. Earl Sasser, Hartford Steam Boiler Inspection and Insurance Company (Harvard Business School, 9-675-088, 1974).

Bechler, K., Prentiss Products Europe: From a National to Pan-Regional Orientation, POM 215.

Boorstin, D. J., *The Discoverers* (New York: Vintage Books [Random House], 1985).

Broadberry, S. N., "Comparative Productivity in British and American Manufacturing During the Nineteenth Century," *Explorations in Economic History*, 31 (3) (1994), pp. 521–548.

Broadberry, S. N., and D. A. Irwin, "Labor Productivity in the United States and the United Kingdom During the Nineteenth Century," *Explorations in Economic History*, 43 (2) (April 2006), pp. 257–279.

Brown, K. A., and N. L. Hyer, "Archeological Benchmarking: Fred Harvey and the Service Profit Chain, circa 1876," *Journal of Operations Management*, 25 (2) (March 2007), pp. 284–299.

Chandler, A. D., Jr., *The Visible Hand* (Cambridge, MA: Belknap Press, 1977).
 Scale and Scope: The Dynamics of Industrial Capitalism (Boston: Belknap Press, 1990).

Christensen, C. M., *The Innovator's Dilemma: When New Technologies Cause Great Firms to Fail* (Boston: Harvard Business School Press, 1997).

Clark, K. B., and T. Fujimoto, *Product Development Performance: Strategy, Organization, and Management in the World Auto Industry* (Boston: Harvard Business School Press, 1991).

Collins, R. S., Stewart Instruments Ltd., POM 112 (1985).

Collins, R. S., and M. Gibbs, ICI – Nobel's Explosives Company (Abridged), POM 241 (February 1, 2002).

Collins, R. S., and R. W. Schmenner, "Achieving Rigid Flexibility: Factory Focus for the 1990s," *European Management Journal*, 11 (4) (1993), pp. 443–447.

"Understanding Persistently Variable Performance in Plants," *International Journal of Operations and Production Management*, 27 (3) (2007), pp. 254–281.

Finkelstein, S., "GM and the Great Automation Solution," Dartmouth Tuck case study. Available at: http://mba.tuck.dartmouth.edu/pages/faculty/syd.finkelstein/case_studies/01.html.

Fisher, M., "What is the Right Supply Chain for Your Product?" *Harvard Business Review*, 75 (2) (March–April 1997), pp. 105–116.

Ford, H., *Today And Tomorrow* (New York: Doubleday, Page and Company, 1926). Productivity Press reprint in 1988.

Frei, F., "Breaking the Trade-off Between Efficiency and Service," *Harvard Business Review*, 84 (11) (November 2006), pp. 92–101.

Gilbreth, F. B., *Motion Study: A Method for Increasing the Efficiency of the Workman* (New York: D. Van Nostrand, 1910).

Goldratt, E., and J. Cox, *The Goal*, (Farnham, UK: Gower Publishing Ltd, 3rd Revised edition, 2004).

Gordon, R. J., "Does the 'New Economy' Measure up to the Great Inventions of the Past?" *Journal of Economic Perspectives*, 14 (4) (2000), pp. 49–74.

Hall, R. E., "Invariance Properties of Solow's Productivity Residual," NBER Working Paper No. 3034 (also Reprint No. r1625), October 1991.

Hall, R. W., *Attaining Manufacturing Excellence* (New York: McGraw-Hill, 1987).

Compression (New York: CRC Press, 2010).

Hammond, J. H., Barilla SpA (A), Harvard Business School case, 9–694–046 (1994).

Hayes, R. H., and S. C. Wheelwright, "Link Manufacturing Process and Product Life Cycles," *Harvard Business Review*, 57 (1) (1979), pp. 133–140.

"The Dynamics of Process–Product Life Cycles," *Harvard Business Review*, 57 (2) (1979), pp. 127–136.

Heskett, J. L., Shouldice Hospital Limited, Harvard Business School case, 9–683–068 (1983).

Hounshell, D. A., *From the American System to Mass Production, 1800–1932* (Baltimore: Johns Hopkins University Press, 1984).

Johnson, E., and T. Clock, Mattel, Inc: Vendor Operations in Asia (2002).

Juran, J. M., and A. B. Godfrey, *Juran's Quality Handbook*, (New York: McGraw-Hill Professional, 5th edition, 2000).

Krugman, P., *The Age of Diminished Expectations: US Economic Policy in the 1980s* (Cambridge, MA: MIT Press, 1992).

Landes, D. S., *Revolution in Time* (Boston: Belknap Press, 1983).

The Wealth and Poverty of Nations: Why Are Some So Rich and Others So Poor? (New York: W. W. Norton, 1998).

Lane, F. C., *Venetian Ships and Shipbuilders of the Renaissance* (Baltimore: Johns Hopkins University Press, 1934).

Venice, A Maritime Republic (Baltimore: Johns Hopkins University Press, 1973).

Lewin, K., *Field Theory in Social Science; Selected Theoretical Papers*, D. Cartwright (ed.) (New York: Harper & Row, 1951).

Mabert, V. A., and M. Showalter, "Logistics of the American Circus: The Golden Age," *Production and Inventory Management Journal*, 46 (1) (2010), pp. 74–90.

Mabert, V. A., J. F. Muth, and R. W. Schmenner, "Collapsing New Product Development Times: Six Case Studies," *Journal of Product Innovation Management*, 9 (3) (September 1992), pp. 200–212.

Miller, J. G., and T. E. Vollmann, "The Hidden Factory," *Harvard Business Review*, 63 (5) (September–October 1985), pp. 142–150.

Mokyr, J., *The Enlightened Economy, An Economic History of Britain 1700–1850* (New Haven: Yale University Press, 2010).

Morgan, I. P., Alpine Tobacco, IMD POM-121 (1986).

Morris, C. R., *The Tycoons* (New York: Henry Holt and Company, 2005).

Ohno, T., *Toyota Production System: Beyond Large-Scale Production* (New York: Productivity Press, 1988).

Omega S. A., Restructuring the Value Chain: the Convergence of Marketing and Manufacturing, written by Research Associate Cathy B. Huycke, under the supervision of Professor Michael D. Oliff, POM 150, 1992.

Pierson, J. L., L. M. Brandt, and M. Ziemba-Davis, "Developing Efficiency in a Total Joint Replacement Practice," personal communication (2008).

Pine, B. J., and S. Davis, *Mass Customization: The New Frontier in Business Competition* (Boston: Harvard Business School Press, 1993).

Prahalad, C. K., and G. Hamel, "The Core Competence of the Corporation," *Harvard Business Review*, 68 (3) (May–June 1990), pp. 79–91.

Reinertsen, D. G., *The Principles of Product Development Flow* (Redondo Beach: Celeritas Publishing, 2009).

Rose, A., *The American Rifle* (New York: Rosewriter, Inc., 2008).

Schmenner, R. W., *Making Business Location Decisions* (Englewood Cliffs: Prentice Hall, 1982).

"Every Factory Has a Life Cycle," *Harvard Business Review*, 61 (2) (March–April 1983), pp. 121–129.

"Escaping the Black Holes of Cost Accounting," *Business Horizons*, 31 (1) (January–February 1988), pp. 66–72.

"The Merit of Making Things Fast," *Sloan Management Review* (MIT), 30 (1) (Fall 1988), pp. 11–17.

"International Factory Productivity Gains," *Journal of Operations Management*, 10 (2) (April 1991), pp. 229–254.

"Looking Ahead by Looking Back: Swift, Even Flow in the History of Manufacturing," *Production and Operations Management*, 10 (1) (Spring 2001), pp. 87–96.

Omega, Autumn 1988, POM 155 (October 22, 1992).

Searle Medical Instruments Group (A) , Harvard Business School Publishing, 9–675–199 (1975).

"Service Businesses and Productivity," *Decision Sciences*, 35 (3) (Summer 2004), pp. 333–347.

Stewart Instruments, Ltd. (Revised), IMD-6–0242 (2002).

Schmenner, R. W., and R. Cook, "Explaining Productivity Differences in North Carolina Factories," *Journal of Operations Management*, 5 (3) (May 1985), pp. 273–289.

Schmenner, R. W., and C. Lackey, "'Slash and Burn' Doesn't Kill Weeds: Other Ways to Downsize the Manufacturing Operation," *Business Horizons*, 37 (July–August 1994), pp. 80–87.

Schmenner, R. W., and B. H. Rho, "An International Comparison of Factory Productivity," *International Journal of Operations and Production Management* (MCB University Press), 10 (4) (1990), pp. 16–31.

Schmenner, R. W., and M. Swink, "On Theory in Operations Management," *Journal of Operations Management*, 17 (1) (December 1998), pp. 97–113.

Skinner, W., "The Focused Factory," *Harvard Business Review*, 52 (3) (May–June, 1974), pp. 113–121.

Instrumentation Laboratory, Inc. , 6–667–008 (1967).

"The Productivity Paradox," *Harvard Business Review*, 64 (4) (July–August 1986), pp. 55–59.

Solow, R., "Technical Change and the Aggregate Production Function," *Review of Economics and Statistics*, 39 (August 1957), pp. 312–320.

"We'd Better Watch Out," New York Times Book Review, July 12, 1987.

Taylor, F. W., *Principles of Scientific Management* (New York and London: Harper & Brothers, 1911).

Verlinden, M. C., Eli Lilly: The Evista Project, Harvard Business School case, 9–699–016 (1999).

Wellian, E., Lego: Consolidating Distribution (A), IMD-6–0315 (2008).

Wyckoff, D., Yellow Freight System, Inc., Harvard Business School case, 9–677–046 (1976).

Index

5 S, 103

accounting, 124, 225, 247, 260
  and productivity, 11
  and swift, even flow, 124–130
Allen, Robert, 69, 72
allocation of overhead, 124
Alpine Tobacco, 237–244
America
  and the Industrial Revolution, 80
American Productivity Center, 18
American system of manufactures, 80, 190
  and clocks, 86
American Tobacco Company, 68
andon, 106
Andrews, Samuel, 65
Arkwright, Richard, 75, 89, 244
Armour, 186
Arsenal, 61
assembly line, 22, 40, 43, 54, 62, 65, 222
automation, 7, 40, 60, 110

B-24 Liberator bomber, 67
backsliding, 256
Barilla, 174–183
barriers to entry, 145
batch flow process, 22, 43
benchmarking, 260
bill of materials, 148
Biomet, 39
Borden Milk, 185
bottlenecks, 29, 161, 255, 260
Britain
  and the Industrial Revolution, 71
buffer lead time, 148
buffers, 151
bullwhip effect, 176–183, 254

Campbell Soup, 185
capacity utilization, 9
  of the economy, 19

Carnegie, Andrew, 67, 90, 245
cells, 54–56, 224
cellular manufacturing, see cells
Chandler, Alfred, 64, 67, 82, 182
chase vs. level production, 122
checklist, 252–256
Christensen, Clayton, 266
circus operations, 96–99
clock
  and continuous improvement, 74
  and the Industrial Revolution, 73, 84
  and machine tools, 79
  and the water frame, 77
Collins, Robert, 226, 256
concurrent engineering, 200
continuous flow process, 21, 43
core competence, 210–212
cost accounting and swift, even flow,
  124–130
cost reduction, 111–112
Crosby, Philip, 17, 101

decoupling inventory, 54
Dell Computer, 34, 51, 87, 229, 245
Deming, W. Edwards, 17, 58
deregulation, 158
Deupree, Richard, 182
distribution system, 172, 186
downstream, 145, 162, 253, 255
Duke, James Buchanan (Buck), 68, 184

Eastman, George, 190
easyJet, 33, 245
economic order quantity, 107, 152
economies of scale, 11, 41, 59,
  244–246
Eli Lilly, 193–198
Enterprise Resource Planning, 13,
  42, 152
entropy, 156
EOQ, see economic order quantity

ERP systems, *see* Enterprise Resource
 Planning
evenness, 26
expediting, 121

factory
 birth of, 77
 factory system, 70
factory focus, *see* focused factory
FedEx, 46, 49
fitting, 80
flexibility, 114–116
flowing stream parable, 105
focused factory, 223–226, 246
foolproof, 17, 52, 103, 104
Ford, Henry, 65, 82, 86, 89, 90, 245
Frei, Frances, 266

Gary, Elbert, 68
General Motors, 66
Gilbreth, Frank, 10
Goldratt, Eli, 56
grouping like things together, 139

H&R Block, 47, 49
H. J. Heinz, 185
Hall rifle, 80
Hall, John, 81
Hall, Robert, 266, 270
Hamel, Gary, 211
Hartford Steam Boiler, 229–232
Harvey, Fred, 82
Hayes, Robert, 43
Hewlett-Packard, 214–217
Holley, Alexander, 68
Hounshell, David, 188

IBM, 145
ICI-Nobel Explosives, 139–145
IKEA, 46, 50
Industrial Revolution, 69–83
 and other countries, 71
 productivity rates, 82
 and swift, even flow, 83
Instrumentation Laboratory, 203–206
interchangeable parts, 66, 80, 84, 86,
 188, 190
inventory, 97, 104, 113, 134, 202
 and swift, even flow, 30
Ishikawa, Kaoru, 17

jidoka, 105
job shop, 20, 43
joint implant surgery, 38
Juran, Joseph, 17, 58
just-in-time, 52, 109

kaizen, 102
kanban system, 114
Kingman's formula, 265

labor cost, 117
labor efficiency, 9–10, 41, 59, 168, 169
labor standards, 148, 150
Landes, David, 69, 72, 90
layoffs of the workforce, 6, 40
lean manufacturing, 52, 57, 99–124
learning curve, 12, 44
LEGO, 173
level production planning, 122, 139
Libby, McNeil, and Libby, 185
line flow process, 22
Little's law, 30
lot size, 107, 166, 181
lot-for-lot, 182

Mabert, Vincent, 97
McCormick Harvesting Machine
 Company, 81, 188
McDonald's, 46
machine speed, 118
machine utilization, 9, 41, 59
managing customers, 161
mass customization, 86–88
mass production, 66, 86
mass service, 48
material flow, 112–114
Material Requirements Planning, 13,
 113, 152
Mattel, Inc., 208–213
metrics, 261
Miller, Jeffrey, 124
Model T Ford, 65
Mokyr, Joel, 69, 72
MRP, *see* Material Requirements
 Planning
muda, 53, *see also* waste
mura, 53
muri, 53

Nucor, 37, 41

Ohno, Taiichi, 53, 67
Omega Watch, 163–169
operations strategy, 219–246, 254
orthopedic surgeon, 3, 38
outsourcing, 207–213, 217
overhead, 30, 116–117

performance measures, 241, 260
periodic reorder system, 153–155
plant charters, 234
plant life cycle, 213
plant manager, 257
postponement, 169
Prahalad, C. K., 211
Prentiss Products Europe, 233–236
preventive maintenance, 119
process flow chart, 133, 252
process matrix, 42
    and clock- and watch-making, 84
process reengineering, 54, 57
process spectrum, 20, 42
procurement, 119–121
product development, 193–203, 217
production planning, 147, 150, 161
productivity
    and capital, 259
    defined, 264
    impact, 3
    impacts on, 5
    importance, 5
    productivity paradox, 247
    and profit, 45, 50, 197, 258
    rates during the Industrial Revolution,
        82
    traps and pitfalls, 6
    and uncertainty, 45
    and variation, 45
product–process matrix, 43
professional service, 48
Protestant ethic, 74
purchasing, 119–121
push vs. pull system, 113, 137, 162,
        166, 255
putting-out system, 71

Quaker Oats, 185
quality, 100, 248, 253
    in the research findings, 59
queuing, 18, 109
Quick Response Manufacturing (QRM), 52

rationalization of production, 237
Reinertsen, Donald, 202
reorder point system, 152–153
replenishment, 167
research findings, 58–61
rigid flexibility, 226
Ringling Bros. and Barnum & Bailey
    Circus, 97
robber barons, 63
Rockefeller, John D., 63, 89, 245
Rolls Royce, 145
Ryanair, 33

scientific management, 102
Searle Medical Instruments Group,
    219–223, 226–228
segregation, 139, 161, 229, 232, 253
service factory, 48, 49
service level, 164
service levels, 165
service matrix, 47
service shop, 48, 49
services, 4, 25, 82, 143, 190, 229–232
    and swift, even flow, 46
servitization, 145, 161, 263
setup reduction, 108
Shewhart, Walter, 17
Shingo, Shigeo, 17, 28
Shouldice Hospital, 93–96
Showalter, Michael, 97
Singer Sewing Company, 188
Single Market, 232, 246
Six Sigma, 17, 52, 57, 89, 226
Skinner, Wickham, 223, 247
Solow, Robert, 13
Southwest Airlines, 33, 49, 51
Spirit Bottling, 151–156
standard design, 86
Standard Oil Company, 63
standard work, 53, 102
Stewart Instruments, 145–150
supply chain, 163–192, 255
Swift & Company, 186
swift flow, 27
swift, even flow
    and clock-making, 83
    and the Industrial Revolution, 71
    as more than other approaches, 56
    and my research, 58
    as theory, 57

defined, 16
its place in explaining history, 88
research findings, 58–61

Taguchi, Genichi, 17
takt time, 53
Taylor, Frederick, 10, 89, 102
Temin, Peter, 67
theory of constraints, 56, 57
throughput time, 27, 135, 142, 148, 155, 159,
    161, 166, 171, 197, 222, 231, 235, 241,
    251, 255
  and cost accounting, 125
  in Lean Manufacturing Philosophy, 112
  in the research findings, 60
time
  in Britain, 74
  and the Industrial Revolution, 73
  and other countries, 74
time and motion study, 10
Timex, 86
tortoise and hare, 31, 112
Total Quality Management (TQM), 52
Toyota Production System, 52, 99–124, 166
Toys R Us, 49

upstream, 165, 169, 191
US Steel, 67
USA Services, 131–139, 232

usual suspects, 6, 40

variation, 17–27, 135, 142, 147, 155, 159, 161,
    165, 171, 176, 197, 206, 213, 221, 231,
    235, 251, 253
  in quality, 17
  in quantities and timing, 18, 23
  for services, 25
  variation in timing vs. variation in
    quantities, 156
Venetian galley, 61
Vollmann, Thomas, 124

wait time, 18
Wal-Mart, 46, 49
Waltham Watch Company, 86
waste, 28–29, 53, 116, 169, 181, 191
  and swift, even flow, 28
watches, see clock
water frame, 75
Weber, Max, 74
Wheelwright, Steven, 43
Wilson & Company, 185
work-in-process inventory (WIP), 21, 24, 30,
    31, 104–106

Yellow Freight, 49, 50, 156–160

Zara, 36, 51